AFTER THE REVOLUTION

PACs, Lobbies, and
THE REPUBLICAN CONGRESS

ROBERT BIERSACK

PAUL S. HERRNSON
University of Maryland

CLYDE WILCOX
Georgetown University

GENERAL EDITORS

D1365279

DISCARD

ALLYN AND BACON
Boston • London • Toronto • Sydney • Tokyo • Singapore

HOUSTON PUBLIC LIBRARY

R0118731903

Vice President, Editor in Chief: Paul A. Smith
Editorial Assistant: Kathy Rubino
Marketing Manager: Jeff Lasser
Editorial Production Service: Chestnut Hill Enterprises, Inc.
Manufacturing Buyer: David Repetto
Cover Administrator: Jennifer Hart

Copyright © 1999 by Allyn & Bacon
A Pearson Education Company
160 Gould Street
Needham Heights, MA 02494

All rights reserved. No part of the material protected by this copyright notice may be
reproduced or utilized in any form or by any means, electronic or mechanical, including photocopying, recording, or by any information storage and retrieval system,
without written permission from the copyright holder.

Internet: www.abacon.com

Between the time Website information is gathered and published, some sites may
have closed. Also, the transcription of URLs can result in unintended typographical
errors. The publisher would appreciate notification where these occur so that they
may be corrected.

Library of Congress Cataloging-in-Publication Data
Biersack, Robert, 1954–
    After the revolution : PACs, lobbies, and the Republican
Congress / Robert Biersack, Paul S. Herrnson, Clyde Wilcox.
      p. cm.
    Includes bibliographical references and index.
    ISBN 0-205-26913-3 (pbk.)
    1. Campaign funds—United States. 2. Political action committees—
United States. 3. Lobbying—United States. 4. Pressure groups—
United States. 5. Republican Party (U.S.: 1854–) 6. United
States—Politics and government—1993– I. Herrnson, Paul S.,
1958– . II. Wilcox, Clyde, 1953– . III. Title.
JK1991.B53   1999
324'.4'097309049—dc21   98-39203
                                       CIP

Printed in the United States of America
10 9 8 7 6 5 4 3 2 1   03 02 01 00 99 98

Contents

CHAPTER 7

CHAPTER 8

CHAPTER 9

CHAPTER 10

CHAPTER 11

CHAPTER 12

CHAPTER 13

CHAPTER 14

Mark J. Rozell

CHAPTER 15

Paul S. Herrnson and Clyde Wilcox

PREFACE

The 1994 elections were a watershed event in U.S. politics, ushering in a new era of partisan politics on Capitol Hill. Following the elections, Republicans possessed a majority of members in the Senate for the first time in eight years and took control of the House for the first time in four decades. Led by House Speaker Newt Gingrich of Georgia, the GOP House majority worked feverishly to translate the party's stunning electoral victory into a policy revolution. Using the Contract with America—the party's 1994 campaign manifesto—as their guidepost, House Republicans sought to enact decades' worth of GOP policy initiatives that had been stifled during the long period of Democratic congressional control. Republican House members succeeded in enacting nine of the contract's ten provisions within a self-imposed deadline of one hundred days during the 104th Congress, but the legislation was bogged down in the Senate, and some elements of the House Republicans' program were vetoed by President Clinton.

Moreover, the Republicans' bellicose rhetoric and unwillingness to compromise with congressional Democrats and the White House left many voters feeling uneasy about the newly ascendant GOP. The Republicans' attempts to cut Social Security and Medicare and to reduce funding for education and environmental protections caught many off-guard, including some voters who had cast their ballots for Republican candidates for Congress. Most voters also blamed congressional Republicans for the stalemate over the 1995 federal budget and the two government shutdowns that resulted from it.

As the 1996 elections began to heat up, a large portion of the U.S. public began to reconsider their opinion of the Republican Congress. Prompted by Democratic Party rhetoric and their own experiences, many voters began to think of the "Republican revolutionaries" as partisan extremists. However, too few voters trusted congressional Democrats enough to return control of the House and Senate to them. President Clinton handily won reelection over Republican nominee former Senate majority leader Robert Dole of Kansas and Reform Party candidate Ross Perot, but his coattails were too skimpy to return control over either chamber of Congress to the Democrats. The 105th Congress convened with ten fewer Republican members of the

House and two more GOP senators. With only an eleven-seat majority in the House, the Republican revolutionaries settled down to a more incremental style of governance, often experiencing the kinds of internal dissension that had led to legislative stalemate under Democratic-controlled congresses.

The Republican Revolution that had changed the dynamics in the House and Senate also had a dramatic impact on the interest groups that do much of their business in the offices and corridors of the U.S. Capitol building. The representatives of unions, abortion-rights supporters, environmentalists, and groups supporting other liberal causes, who had enjoyed substantial access to Congress's leadership when Democrats controlled the House and Senate, suddenly found themselves shut out of the power centers on Capitol Hill. By contrast, lobbyists for business groups, pro-life forces, gun-rights activists, and other conservative groups, who formerly had only limited input into the policy process under the era of Democratic control, were invited to meetings with congressional leaders and the chairs of congressional committees to plan legislative strategy.

After casually observing some of the changes taking place in Congress and in various interest groups, we decided that more detailed and systematic study was in order. What impact would the Republican majority in Congress have on the contributions and campaign efforts of interest groups? Would the managers of business PACs suddenly change their strategies and shift the bulk of their contributions from Democratic to Republican incumbents? Would liberal groups rise to the challenge and pump more money into the campaigns of Democratic candidates? Would these groups donate this money to Democratic challengers and open-seat candidates, or would the groups focus on protecting the Democratic incumbents who survived the 1994 Republican juggernaut? Perhaps the groups' members would have become so demoralized that they would be unable to raise sufficient funds to accomplish either goal. How would conservative groups react? Would they be able to sustain their already high contribution levels and campaign efforts following the Republican victory? Would they focus their efforts on protecting GOP incumbents, especially first-term House members, or would they devote most of their resources to expanding the Republicans' congressional majorities? What about these groups' representatives on Capitol Hill—what adjustments in lobbying strategy would they make in response to the new partisan balance in Congress?

In order to address these questions, we selected a diverse group of PACs and lobbies that represent different political, economic, and social interests. The groups differ in wealth, size, and organizational structure. They also vary in their responses to the Republicans' winning and maintaining control of Congress. We then assembled a team of political scientists who possess expertise in interest group politics and asked each researcher to conduct an in-depth case study of one group. We provided these researchers with a common set of questions and asked them to conduct several interviews during the course of the 104th Congress and shortly after the 1996 elections. We also encouraged them to follow their own instincts in order to learn about the nuances of their group's adjustment to the new realities on Capitol Hill.

The resulting book was written with a variety of audiences in mind, including undergraduate students, scholars, and political practitioners who specialize in congressional elections, interest group politics, and campaign finance. As a set, the chapters portray interest groups that have diverse goals and capabilities. Each group's responses to the new alignment on Capitol Hill were influenced by its goals, internal structure, and relationships with members of Congress and other groups. These case studies demonstrate how an illustrative set of PACs and lobbies responded to major political change.

As with any collaborative effort, this book would not have been possible without the cooperation of many individuals. We must first thank our academic colleagues who participated in the project. We also want to acknowledge the PAC directors, lobbyists, and other political practitioners who were willing to discuss with us the changes they participated in and observed. We also thank the reviewers who offered helpful suggestions for improving the manuscript: Anthony Corrado, Colby College; John C. Green, University of Akron; and John R. Wright, George Washington University. Finally, we thank Peter Burns, Sean Cain, Peter Francia, and Rachel Goldberg for assisting us in turning the manuscript into a book.

We dedicate this book to some of the professors who took special efforts to nurture our interest in politics and make our undergraduate educational experiences rewarding. Dick Bingham mentored Robert Biersack at Marquette University; Judith Best mentored Paul Herrnson at the State University of New York College at Cortland and Paul Smith mentored him at Binghamton University; Benjamin Snyder and Patricia Self played a similar role for Clyde Wilcox at West Virginia University.

INTRODUCTION

Robert Biersack and Paul S. Herrnson

In October of 1994, as Republican leaders of the House of Representatives began to think that they might capture control of the House for the first time in forty years, they placed the PAC community on notice of the possible consequences of this outcome. Having long felt cheated because business-oriented PACs gave significant financial support to congressional Democrats, House Republican leader Newt Gingrich (R–GA) declared that PACs that failed to participate in the coming "revolution" would face "a long, cold two years in Washington" (Babson and St. John 1994, 3456).

Most corporate, trade, and other probusiness PACs failed to heed this warning. Only a few became more supportive of Republicans, and most of these gave only slightly more money to GOP candidates and waited until the latter stages of the 1994 campaign season to do so. Following the Republicans' stunning takeover of both houses of Congress, there was much talk in the capital about the sea change in the flow of money that would likely come about in future elections. The flow of PAC contributions that took place immediately after the election encouraged some political observers to speculate that Democratic candidates for Congress might be able to raise only a tiny fraction of the funds they had raised from PACs in the past (Salant and Cloud 1995).

Some also predicted that the "Republican Revolution" in Congress would result in a parallel revolution in the interest group community. Unions, environmentalists, feminists, and other liberal groups would become outsiders for the first time in a generation, while antitax groups, pro-gun organizations, champions of deregulation, and other conservative groups, which previously had only limited access to the system, became the new insiders. Organizations would need to change their tactics in response to this new reality, for union lobbyists could no longer count on easy access to committee chairs, while the Christian Coalition might no longer need to pressure members with floods of phone calls and faxes.

1

This book examines the impact of the 1994 elections and the Republican takeover of Congress on PACs and lobbies that participate in national politics. All revolutions have an impact on how governments and the groups that support them conduct their business, and they all produce winners and losers among those who supported different causes. In the chapters that follow, we examine how different groups of winners and losers reacted to the Republican takeover of Congress. The takeover did not fundamentally change the way that interest groups do business on Capitol Hill, but it did have a major impact on the operations of many individual groups. When the 104th Congress convened in January 1995, a new world of possibilities had opened for business organizations and conservative groups, while the old avenues of influence began to close down for many unions and liberal organizations. Many groups had to rethink the well-established patterns of activity they had used to influence the legislative process when it was under Democratic control, leading several to alter their strategies and tactics.

The Rules of the Game

The basic rules that govern the participation of corporations, labor unions, and other interest groups in federal elections are codified in the Federal Election Campaign Act of 1974, its amendments, and associated regulatory decisions and court rulings (collectively known as the FECA). The law allows all kinds of organizations to create voluntary political institutions (popularly called political action committees or PACs) to raise funds from group members and contribute them to candidates for federal office. Corporations, unions, and membership groups can use their corporate profits, union dues, or membership fees to pay for their PACs' overhead. Ideological and issue-oriented PACs that do not have organizational sponsors, sometimes referred to as "nonconnected PACs," do not enjoy this luxury and must finance their operations with the funds they collect from their contributors. These PACs' major advantage is that they can solicit contributions from any individual, whereas other PACs can only ask the members of their parent organizations for money.

Individuals are permitted to give up to five thousand dollars each year to a PAC, but PACs sponsored by corporations, unions, and groups with regular members can only receive contributions from certain "members" of the organization. Thus corporations can solicit contributions only from management and executive employees or stockholders, and unions and other membership groups can only accept donations from members. Individuals who contribute to a PAC can also give an additional contribution to a designated candidate using the PAC as the vehicle to deliver that contribution. These contributions count only against the one-thousand-dollar-per-election limit on an individual contribution to the candidate; they do not count toward the PAC's contribution limit.[1] In addition, some PACs, most notably EMILY's List, which helps elect Democratic women, collect checks from their members and physically present them to candidates. This process, known as "bundling," allows PACs to collect funds for candidates that are in excess of the contribution limit. Ideological groups are not the only ones that bundle, and many corporations will encourage executives to buy seats at the company table at fund-raising dinners for key policy-makers, thereby magnifying the effects of any contribution from the company PAC.

Any PAC that has existed for at least six months, has received contributions from at least fifty people, and has made contributions to at least five federal candidates is entitled to contribute up to five thousand dollars to any federal candidate for each election in which that candidate participates.[2] This allows PACs to give a maximum contribution of ten thousand dollars per candidate in most congressional elections because primary and general elections count as separate races.[3] PACs can make contributions in the form of cash or in-kind services consisting of polls, phone banks, and other commodities or activities. They can also make unlimited expenditures to advocate the election or defeat of a federal candidate as long as those expenditures are not coordinated with the candidate's campaign.

Moreover, recent court rulings allow interest groups to spend treasury funds, sometimes referred to as "soft money" because they are raised and spent outside of the FECA's regulatory framework, in ways that can influence federal elections. These funds can be spent on political communications as long as they do not expressly advocate the election or defeat of a specific candidate.[4] Unions, corporations, trade associations, and other groups can mount television, radio, direct-mail, and telemarketing campaigns to distribute information about the positions of federal candidates on issues in ways that can help or harm those candidates' electoral prospects. During the 1996 elections, the American Federation of Labor–Congress of Industrial Organizations (AFL-CIO) spent $35 million on television and radio ads to make the case that Republican members of Congress had tried to cut spending on Medicare, education, and environmental protections in order to pay for a tax cut for the wealthy. Much of this money was spent in ways intended to harm the prospects of marginal Republicans, many of whom were House freshmen. A group of business groups headed by the National Federation of Independent Business, known as "The Coalition," spent $5 million on ads to defend these members. These "issue advocacy" campaigns were legal because they did not directly call for a candidate's election or defeat. The use of issue advocacy campaigns grew exponentially during the 1996 elections. Issue advocacy differs from independent expenditures in two important respects: It is not disclosed to any federal agency, and the money that pays for this activity can come directly from interest group treasuries.

The rules governing lobbying in Washington were revamped more recently than those governing campaign finance. In 1995, Congress passed the Lobbying Disclosure Act, which requires lobbyists to register with the Clerk of the House and the Secretary of the Senate and file semiannual reports about their lobbying activities. The new law is a significant improvement on existing regulations: For example, it includes in its definition of lobbying communications from group representatives to congressional staff and executive branch officials. Yet it does not include grassroots lobbying under its disclosure requirements, and requirements for disclosure of coalition activity are not entirely effective. Also in 1995, first the House and then the Senate passed separate resolutions imposing limits on the gifts and meals that legislators and their aides can accept from lobbyists. The gift bans also prohibit members and staffs from accepting travel to leisure or recreational events. One of the ironies of the gift bans is that lobbyists can continue to wine and dine members if they report the expenditures for meals as in-kind contributions to the members' campaign committees. Another irony is that campaign fund-raising events have become more important venues for informal meetings between legislators and lobbyists. Other changes in lobbying had to do with the executive branch reforms that were issued by President Clinton in January 1993. These include an increased cooling-off period for postemployment lobbying by executive branch officials, from one to five years, and a lifetime prohibition against former executive branch officials working as agents on behalf of foreign governments and political parties (Shaiko 1998).

The Players

The number of PACs grew rapidly after the 1974 amendment to the FECA codified their existence and the Federal Election Commission's 1975 SUN-PAC Advisory Opinion allowed sponsoring groups to pay their PACs' overhead (see Figure 1.1). The number of PACs skyrocketed from 608 committees at the end of 1974 to 4,009 in 1984, and then grew more slowly to 4,528 in 1996. Most of the growth took place among business-related PACs, including those sponsored by corporation and trade associations. The number of ideological PACs also grew dramatically. The number of labor union PACs grew the least because many unions already had PACs in 1974, and because there are far fewer unions than corporations in the United States.

PAC contributions also grew at a rapid rate during the 1970s and early 1980s, followed by slower growth (see Figure 1.2). Corporate and trade association PAC contributions increased the most during the 1990s and accounted for most of the PAC donations made in 1996. Labor PAC contributions grew at a somewhat slower rate, and labor contributed significantly

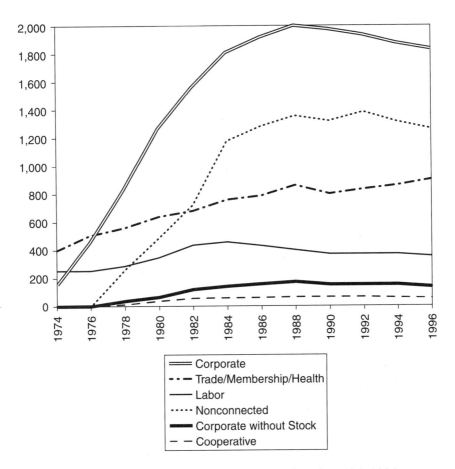

Figure 1.1　Growth in the Number of Registered PACs, 1974–1996

less than did their corporate counterparts. By 1996, PACs provided nearly 40 percent of all funds raised by House incumbents in contested elections, and 22 percent of all Senate incumbents' receipts (Herrnson 1998, 139, 154).

The PAC community is dominated by a few large committees. Of the 4,528 PACs in existence in 1996, nearly a third made no contributions at all to federal candidates, while 180 gave $250,000 or more, more than 57 percent of all contributions made by PACs. The 33 largest PACs gave more than one-third of all PAC contributions, while the smallest 2,200 active committees made less than 13 percent of all PAC contributions. Thus, a majority of active PACs give only small sums to a handful of candidates, while a small number give large amounts to candidates in many races.

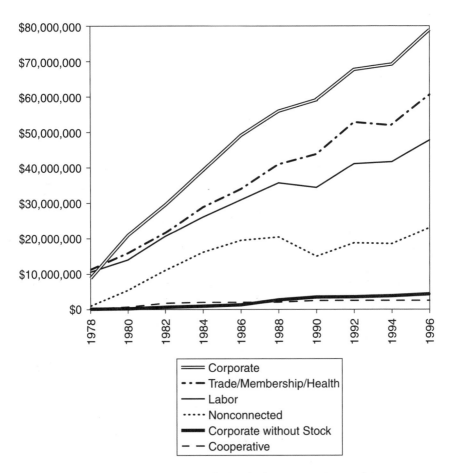

Figure 1.2 PAC Contributions in Federal Elections, 1978–1996

PACs have increasingly given to incumbents over time. During the 1978 elections, PACs gave 57 percent of their contributions to incumbents, 22 percent to challengers, and 21 percent to open-seat candidates. By 1994, the proincumbent orientation of PAC contributions had become even more pronounced, with incumbents receiving 79 percent, challengers 10 percent, and open-seat candidates only 11 percent of all PAC dollars. Because there were more Democratic than Republican incumbents, the Democrats increasingly benefited from the PACs' largesse.

Organized interests participate in elections in a variety of ways besides PAC activity. Think tanks, such as the Heritage Foundation, give candidates issue research. Labor unions have traditionally carried out fieldwork for

Democrats, and business groups have assisted Republicans. The American Israel Public Affairs Committee, which seeks to promote a secure Israel and strong American–Israeli relations, helps candidates raise money but does not make campaign contributions. Churches and church-based organizations in African American and ethnic communities have long histories of political activism. Environmental groups and the Christian Coalition are relative newcomers to electoral politics, but their voter guides and voter-mobilization efforts have played important roles in recent congressional elections (Herrnson 1998; Rozell and Wilcox 1998).

Some interest groups that are not supposed to participate in federal elections do so, albeit in an indirect fashion. A number of charitable, educational, civic, and other tax-exempt groups (classified as 501(c)(3) and 501(c)(4) organizations in the federal tax code) have recently begun to carry out activities designed to indirectly influence congressional and other elections. Among these groups are GOPAC, the Abraham Lincoln Opportunity Foundation, and the Progress and Freedom Foundation, which were part of House Speaker Newt Gingrich's political operation; Americans for Tax Reform, a group that has close ties with the Republicans; and Vote Now '96, a voter-registration group that focuses on demographic groups that are traditionally loyal to Democrats. Federal tax law and federal election law allow tax-exempt groups to spend money for public education, including education about political candidates and issues, and these laws allow PACs to contribute money directly to federal candidates and spend money to directly promote their election or defeat. Although the lines between what constitutes educational and election activity have blurred in recent years, the law encourages interests to create a variety of interrelated groups, each of which uses different activities to promote their common causes (Herrnson 1998, 127).

The lobbying community, which had been in existence well before the birth of the first modern PAC, has not changed drastically as the result of the FECA, the Lobbying Disclosure Act, or the House and Senate gift bans. The growth in the size and reach of the federal government and economic, social, and technological change have probably had a greater impact on lobbying than political reform (Truman 1951). Prior to 1920, the United States Steel Corporation was the only U.S. company to have a permanent office in Washington. By 1940, a mere 5 corporations had created Washington offices. Favorable economic climates and government expansion led more than 175 corporations to set up permanent offices in the nation's capital (Epstein 1969, 90–91). It has been estimated that by 1996, more than 600 U.S. corporations maintained full-time offices in Washington. The number of trade associations grew even more rapidly. In 1955 there were about 5,000 national associations in Washington; in 1975 there were 13,000; and in 1996 the number reached more than 23,000, plus an additional 64,000 regional, state, and local associations (American Society of Association Executives 1996, 1). Labor unions also have a strong presence in the nation's capital. The AFL-CIO represents more than 80 national and international unions. Numerous individual unions also maintain their own permanent Washington offices. In addition, there are more than 2,000 public interest groups and membership organizations that maintain public relations offices in Washington.

Many groups that are unwilling or unable to maintain a permanent lobbying office in Washington, and some groups that do, use hired guns to present their viewpoints to federal lawmakers. The number of multiple-client lobbying firms, lawyer-lobbyist groups, and public relations/lobbying firms in Washington has mushroomed in recent years. Firms such as the Duberstein Group, Patton, Boggs, and Blow, and Hill and Knowlton Worldwide play important roles in writing legislation and building the coalitions needed to pass or defeat bills in Congress. It is now possible to hire firms that specialize in lobbying specific committees, in creating coalitions to lobby in concert, or to mobilize group members in real or manufactured grassroots campaigns (Shaiko 1998).

Interest Group Strategies

PACs and other interest groups that participate in elections, either directly through contributions or indirectly through mounting issue advocacy campaigns, pursue a variety of goals. Most PACs that represent business interests, particularly corporations, give contributions to incumbents in order to gain or maintain access to lawmakers who are in a position to influence the policies that regulate or foster their business activities. Ideological and many labor PACs are more interested in influencing the composition of Congress than maintaining access to incumbents. For this reason, they give contributions to candidates who share their views, and they target a significant share of their resources toward candidates in close races, including promising nonincumbents. Most of these PACs are strongly aligned with one of the two major parties.

Of course, nearly all PACs give at least some money to incumbents. Unions, for example, give some contributions to maintain access to powerful incumbents and others to elect sympathetic new members, and even ideological PACs give to incumbents who carry their agenda to the floor. Moreover, a small number of large corporate and trade committees contribute to some nonincumbents. These PACs contribute to a few congressional nonincumbents because they are members of a state legislature, and they give to others in response to solicitations that are made on the candidates' behalf by party leaders.

Institutional considerations also influence PAC decision making. PACs with small treasuries can only support a small number of candidates before they exhaust their funds. Wealthy PACs can afford to give contributions to more candidates and this makes their decisions more complicated (Wilcox 1989). Some groups, such as the National Association of Realtors' PAC, have enough resources to give the maximum allowable contribution to all of their preferred favored candidates and make significant donations to others who are lower on their priority list.

The organizational structure of a PAC and its sponsor can also influence PAC decision making. Whether an organization has a broad geographic base or focuses its activities in a smaller area is important, as is the number of political interests that belong to an organization and the degree of harmony among them. The level of membership involvement in PAC decision making can have a major impact on the distribution of PAC contributions. PACs that have broad geographic memberships are comprised of individuals who have less than identical goals; these PACs allow for significant membership involvement in PAC decision making and are less likely than others to focus only on "inside the beltway" considerations, such as subcommittee assignments, that are deemed important by the organization's lobbyist (Wright 1985). When a PAC's members demand that it support their local House members and senators, they can reduce the amount of funds that are available to contribute to legislators who are in a position to have a direct impact on the PAC's interests.

The amount of information available to committee leaders can also influence PAC decision making. PACs located in the Washington, DC, area are able to avail themselves of more information about the dynamics of individual campaigns than are others. Washington-area PACs are able to attend briefings conducted by the Democratic and Republican congressional campaign committees and various "lead PACs," such as the National Committee for an Effective Congress, the AFL-CIO's Committee on Political Education (COPE), and the Business–Industry Political Action Committee (BIPAC). They can also garner information at fund-raising events and less formal occasions that regularly take place on Capitol Hill.

Finally, the context provided by an individual election season can influence PAC decision making. During election years that favor one party, that party usually fields a strong group of challengers and open-seat candidates. As a result of the political context and their own political experience and skills, these candidates are able to attract significant money from PACs that pursue ideological goals or a combination of ideological and access-oriented objectives. Challenger and open-seat candidates of the other party, by contrast, usually raise little in PAC funds (Jacobson and Kernell 1983). Incumbents who are in jeopardy of losing their seats usually raise an abundance of PAC dollars, regardless of whether their party is advantaged or disadvantaged by the electoral context.

Interest groups also use a wide array of strategies and tactics in lobbying Congress. Virtually all of them use "insider" techniques, such as testifying at congressional hearings, contacting government officials at their offices and in informal settings, and providing officials with research results and technical information. Approximately 85 percent also help draft legislation, consult on legislative strategy, and enter into coalitions with other groups. About 80 percent use "outsider" techniques, including organizing letter-writing campaigns and other grassroots efforts. Less than one-third run advertisements in the media to publicize their issue positions (Schlozman and Tierney 1986, 149–150).

Although most groups use each of these strategies on occasion, there are real differences in the types of groups that can use each strategy. This is true for several reasons. First, each strategy requires different resources. Inside strategies work best for organizations with substantial financial resources that guarantee access or for groups with substantial policy expertise, and they work least well for ideological groups that seek to persuade government to endorse a set of behavioral norms. Outside strategies work best for organizations with many members with intense preferences, and least well for "think tanks" and corporations that have no real membership.

In addition, an organization's policy goals influence the kinds of strategies it chooses to employ. Some groups seek policies with narrow benefits and diffuse costs, and thus seek to keep the scope of the conflict limited and the definition of the issue narrow. Corporations and trade associations usually seek to lobby quietly, testifying before Congress and meeting with committee and party leaders to make the case that a tax break or some other policy would enable their industry to grow and result in the creation of hundreds of thousands of new jobs. When the tobacco lobby succeeded in winning a $50 billion tax credit in the 1997 budget bill, for example, they did so by working behind the scenes with the party leaders in the House and Senate.

A trade association that opposes the imposition of a new tax on its product, by contrast, would probably use a combination of insider and outsider techniques. The National Beer Wholesalers Association, for example, directly lobbied members of Congress and sent out more than three thousand faxes instructing its members to call the White House and their representatives in the House and Senate in order to express their opposition to a tax increase that the Clinton administration was considering as part of its 1993 deficit reduction program (Drew 1997, 16).

In contrast, ideological groups frequently pressure Congress by burying its members in mail, phone calls, and faxes. The Christian Coalition and the National Rifle Association (NRA) are known for their ability to mobilize their membership in a short time to communicate with their representatives and senators. Yet even these groups use a mix of inside and outside strategies: The NRA played a crucial role in organizing House hearings into Bureau of Alcohol Tobacco and Firearms "excesses" in 1995 and 1996, and the Christian Coalition was a part of the team of interest groups that wrote the implementing legislation for the Contract with America (Gimpel 1998).

Finally, a few organizations invest significant resources in media advertising, in effect lobbying the public to contact their members. The Health Insurance Association of America's ability to defeat the Clinton administration's health care reform plan using television ads featuring two fictitious characters, Harry and Louise, voicing their concerns about the program is a case in point. Popular support for national health insurance was strong until these advertisements succeeded in raising public fears of the possible negative consequences of reform (Connolly 1993).

The Impact of Partisan Change

Political activity in Washington reflected a stable set of assumptions from the 1970s through 1990: (1) incumbents would win more than 90 percent of all House races and roughly 75 percent of all Senate contests, (2) Democrats would continue to maintain procedural control of the House, and (3) Democratic control of the Senate would be interrupted by occasional Republican takeovers. As a result, most PAC contributions, including those made by businesses, flowed to incumbents, most of whom were Democrats, and most lobbyists sought to ingratiate themselves with the Democratic committee and subcommittee chairmen and party leaders who controlled the congressional agenda.

Democratic control did not result in Republican legislators being ignored by PACs and lobbyists. On the contrary, GOP members routinely received large sums of PAC money, especially from corporate interests, and worked closely with the interest group representatives who sought their assistance. However, as Congress's seeming "permanent minority," GOP members, especially in the House, were not the primary focus of interest group contributions or lobbying (Connelly and Pitney 1994).

After the 1992 election, however, some of the norms that had evolved in the realms of campaign finance and lobbying began to weaken. The emergence of conservative firebrand Representative Newt Gingrich as the House Republican whip resulted in GOP members of the lower chamber becoming less accommodating to the Democratic majority. In the 1994 campaign, GOP leaders perceived an opportunity to seize control of Congress, for Clinton was generally unpopular, and voter dissatisfaction was high. Republicans nationalized the campaign around the ten issues featured in their Contract with America and issued blistering attacks on the Democrats as the party of big government, corruption, and "politics as usual" in Washington. They also sought greater financial and political support from PACs and lobbies in 1994, but with only limited success.

Few Washington insiders other than Gingrich anticipated the Republican tidal wave of 1994. Moreover, PAC managers are not known for taking risks. Very few contributed significant sums to Republican challengers or withheld money from Democratic incumbents during the 1994 elections. Congressional incumbents collected 72 percent of all PAC contributions, while challengers and open-seat candidates raised only 10 and 18 percent, respectively. The partisan distribution of PAC money was 62 percent to 38 percent in favor of the Democrats. The pattern of PAC contributions in 1994 did not significantly deviate from previous elections. The Republican freshman class of 1994 made its way to Capitol Hill with little help from the PAC community.

Following the 1994 elections, the three assumptions that had guided most interest group activity in Washington appeared to be turned on their heads. Thirty-five sitting House members, including the Speaker, and two senators—all Democrats—had been defeated in the general election, and Republicans were in control of both the House and Senate. Whether the GOP would be able to maintain its congressional majorities remained an open question as the 1996 elections approached. The uncertainty of the 1996 elections, however, did little to slow down the pace of change in the historic 104th Congress.

The Battle over Congress

The 1996 elections posed some major challenges to PACs and the broader interest group community. The possibility that partisan control over Congress could once again change meant that the stakes were unusually high. Conservative groups had enjoyed unprecedented influence under the Republican-led Congress. Groups such as Americans for Tax Reform, the National Federation of Independent Businesses, and the Christian Coalition, which had been shut out of the lawmaking process when the Democrats were in control, were given a major role drafting legislation under the GOP's leadership. Liberal groups, including unions, teachers, and environmentalists, had the opposite experience. Organized interests allied with the two parties learned the lesson that their ability to accomplish their legislative goals depended largely on which party controlled Congress's agenda. For these groups, the lines over which the 1996 elections would be fought had been neatly drawn. Each would work especially hard to help their party win as many congressional seats as possible.

The lines were not so neatly drawn for other groups, however. Numerous corporations and trade associations had been giving both to Democratic and Republican incumbents since the early 1980s. The tobacco industry, the American Medical Association, and the National Association of Realtors were notorious for playing on both sides of the fence. Many of these unaligned groups had been supporting incumbent Democrats because they controlled the congressional agenda even though the groups' economic interests suggested they would support Republican challengers. Following the Republican takeover of Congress, these groups switched the bulk of their contributions in favor of GOP candidates, but they did not completely abandon Democratic incumbents. Their mixed giving patterns persisted partly because they recognized the advantage of having access to members of both parties and partly because of the uncertainties surrounding which party would control the 105th Congress. The fund-raising efforts President Clinton made on behalf of some Democratic congressional candidates also probably influenced the contributions of many PACs.

How did different kinds of PACs respond to the Republicans' ascendance on Capitol Hill? Did business-oriented PACs that had previously pursued access-oriented strategies abandon Democratic members of Congress who had been shorn of committee chairmanships and other positions of influence in order to support Republicans who shared their free market anti-regulation principles and now held the reins of power in the legislature? Or did these PACs continue to pursue an access-oriented strategy that dictated that they give contributions to both Democratic and Republican incumbents? Did labor PACs continue to pursue highly partisan "mixed" strategies that resulted in their contributing virtually all their funds to powerful Democratic incumbents and promising Democratic challengers and open-seat contestants? Or did they begin to siphon off some of the money that they had previously given to Democrats in order to gain access to Republican committee and subcommittee chairmen and party leaders?

How did lobbying groups react to the Republican takeover? Was the coalition of business groups, antitax proponents, opponents of federal regulation, pro-gun forces, and Christian conservatives, which in the past had helped to defeat Democratic legislation, able to remain united behind a Republican legislative agenda, or did it disintegrate as a result of internecine warfare? What about the labor unions, environmentalists, social welfare advocates, and other liberal groups that had often squabbled among themselves, sometimes undermining congressional Democrats' ability to pass laws that would have benefited these groups? Were they able to unite in opposition once they found themselves outsiders in a Republican-controlled Congress? How did these groups change their strategies as their access to policy makers changed?

Overview of the Book

The chapters that follow address these and other questions about how interest groups reacted to the Republican Revolution by examining the responses of an illustrative set of PACs and lobbies. The authors of these chapters used data from the Federal Election Commission (FEC) to analyze the contributions made by each interest group. They conducted one or more semistructured interviews with interest group leaders to learn about changes in the groups' strategies.[5] The interviews were guided by a common set of questions to ensure that all of the major topics were addressed.

The groups examined in this book include a variety of corporations, trade associations, labor unions, and ideological membership organizations. The first four chapters examine those groups that clearly benefited from the Republican takeover of Congress. The National Federation of Independent Business (NFIB), which represents the interests of small business, was one of the biggest winners. After the Republican takeover, the NFIB gained major access to the leadership of Congress. The group was able to take a key role in writing probusiness legislation, including tax relief, regulatory reform, and the implementing legislation associated with the Contract with America.

The Republican takeover was also a major achievement for the Business–Industry Political Action Committee (BIPAC). BIPAC is primarily an election-oriented group. It does not lobby Congress. After fulfilling its raison d'être, the election of a probusiness Republican Congress, BIPAC began to reformulate its mission to focus on protecting probusiness Republicans who are in jeopardy of losing their seats.

Prior to the Republicans' ascendance on Capitol Hill, the American Medical Association (AMA) had access to lawmakers of both parties, but it had to spend a great deal of time fending off reform proposals that were advanced by the elderly, unions, and other liberal constituencies. Once the GOP took control, the balance of power shifted in favor of the medical community. The AMA began to enhance its influence in the ongoing deliberations over reforming the health care delivery system.

The last big winner covered in the book is the NRA, which is the nation's strongest pro-gun lobby. For years the NRA had been fighting a rear guard action against a Congress dominated by pro-gun control Democrats. It lost some battles, such as when the 103rd Congress passed the Brady Bill Handgun Violence Prevention Act, which placed new restrictions on the sale of handguns. With the Republican takeover, the NRA found itself in a position to mount a frontal assault on laws limiting gun ownership. The group played a key role in arranging congressional hearings on gun control issues, but it was unable to repeal the ban on assault weapons and other key regulatory provisions.

The next six chapters present case studies of groups that were among the biggest losers following the GOP takeover. January 1995 was a rude awakening to many interest groups that had strong ties to the Democratic Party and had enjoyed easy access to policy makers. Some, like organized labor, found themselves totally frozen out of the policy process. Others, such as environmental and liberal social groups, had some access to the GOP's moderate wing, but Republican conservatives controlled the agenda in the House and exerted increasing power in the Senate as well. These groups suddenly found themselves forced to try to create coalitions to defeat bills that they had no voice in crafting.

Organized labor, represented in this volume by the AFL-CIO's COPE and the UFCW, were major losers in the Republican Revolution. For roughly forty years labor lobbyists could meet with majority party leaders and committee chairs whenever they wished. Once the Republicans came to power, they shut labor out of policy deliberations. Moreover, the agenda of the new Congress was filled with legislation that labor opposed, from changes in pension laws to worker-safety provisions. Although the new Congress did pass an increase in the minimum wage under strong pressure from the White House, backed by strong public support, labor won few other victories in the 104th Congress. Moreover, the autonomy and political influence of labor came under direct assault under the 105th Congress when GOP leaders sought to prohibit unions from using their members' dues to pay for political activities unless individual workers approved the spending in advance.

Environmental groups, represented here by the Sierra Club and the League of Conservation Voters, were also big losers when the GOP gained control of Congress. The new majority in the House moved quickly to ban unfunded mandates, which would have severely limited state and local enforcement of existing environmental laws. It also passed regulatory reform that would have made it very difficult to pass any new national environmental regulations and that called into question many existing statutes. Antienvironmental policies were also liberally distributed throughout a variety of bills.

Unlike labor, environmentalists were not totally shut out of the new Congress, but their access was significantly curtailed. Moreover, they found themselves fighting against a number of major bills and myriad provisions in other legislation while facing generally hostile party leaders and committee and subcommittee chairs. Environmentalists did manage to appeal to public opinion, and polls in late 1995 and early 1996 showed that many Americans were deeply concerned about the nature of legislation passed by and considered by the new Republican majority.

The newly elected Republican members were disproportionately social conservatives, often with close ties to a Christian Right or pro-life organization. Groups that advocated liberal positions on social and moral issues were also major losers in the new Congress. Pro-choice groups like the National Abortion and Reproductive Rights Action League (NARAL) found themselves on the defensive, but they did have access to some pro-choice Republicans. Pro-gay and lesbian groups, such as the National Gay and Lesbian Victory Fund, were also disadvantaged by the new Congress but were able to retain some access to policy makers who were themselves openly (or not openly) gay or lesbian, who represented areas with significant gay and lesbian populations, or who, like Speaker Newt Gingrich, had gay or lesbian relatives.

Although liberal groups retained some access to Republicans and strong support among Democrats, they faced a Congress controlled by a party whose center of gravity had swung far to the right on social issues. House Republicans had not included abortion or gay rights in their Contract with America, but the new Republican Congress did pass a ban on certain late-term abortions, which Clinton vetoed, and the Defense of Marriage Act, which Clinton signed. Liberal groups worked with GOP moderates and most Democrats to try to defeat legislation but were unable to influence the content of bills.

The final three case studies focus on groups whose ability to promote their agenda did not appear to improve or suffer immediately after the Republicans came to power, or whose long-term fate is uncertain. AT&T, the telecommunications giant, has generally supported incumbents of both parties and thus gave a majority of its contributions to Democrats for many years. The company fared reasonably well under Democratic control, but in 1995 the new Republican majority passed a major telecommunications bill that adversely affected the company's interests and led to a major corporate restructuring. Yet the long-term fate of AT&T under the new Republican Congress is less certain because, following the GOP takeover, AT&T's PAC began to contribute a majority of its funds to GOP incumbents and to focus on establishing ongoing ties to Republican leaders.

The Realtors have traditionally maintained good relations with Democratic and Republican lawmakers and thus were not significantly affected by the change in control of Congress. The organization has recently restructured its contribution strategy to give local activists a greater role in contributing and lobbying, and this grassroots contact by business-oriented citizens assures the Realtors that they will have the ear of policy makers, regardless of who controls Congress.

Finally, WISH List finds itself in an ambiguous position after the Republican Revolution. On the one hand, this explicitly Republican group now has access to the majority party in Congress, but that party is increasingly pro-life and has pushed for legislation that WISH List opposes. Ironically, the Democratic Congress was more favorable to WISH List's policy agenda than the new GOP majority. WISH List seeks to elect pro-choice Republican women in a time when the party is dominated by pro-life forces and is moving in a conservative direction on abortion. Its battles are mostly fought in Republican party primaries, where it has enjoyed only limited success.

Notes

[1]Primaries, general elections, and runoffs are each considered separate elections under the FECA.

[2]Groups that do not meet these qualifications are limited to the same one-thousand-dollar contribution limit as individuals.

[3]PACs can spend an additional five thousand dollars in the event of a runoff.

[4]See, for example, *Federal Election Commission v. Christian Action Network*, 92 F. 2nd 1178 (4th Cir. 1996).

[5]In the case of the American Medical Association, the group's lobbyists and PAC director refused repeated requests for an interview. However, the author was able to speak with other members of the organization.

FROM WALL STREET TO MAIN STREET: THE NATIONAL FEDERATION OF INDEPENDENT BUSINESS AND THE NEW REPUBLICAN MAJORITY

Ronald G. Shaiko and Marc A. Wallace

The Republican Party is the party of small business, not big business; the party of Main Street, not Wall Street. *Republican National Committee Chairman Haley Barbour, Election Night 1994.*

The strength of America is not on Wall Street but on Main Street, not in big business but in small business with local owners and workers. *Representative J. C. Watts (R-OK), Republican Response to President Clinton's 1997 State of the Union Address.*

Of all the organized interests featured in this volume, the National Federation of Independent Business (NFIB) has the closest working relationship with the Republican leadership in Congress today. This relationship has developed significantly during the past five years as the political interests of small business America and those of the architects of the Republican Revolution in Congress have become more closely aligned. Following the defeat of George Bush in 1992, the Republican leadership in the House of Representatives in particular sought to clarify the message that would guide them to majority status in Congress. A significant part of that message included a clear delineation between small business entrepreneurs in cities and towns across America and the large multibillion-dollar corporations that were producing record profits while simultaneously laying off thousands of employees in widespread "downsizing" efforts.

The catalyst in the formulation of the Republican message was the battle over the Clinton Health Care Plan in 1993 and 1994. The Clinton vision of national health care provided the Republican Party leadership in Congress with the opportunity to present the starkest of contrasts between the public philosophy of President Clinton and the Democratic Party and their vision of the proper relationship between the federal government and the American public as it related to national health care. The NFIB played an integral role in articulating the consequences of proposed federal mandates on health care provision. Working in concert with Republicans in Congress and like-minded organized interests, the NFIB set out to mobilize its more than six hundred thousand small business owners, who collectively employ more than seven million workers and account for more than $750 billion in annual revenues.

Unlike those lobbying interests representing corporate big business in the health care debate, small business interests were more clearly positioned to present a coherent case against the proposed Clinton Plan. For the vast majority of NFIB members across the country, the imposition of federal mandates on employee health care benefits translated into financial disaster. With single-digit profit margins in many cases, a significant number of small businesses would be forced to close their doors, unable to provide mandated benefits without going bankrupt in the process. The NFIB message from small business America, disseminated through a nationwide grassroots mobilization effort, was a crucial element in the collapse of the Clinton Health Care Plan. The success of the NFIB in the Clinton Health Care battle translated into clear access to the Republican leadership in both houses of Congress as well as significant input into the policy agenda of the Republican Party. This success in the policy arena for NFIB also served as the impetus for an organizational transformation that has directed additional resources and leadership attention toward the political mobilization of NFIB, both in Washington and from across the country through its elaborate grassroots network.

The NFIB is not a new political force in U.S. politics. Established in 1943, the organization has maintained a membership of at least five hundred thousand members for more than two decades (NFIB 1985, 11). Nonetheless, its Washington presence has increased significantly in just the past five years. Even more recently, the organization's political action committee, created in 1977—National Federation of Independent Business/Save America's Free Enterprise (SAFE) Trust—grew exponentially between the 1994 and 1996 elections, with further growth expected in the 1998 contests.[1] Prior to the 1996 elections, SAFE Trust had contributed roughly $300,000 to congressional candidates in each of the preceding four election cycles, with a slight increase in 1993–1994 to $370,000. In the 1996 contest, SAFE Trust contributed more than $1 million to congressional candidates. This increase is illustrative of the broader shift in organizational focus toward Washington politics and the political activation of NFIB members at the federal level.

Prior to the 1990s, NFIB had long established itself as an organization focused on representing the interests of small business America in state capitals across the nation. At the dawn of the new millenium, the NFIB remains committed to its political presence at the state level. To that end, in addition to its federal PAC, SAFE Trust, it also maintains political action committees in thirty-five states and has full-time state directors in all fifty states. Even with its energized efforts in Washington, through budget and staff increases in the last few years, the NFIB remains a key actor in most state capitals.[2] The rise to power in Washington politics, however, has occurred much more recently. In this chapter, we will explore the growth of NFIB over the past five years as it has risen to become one of the key allies and advisers to the Republican leadership in Congress today.

Organizational Maintenance and Political Representation

The organizational foundation of the NFIB is derived from small businesses. Although large corporations are important nationally and internationally, small businesses are more important locally and regionally because they provide a disproportionate number of jobs in the United States (Birch 1987; Fasig 1996). In addition, small businesses have strong ties to and vested interests in the communities in which they operate. The people who own the businesses on Main Street, including the auto mechanic, the barber, and the local grocery store owner, are the sponsors of the neighborhood little league sports teams and a wide variety of community events. It is from this diverse network that the NFIB has cultivated its political influence initially at the state level before making inroads at the federal level. Unlike a professional or trade association that draws members from a single industry or profession, the NFIB membership is comprised of small business entrepreneurs from across the entire economic spectrum. Because of its big-tent approach, the NFIB currently boasts a membership of more than six hundred thousand businesses, comprised primarily of service and retail companies, but construction and manufacturing businesses also have a strong presence (Fasig 1996). The majority of NFIB member businesses have fewer than ten employees and generate annual revenues of less than $1 million. Although all businesses are represented equally, membership dues are based on a sliding scale ranging from $100 to $1,000, depending on the annual revenues of each member company.

It is ironic that the National Federation of Independent Business, as a nonprofit business association, is too large to be considered a small business enterprise. With a staff of more than 800 employees and an annual operating budget of more than $70 million, the NFIB is hardly the "mom-and-pop" organization incorporated by founder Wilson Harder and his wife Dode on May 20, 1943 (NFIB 1985, 2).[3] The bulk of the NFIB staff is comprised of a national sales force of more than 600 employees, charged with making up to ten calls on small business owners each day across the country in order to retain existing members and solicit new business memberships. Like most membership organizations, the NFIB loses some portion of its membership each year. In recent years, the NFIB experienced turnover rates in membership of 20 percent. This level of turnover is quite competitive among national trade and professional organizations. Nonetheless, it requires the NFIB to attract roughly 120,000 new members each year simply to maintain its membership base, no small task. The remaining employees are located at the NFIB national headquarters in Nashville, Tennessee, and in the Washington, DC, office. Approximately 125 employees work in Nashville, while about 60 employees operate the government relations arm of NFIB in Washington. In addition, there are 50 state directors who coordinate the political advocacy efforts in each state with the Washington office.

Compared with the vast variety of nonprofit trade and professional associations, the NFIB is one of a growing number of "full-service" organizations (Shaiko 1991). As a nonprofit business organization regulated by the Internal Revenue Service (IRS), the parent association, NFIB, operates as one of more than fifty thousand "business leagues" in the United States (see, e.g., Smucker 1991; Weisbrod 1988). In addition, the NFIB operates a nonprofit tax-exempt foundation, *The NFIB Education Foundation*, used to educate members on organizational matters and conduct research on the policy preferences of members; the foundation also operates a college scholarship program for children of small business owners. During the 1996 elections, the NFIB PAC, SAFE Trust, was linked to the parent organization. By the end of 1997, however, the Washington office of NFIB will be reconstituted as a "social welfare" political advocacy organization for Internal Revenue Service purposes, separate from the parent organization; SAFE Trust will be linked to the new political arm for the 1998 elections. This new organizational structure will facilitate separate and distinct political fund-raising efforts, as opposed to membership solicitations for the parent organization.

Whether mobilizing for political purposes or simply seeking to maintain memberships, the NFIB has developed a communications network with its members that is the envy of the political community in Washington. In all membership organizations, leaders must create a feeling of belonging in order to link members with the organization, or they must offer an economic transaction in which the benefits for potential members outweigh the organizational costs of membership (Aldrich 1979; Hirschman 1970; Olson 1965; Wilson 1995). The NFIB seeks to link members to the organization in a variety of ways.

Like most organizations, the NFIB provides premiums for belonging, selective benefits received by "members only." These premiums include a subscription to *Independent Business*, a bimonthly magazine that includes useful insights for business management and expansion, spotlights NFIB members, and discusses the federal legislative agenda. To keep members informed about pending legislation on Capitol Hill, the NFIB also distributes *Capitol*

Coverage: Report from the Front Lines, a bimonthly publication focused on congressional and White House activities as well as the successes and failures of the legislative efforts conducted by NFIB lobbyists. Issue updates and *Action Alerts* are also distributed to members in addition to *Capitol Coverage* and *Independent Business.* Members also receive subscriptions to *State Capitol Coverage,* a newsletter that provides updates on legislation pending in their state capitals. The organization also publishes a congressional report card, *America's Small Business Report Card,* that provides ratings of members of Congress, based on their votes on key small business issues. The key issues and positions are established by the NFIB membership through in-depth surveys and Mandate Ballots (NFIB 1995a). In addition, the NFIB offers a variety of discount packages on car rentals, airline travel, hotels, and insurance coverage as well as an NFIB affinity credit card.

Conferences and conventions for members provide additional means through which they obtain useful business information as well as political intelligence. A satellite conference held in April 1996 trained NFIB members in political action. The satellite conference linked five hundred members in eighteen cities in ten states, including Alabama, Florida, Indiana, Massachusetts, Minnesota, South Carolina, and Texas (Dugan 1996). In October 1996, *Campaign '96—How Small Business Can Impact the 1996 Elections* was held in the nation's capital. Some of the topics at these conferences included campaign management, organizing grassroots campaigns, talking to the press, using the member's business to aid candidates, endorsing a candidate with other businesses through local advertisements, and running for office (Dugan 1996; NFIB 1995b). Throughout the year, Small Business Days are held in state capitals across the country and in Washington, allowing members to be their own lobbyists for a day. These lobby days empower NFIB members and provide direct contacts with their elected officials. NFIB membership participation in these "members-only" activities also provides opportunities for networking among members with similar business interests.

Participation in the internal political decision-making process also serves to link some portion of the NFIB membership to the organization. Response rates to the organization's Mandate Ballots rarely exceed 20 percent. The ballots energize and activate the politically attentive core of the NFIB membership. It is important to note that with a membership of six hundred thousand, it is not necessary to mobilize every member to be politically effective. In fact, most of the political activity in Washington that is linked to grassroots mobilization involves only a small portion of most memberships. Knowing well that mass mobilizations are both costly and, at times, unwieldy, the NFIB has identified various segments of its membership that are predisposed to conduct certain political activities beyond voting on election day.

The core NFIB grassroots constituency consists of between four and five thousand member activists who serve on Guardian Action Councils across the country. NFIB leaders maintain almost constant contact with these key political activists through their fax and e-mail networks; these members provide specific policy input for NFIB leaders. Below the Guardians, NFIB maintains a "key contact list" of approximately fourteen thousand member activists who are willing to write or call legislators on small business policy issues, write editorials in local newspapers, and testify before legislative committees at the state or federal level; this list also includes members with personal relationships with key elected officials. A broader segment of the membership base includes those members who are willing to contribute to SAFE Trust. In the 1996 elections, over twenty-five thousand NFIB members contributed more than $2 million to the NFIB PAC.[4] Beyond the financial donor segment, larger blocs of members are easily identified through computer analyses of membership files. Beyond contacts with members through direct mail, the NFIB has developed fax and e-mail networks, as more than 80 percent of members have fax capabilities and 60 percent own computers with modem links (Danner 1997b). The NFIB also maintains a toll-free 800 number for members to communicate directly with the organization. Most recently, in September of 1996, NFIB joined the global community on the Internet when it launched its web site: For each of the more than six hundred thousand members, never does a month pass without at least one contact from the NFIB.

Indeed, the NFIB is successful at lobbying state and federal governments through its membership because its grassroots communications network provides a direct linkage between NFIB leaders and members. With this foundation, the NFIB has the leverage to command the attention of state and federal legislators. For several decades, small businesses have been credited with creating the majority of new jobs in America (Birch 1987; Fasig 1996). By some accounts, small businesses are responsible "for providing work for members of 42 percent of American households" (Weisskopf 1996a). This trend is unlikely to subside in the future, for in any congressional district, "the largest employer collectively is small business" (Fasig 1996). With more than one thousand NFIB members in each congressional district, on average, employing seven million citizens nationwide, the organization has earned a considerable amount of respect in Congress, especially with the Republican leadership in both houses.

The chief House lobbyist for the NFIB, Mark Isakowitz, notes that the results of the Mandate Ballots and the narrative comments from its membership are provided to the appropriate member of Congress to demonstrate small business support for or opposition to a pending bill (NFIB 1996, 4). The grassroots prowess of NFIB means that when its representatives talk, "Members of Congress are going to listen" (Henry 1996). This was clearly demonstrated in the battle over the employer mandate provision of the national health care debate, mentioned earlier. Mobilizing its small business army, the

NFIB illustrated the projected damage of this provision by sending a four-page color brochure to its members, educating them about the potentially negative financial impact of the proposed plan (NFIB 1994). The brochure provided a section for calculating the total cost of the mandate based on the total number of full- and part-time employees for each member business. True to its grassroots mobilization approach, the brochure provided the office addresses and telephone numbers for members of the House and Senate. After calculating the expected costs of the provision, members were urged to use the enclosed addresses and phone numbers to contact their elected representatives and convey their criticisms. The successful opposition strategy undertaken by the NFIB in the health care debate prior to the 1994 congressional elections served as a catalyst for greater political mobilization of the NFIB membership and propelled NFIB to the forefront of federal lobbying efforts for the small business community.

Donald "Dan" Danner, NFIB vice president for federal government relations and head of the Washington office, believes that NFIB is successful in the public policy-making process due to three main factors. First, size matters, particularly with six hundred thousand small business owners nationwide, each of whom is faced with meeting a payroll; complying with local, state, and federal regulations; and competing daily for his or her economic livelihood. Second, the NFIB leadership educates and informs its members on a wide variety of issues relevant to small businesspeople on a regular basis and, as important, listens to the views of their members when developing policy agendas and political strategies. Third, NFIB members consistently demonstrate their commitment to small business America and are willing to undertake additional responsibilities, including political involvement, in order to preserve their economic viability (Danner 1996).

The success of NFIB in the health care debate was grounded in the overwhelming consensus (95 percent opposition to employer mandates) among NFIB members regarding the detrimental impacts of the Clinton Plan. On other salient issues before Congress in recent years, the NFIB has remained on the sidelines, due to a clear lack of policy consensus among its members. For example, the NFIB took no position on the North American Free Trade Agreement (NAFTA) as roughly one-third of members supported the initiative, one-third opposed, and the remaining one-third perceived little or no impact on their businesses. While Danner and other NFIB leaders could not identify a precise percentage of membership support necessary for NFIB action, a clear consensus of at least two-thirds to three-quarters of interested members seems to move an issue onto the NFIB agenda. It is clear that the organizational structure of NFIB serves to facilitate a unified voice among leaders and members in the process of political representation in the policy-making process as well as to allow NFIB members the ability to constrain the policy agenda of NFIB leadership.

Leadership Transformation and Linkages to the Republican Party

The organizational relationship outlined above is now fully implemented as a result of a significant change in the leadership of NFIB, beginning in 1992. In November of 1991, longtime NFIB president and chief executive officer, John E. Sloan, Jr., died. His replacement, S. Jackson "Jack" Faris, transformed the organization in a number of important ways. First, he moved the national headquarters from San Mateo, California, to Nashville, in his home state of Tennessee, during his initial year as president. Second, he revitalized the Washington political operation. Third, he hired political staff that elevated the status of NFIB within the Republican ranks of Congress and within the Republican Party leadership. Fourth, he orchestrated the political activation of an ever-growing number of NFIB members during the last two elections through his outspoken advocacy of small business issues. Unlike his predecessor, Faris does not shy away from the media and is quick with the quotable quote, for example: "Our members want the federal government off their backs, out of their pockets, and off their land" (Skrzycki 1995). Finally, Faris added to the NFIB arsenal a personal linkage to the Republican Party apparatus, having served as head of the Republican National Finance Committee prior to joining NFIB.

Other NFIB staff were also well connected to the GOP. Chief lobbyist John Motley represented the NFIB in the "Thursday Group," a coalition of roughly a dozen business groups and conservative organizations created in early 1995 by Representative John Boehner (R–OH), the chairman of the House Republican Conference.[5] During the first one hundred days of the 104th Congress, "the Thursday Group functioned as the Revolution's boosters and its board of directors" and served to mobilize grassroots support for each of the items in the Contract with America (Judis 1996).[6]

Two other key members of the NFIB lobbying shop were Marc Nuttle and Jeff Butzke, who were hired in 1993 and 1995, respectively. Nuttle had been the executive director of the National Republican Congressional Committee (NRCC) from 1989 to 1991 and was instrumental in convincing J. C. Watts (R–OK) to run for Congress in 1994 (Shribman 1995, 3).[7] Butzke had run a consulting firm that worked for Republican candidates in local, state, and federal elections and had run against Representative Tom Downey (D–NY), unsuccessfully. Butzke orchestrated direct-mail fund-raising and helped SAFE Trust PAC increase the number of NFIB PAC donors from fourteen thousand in the 1994 election cycle to more than twenty-five thousand in the 1996 cycle (Danner 1997b; Lundegaard 1996).

While the dramatic increase in fund-raising by Butzke allowed the NFIB to expand its political operations, the PAC activities of the 1994 elections marked the transformation of NFIB into one of the key actors in the 104th

Congress. The efforts of Nuttle, Motley, and the political staff of NFIB in the 1994 congressional elections included campaign contributions of $371,625 to 232 congressional candidates; 89 percent of the candidates receiving SAFE Trust support were Republicans, who received 91 percent of the contributions. The giving strategy of NFIB was clearly linked with the Republican mission of capturing both houses of Congress as just over 60 percent of all contributions went to challengers or candidates in open-seat races in the House and Senate. When the dust settled on election night in 1994, the NFIB "had given money and manpower to eight of every ten Republican winners in closely contested races, including the large, breakthrough class of freshmen" (Weisskopf 1996, A1). By strategically targeting the $370,000 PAC war chest as well as an additional $1 million budget for political activities involving NFIB members, Nuttle helped to orchestrate the Republican Revolution of 1994. Following the 1994 elections, Nuttle concluded: "We sailed out to sea in a raft with a sail and rode a tidal wave into shore" (Weisskopf 1996, A1).

Many freshman members of the 104th Congress praised the NFIB and its members for their efforts during the elections. Senator Rick Santorum (R–PA), the beneficiary of an estimated three hundred thousand dollars in NFIB support through member and PAC contributions, also benefited from the grassroots support drawn from the more than thirty thousand NFIB members in Pennsylvania. "They filled the gaps in the campaign organization, provided enthusiastic volunteers and helped us develop a base of small donors," said Santorum, who defeated incumbent Democrat Harris Wofford. Senator James Inhofe (R–OK) was originally viewed as a decided underdog in the open-seat Senate race in Oklahoma against Dave McCurdy (D–OK), based on the flow of Washington PAC money. With the support of NFIB, money and volunteers began to flow toward Inhofe. He concluded: "The support was there in a lot of places it wasn't before, and I attribute that to the fact that NFIB supported me." On the House side, Representative George Nethercutt (R–WA), who defeated Speaker of the House Thomas Foley (D–WA) by less than four thousand votes, was quite certain of the impact of NFIB on his race: "If I had big business endorsements and he had NFIB, he would've won. It showed I was for the little guy, the small donor, the small business person who is affected by what I do on a day-to-day basis. They [NFIB] can win and lose races for you. It sure showed in mine" (Weisskopf 1996a).

The 104th Congress and the 1996 Elections

The NFIB was perfectly situated to work with the new Republican leadership once the GOP controlled Congress. The goodwill toward NFIB was widespread as scores of new and returning members of both houses had relied on the NFIB for financial and grassroots support during the 1993–1994 election campaign. The NFIB literally had a "seat at the table" as the process of gaining passage of the items in the Contract with America began (Gimpel 1996). Newly elected Speaker of the House Newt Gingrich (R–GA) charged House Conference Chair John Boehner with mobilizing support for the Contract with organized interests sympathetic to the Republican agenda. Admission into Boehner's Thursday Group was predicated on the total support of all items in the Contract by each organization, whether or not some of the items concerned the memberships of the interest groups. The NFIB was willing to make such a commitment to the Republican leadership.

The dividend paid to NFIB and other groups now directly linked to leadership core was access, input into the selling of the Contract to the American public and, more importantly, input into the policy agenda for the remainder of the 104th Congress. Beyond the ten items in the Contract with America, the NFIB agenda for the new Congress was expansive and included major items such as regulatory reform, product liability reform, workplace flexibility, and small business tax relief. With the Republicans controlling the committee agendas, the NFIB increased its formal presence in committee hearings. In the first session of the 104th Congress, NFIB representatives testified on fifty-three separate occasions, far surpassing the number of committee appearances before congressional committees in any Congress controlled by Democrats (Danner 1997a). In the 104th Congress, the NFIB was successful in gaining passage of just over 70 percent of its agenda items, a substantial increase over its success with a more limited agenda in the Democratic-controlled 103rd Congress.

Even when the NFIB lost a legislative battle, it enjoyed some measure of success. Perhaps the best example of winning while losing is the minimum wage bill, H.R. 3448, that increased the minimum hourly wage by 90 cents to $5.15 over a two-year period. Although NFIB opposed any increase in the minimum wage, the Republican leadership in both houses agreed to include several "sweeteners" in the legislation that would make the inevitable passage of the bill more palatable to small business America.[8] Amendments added to the minimum wage bill, including several key changes in pension law that benefit small and large businesses and an increase in the equipment purchase deduction for small business owners, netted NFIB member companies and small business retailers and manufacturers more than $10 billion in tax relief over the next decade (Pianin 1997, A8).

In the midst of their legislative success, NFIB leaders were gearing up for the 1996 elections. Speaking nine months prior to the November elections, Danner estimated that NFIB would be involved in approximately 225 congressional races with PAC contributions of roughly $750,000 (Danner 1997a). By election night, Danner's predictions had been surpassed by a significant margin. In the end, NFIB had amassed a $3.5 million political war chest that included just under $1.1 million in PAC contributions in 275 congressional races.

SAFE Trust PAC in the 1996 Elections

The NFIB modified its strategy to protect Republican freshmen who had supported its legislation in the 104th Congress. As a result, the 60:40 ratio of giving to challengers and candidates in open-seat races versus incumbents in 1994 was changed to a 50:50 ratio in 1996, with half of the NFIB PAC contributions (almost $550,000) going to incumbents, approximately 30 percent to candidates in open-seat races, and the remaining 20 percent to challengers.

The evaluations and recommendations of the NFIB political staff and an incumbent's voting record on key small business votes determined who receives NFIB support. Members of Congress must have supported the NFIB legislative position on at least 70 percent of roll call votes chosen by NFIB. In the 104th Congress, NFIB identified thirty-seven House votes and twenty-nine Senate votes as key votes to be calculated in the NFIB ratings score card; sixty-seven members of the House and seventeen Senators received perfect scores of one hundred; all were Republicans. An additional fifty-three House members and ten Senators voted against NFIB positions only once. For this Congress, NFIB had the almost total support of more than one-quarter of the members of each chamber or more than half of the votes necessary to pass any piece of legislation. Few organizations with issue agendas as broad as NFIB can claim such a loyal and large support base.

While an NFIB support score of seventy is a necessary condition for Republicans in Congress to receive PAC support, it is not sufficient. The political staff evaluates each incumbent and his or her campaign needs.[9] For the 1996 elections, SAFE Trust PAC contributed to Republican House members who had received NFIB support scores averaging ninety-three and to Republican Senators with higher scores that averaged ninety-five. House Democrats running for reelection were judged by a different standard.[10] In less than 7 percent of races in which NFIB was involved did SAFE Trust support a Democrat. Of these nineteen races, twelve involved incumbent Democrats. These twelve House members received NFIB support scores of seventy, on average, ranging from a high score of ninety-seven received by Ralph Hall (D–TX) to a low of fifty-four received by David Minge (D–MN). Four additional NFIB-funded House Democrats fell below the seventy mark in the 104th Congress ratings, although these four members and Minge had met the threshold in the 103rd Congress ratings.

In the 104th Congress, 98 percent of Republican members of Congress met the NFIB requirements compared to only 7 percent of Democrats (Bukro 1996). Even though it gave 95 percent of its support to Republicans, the NFIB did not escape the wrath of the Republican congressional and party leadership, who viewed this practice as an attempt by the NFIB to establish a safety net in case the Democrats regained control of one or both houses of Congress (Cooper 1997). NFIB foundation manager, Dan Danner, responded to the Republican charge by stating: "The NFIB has always been a probusiness organization, not an arm of the GOP" (Gilbert 1996). Jeff Butzke added that the group's acronym stands for "the National Federation of Independent Business, and not the National Federation of Republican Business" (Gilbert 1996).

NFIB giving to challengers and candidates in open seats involves close scrutiny of the fund-raising potential, political viability, and any relevant polling data for each candidate prior to committing resources to a campaign (Weisskopf 1996). Obviously, small business ownership and NFIB membership are looked on favorably. The staff also analyzes the voting record of the incumbent when deciding to fund challengers. The NFIB is predisposed to support challengers when incumbents receive NFIB scores of less than forty (NFIB 1985, 18). In their search for quality challengers and candidates for open-seat races, the informal Republican Party/PAC network proved to be quite helpful. With Nuttle moving around the country with the Dole/Kemp campaign and his former ties to the NRCC, and Butzke with established ties to Republican political consultants involved in hundreds of races in the cycle, few races avoided the scrutiny of the NFIB.

Once the political staff has identified the races in which they are going to participate, they must decide on the amount of PAC support to provide as well as the forms of support: direct PAC contributions, in-kind direct PAC contributions, or independent expenditures. In the 1996 elections, SAFE Trust PAC contributions were limited to direct financial contributions and in-kind contributions to candidates, with the exception of one independent expenditure of four thousand dollars in the successful reelection campaign of freshman Jon Fox (R–PA). In 76 of the 275 congressional races in which SAFE Trust was involved, PAC contributions took the form of in-kind media advertisements produced and paid for by NFIB, with the direct input of each candidate campaign organization, or a combination of cash contributions and in-kind media advertisements.

These 76 contests were among the 113 congressional races designated for "major involvement" by NFIB in 1996. Major involvement translates into campaign efforts well beyond the activities of SAFE Trust, including efforts conducted by the NFIB parent organization that fall beyond the purview of the Federal Election Commission (FEC). These efforts include holding press conferences, organizing meetings between candidates and NFIB members, organizing volunteer recruitment and get-out-the-vote efforts through direct mail and telemarketing, mailing of "foldout" candidate materials to members, and organizing and hosting fund-raising events. The NFIB also conducted political action training sessions for two thousand member activists during the cycle. Such organizational activities are subsumed under the heading of "internal communications."

NFIB and Internal Communications

The FEC regulates only those activities deemed to be electioneering—direct or indirect support for or opposition to a candidate in an election for federal office. Internal communications between leaders and members of an organization, whether partisan in nature or strictly educational, are exempted from scrutiny by the FEC. Hence, the costs of providing such information to members in congressional districts across the nation are not counted against the ten-thousand-dollar primary and general election spending limit placed on PACs, nor are they recorded with the FEC as independent expenditures. In 1996, the NFIB conducted direct-mail and telemarketing volunteer recruitment campaigns in more than 100 congressional districts that included the mailing of 197,051 volunteer letters to NFIB members in 103 congressional districts. Beyond the recruitment of campaign volunteers, NFIB also mailed 239,979 foldouts, suitable for display in storefront windows, to NFIB members in 131 districts. The distinction between a foldout and a campaign poster is important. Campaign posters are created with the intent of mobilizing public support for or opposition to candidates and would constitute an independent expenditure or a direct in-kind contribution to the campaign. However, an internal communication directing a member to vote for a certain candidate, in the form of a foldout brochure, does not constitute a regulated action, even if the NFIB member then places the foldout in the front window of his or her business. By our conservative estimates, NFIB easily spent more on its internal communications and training efforts than the $1.1 million it contributed directly to candidates through SAFE Trust in the 1996 elections. The NFIB also joined forces with several key Republican business allies to do battle with the AFL-CIO and its $35 million "issue advocacy" campaign. These groups were called to arms by Thursday Group leaders Representative Boehner and Senator Coverdell and given marching orders by RNC Chair Haley Barbour: "We want to stop the lies. These union bosses are tax-and-spend liberals who will stop at nothing to buy control of the United States Congress" (Crabtree 1996). On May 6, 1996, "The Coalition—Americans Working for Real Change" was formed by NFIB, the U.S. Chamber of Commerce, the National Association of Manufacturers, the National Restaurant Association, and the National Association of Wholesaler–Distributors (Stone 1996a). By the end of the summer, more than thirty business groups had joined the effort to counteract the AFL-CIO campaign.

NFIB, The Coalition, and Issue Advocacy in 1996

The key difference between issue advocacy campaigning and electioneering or candidate advocacy lies in the nature of the message presented in television, radio, or direct-mail efforts. Labor unions as well as corporations are prohibited from using union dues or corporate dollars in election campaigns. However, both unions and corporations are free to use their funds from their organizational budgets to conduct grassroots lobbying efforts that support or oppose policy proposals before the Congress or the White House. Such grassroots media campaigns have been used for years to sway votes on Capitol Hill. The health care battles of 1993 and 1994, for example, were highlighted by media campaigns intended to mobilize public opinion at the grassroots level. The most widely cited example of this phenomenon was the issue advocacy campaign that the Health Insurance Association of America (HIAA) used to introduce "Harry and Louise" and their concerns about the Clinton Plan to the general public.

Beginning in early 1996, the AFL-CIO launched its first wave of television commercials that targeted vulnerable Republican incumbents in the House, many of whom were freshmen. The ads urged viewers to contact members of Congress but did not specifically advocate the legislators' election or defeat. Bombarded by negative commercials for several months, these vulnerable Republicans turned to their congressional and party leaders for help. Between May and October of 1996, The Coalition managed to raise and spend $5 million to counter the issue advocacy campaigns of the AFL-CIO. It is important to note that two of the five key interest groups involved in funding and orchestrating the efforts of The Coalition—the Chamber of Commerce and the National Association of Manufacturers—do not operate PACs. Thus, their political activities were not reported to the FEC.

The Coalition, while outspent by the AFL-CIO, had the advantage of knowing when and where the Labor commercials were going to air, as the media buys were traceable through the Polaris tracking system. With limited resources, the political leaders of the five major groups, under the pro bono direction of Chuck Greener, senior vice president of Porter/Novelli (a Washington lobbying firm and former RNC political operative), strategically planned the issue advocacy campaign to counteract the AFL-CIO advertisements. The NFIB provided district-by-district intelligence reports and the National Restaurant Association was the largest financial contributor to the effort with its $1 million donation.

The Coalition targeted thirty-seven House races with issue advocacy campaigns. It aired six basic versions of television and radio issue advertisements, adapted to each congressional district. In all, The Coalition purchased television and radio air time sufficient to run six thousand television and seven thousand radio commercials. In addition, Coalition partners mailed a total of two million letters to their members in the targeted districts during the final two months of the campaign (Nichols 1997). In comparison, the AFL-CIO ran twenty-seven thousand television commercials in its year-long campaign and spent more than $100,000 in each of more than thirty congressional districts, including more than $1 million against freshman J. D. Hayworth (R–AZ) (Crabtree 1996).

The Election Aftermath and Prospects for NFIB

Despite the rumblings from Republican leaders regarding NFIB's contributing 5 percent of its funds to Democrats in the 1996 elections, the organization remained one of the closest allies of the Republican leadership during the 105th Congress. The NFIB mirrored its legislative success in the 104th Congress on election day 1996, with 70 percent of NFIB-supported candidates (191 of 275) gaining seats in the 105th Congress. Of the 113 very competitive races that were designated for "major involvement," 61 NFIB-backed candidates were winners. Thirty of these races, five in the Senate and twenty-five in the House, won by margins of six points or less. NFIB efforts in four of these elections, the Colorado Senate race and the House races in the 6th District of Arizona, the 20th District of Illinois, and the 3rd District of Kentucky are illustrative of the major involvement undertaken through SAFE Trust PAC, the internal communications of NFIB, and the grassroots support of NFIB members in hotly contested congressional races in 1996 (see Table 2.1). When all of the votes were tallied, thirteen NFIB members were elected to the House and four to the Senate, with NFIB continuing to enjoy its place in the inner circle of the Republican leadership in Congress (Dine 1996a).

Unlike the NFIB, big business interests did not fare as well in the 1996 elections. Taking a more pragmatic approach, a number of major corporate PACs divided their contributions more evenly among Republicans and Democrats. These actions did not escape the scrutiny of Haley Barbour and the Republican leaders in Congress. Within days after the election, Barbour offered a scathing critique of the actions of big business:

> With most of big business, the 1996 election was business as usual—no special effort, giving to both sides, bipartisanship. Some groups like the Business Roundtable (BRT) did things that actually helped Clinton and hurt Republicans.... BRT actually helped Clinton defeat the balanced budget in 1995, and its efforts hurt Republicans throughout (Barbour 1996).

While closely aligned with the Republican Congress, the NFIB has not precluded working with the Clinton White House. For example, the NFIB

Table 2.1 Examples of NFIB Major Involvement in 1996 Congressional Elections

NFIB-Supported Candidate	Vote Percent	Opponent	Vote Percent	State	Election
Wayne Allard (R)	51	Ted Strickland (D)	46	CO	Senate

- 10,709 foldouts sent to NFIB members
- 13,240 volunteer letters sent to NFIB members
- $4,500 SAFE Trust cash contribution in primary
- $5,000 SAFE Trust in-kind contribution (TV commercial)
- Two NFIB member press conferences held
- "Walk Down Main Street" event with NFIB members

J. D. Hayworth (R)	47	Steve Owens (D)	47	AZ–6	House

- 1,090 foldouts sent to NFIB members
- 1,090 volunteer letters sent to NFIB members
- $4,400 SAFE Trust contribution in primary for radio ads
- $5,000 SAFE Trust in-kind contribution in general (radio ad recorded by NFIB member Joy Staveley)
- Seven-city press tour with NFIB members in district
- Fund-raiser hosted by NFIB member Bennett Kopp
- NFIB press release announcing support

John Shimkus (R)	50	Jay Hoffman (D)	50	IL–20	House

- 1,705 foldouts sent to NFIB members
- 1,705 volunteer letters sent to NFIB members
- $5,000 SAFE Trust in-kind contribution in general (radio ad recorded by NFIB member Judy Hughes)
- Three NFIB member meetings held
- Four NFIB member press events held
- NFIB press release announcing support
- Fund-raiser hosted by Guardian Action Council member Linda Vala

Anne Northrup (R)	50	Mike Ward (D)	50	KY–3	House

- 930 foldouts sent to NFIB members
- 930 volunteer letters sent to NFIB members
- $2,500 SAFE Trust cash contribution in primary
- $4,636 SAFE Trust contribution in general (paid for candidate-produced small business TV ad)
- Letters sent to invite NFIB members to fund-raiser
- Press conference announcing support
- Candidate wrote guest column in state *Capitol Coverage*

was amply represented among the two thousand participants in the 1995 White House Conference on Small Business. It also established a working dialogue with Erskine Bowles, who was a North Carolina businessman prior to joining the Clinton administration as director of the Small Business Administration and later became White House Chief of Staff. NFIB president Jack Faris argues that there are several key actors in the White House who "consider us enemies," but he views Bowles as "a real bright spot in this administration." Faris adds:

> He has signed the front of a check, so he knows what that feels like. I don't believe he will tolerate one person on his staff not dealing straight-up with every honest organization trying to deal with the administration (Dine 1996a).

As for the future role of the NFIB in elections, Faris argues:

> We haven't even gotten started yet. We think we could have more impact than either political party. The interest level of small business in politics is greater than it ever has been (Dine 1996b).

He characterizes the electoral activities of the NFIB in the 1996 elections as "baby steps." Rather than training two thousand small business owners in political action in 1996, he foresees twenty thousand NFIB members active in political campaigns by 2004 (Dine 1996b). With enduring ties to the Republican leadership in Congress and an established political operation in Washington that has grown exponentially in the last election cycle, the activist NFIB of the twenty-first century envisioned by Faris is quite likely to become a political reality.

Notes

[1] In its first election cycle, 1977–1978, SAFE Trust contributed $9,688 to fifty-four congressional candidates. In 1982, NFIB created its first five state PACs.

[2] A Lexis–Nexis search conducted on the National Federation of Independent Business in the first three months following the 1996 elections generated 340 news stories (November 15, 1996, to February 15, 1997). Almost two-thirds of the stories involved the NFIB in state legislative advocacy efforts.

[3] In 1943, the Harders incorporated a business known as the National Federation of Small Business (NFSB) and were the sole stockholders in the new enterprise. In April of 1949, NFSB became the National Federation of Independent Business and was reconstituted as a nonprofit organization. The Harders exchanged all of the NFSB assets with the new NFIB for the sum of ten dollars (NFIB 1985, 5).

[4] In calendar year 1996 alone, SAFE Trust received contributions from 23,668 NFIB members totaling $1,968,153. The average contribution to SAFE Trust in the 1995–1996 election cycle was slightly over $80.

[5]Motley left the NFIB in June 1995.

[6]The membership in the Boehner "Thursday Group" originally included NFIB, the U.S. Chamber of Commerce, the National Association of Wholesalers and Distributors, the National Restaurant Association, the National Association of Home Builders (NAHB), the Christian Coalition, Citizens for a Sound Economy, and Americans for Tax Reform. Today, the Thursday Group is codirected by Senator Paul Coverdell (R–GA) and also includes the National Association of Manufacturers, Food Distributors International, Associated Builders and Contractors, and the National Retail Federation. The NAHB was removed from the Thursday Group for a period in 1996 following the firing of its head lobbyist, Bob Bannister. NAHB regained membership in 1997.

[7]Nuttle joined Robert Dole's campaign staff in late 1995 but continued to advise the NFIB.

[8]The minimum wage bill passed the House by a vote of 266–162 and was approved in the Senate by a 72–24 margin. The bill was signed into law by President Clinton on August 20, 1996.

[9]In the 1995–1996 cycle, eight House Republicans received perfect scores of one hundred yet received no support from SAFE Trust PAC: Everett (R–AL), Herger (R–CA), Mounzullo (R–IL), Hoekstra (R–MI), Knollenberg (R–MI), Portman (R–OH), Pryce (R–OH), and Spence (R–SC). Everett, Hoekstra, and Pateman do not accept PAC contributions.

[10]No Democrats in 1996 Senate races received NFIB support.

C H A P T E R   3

BIPAC: WORKING TO KEEP A PROBUSINESS CONGRESS

Candice J. Nelson and Robert Biersack

In November of 1994, for the first time in forty years, Republicans were elected to majority control of both the U.S. House of Representatives and the Senate, creating a Congress that was more favorable to business interests than any in recent memory. In early 1996, however, it appeared that the first truly probusiness majority in many years might not be returned to office because polls showed public dissatisfaction with the policies of the new Congress. The Business–Industry Political Action Committee (BIPAC) had been a leading advocate of probusiness political activity throughout the modern campaign finance era by providing critical information and guidance to other business PACs about which candidates to support, but the 1996 elections offered new electoral opportunities and challenges. Court rulings had allowed groups to spend unlimited amounts to advocate issue positions in advertising that might help or hurt certain candidates, and the AFL-CIO had announced that it planned to spend $35 million targeted against seventy-five business-oriented Republican members of Congress. BIPAC played an important role in organizing the electoral efforts of the business community in the 1996 elections in this new electoral environment.

Organization and Decision Making

BIPAC was formed in 1963 to elect to Congress candidates who "strongly support policies that will strengthen the free enterprise system, advance the needs of American business, create jobs, and promote economic growth and opportunity" (www.bipac.org/mission.htm). BIPAC tries to accomplish its goals through its Action Fund, which makes contributions to congressional candidates, and the Business Institute for Political Analysis (formerly the Education Fund), which researches candidates and makes its research available through publications, conferences, and briefings. Decisions on which candidates to support are made by a six-member Candidate Review Board, which has at least one Republican and one Democratic member (Budde 1996a).[1] Candidates receive support from BIPAC based on three criteria: preponderance of support for business interests, a competitive race, and the need for money.[2]

The 1994 Elections

The business community fared well in the 1994 elections, but ironically 1994 was a difficult year for BIPAC. The organization lost the support of some longtime members and found its role as the leader of the business community's electoral efforts eroding. Bernadette Budde, senior vice president of BIPAC, believes BIPAC lost the support of some organizations in 1994 because some "became fixated in the legislative arena" (Budde 1996a). For example, both a large pharmaceutical company that was an early supporter of BIPAC and a large health care provider stopped contributing to BIPAC in 1994 because they wanted to focus all of their resources on lobbying against President Clinton's health care legislation. As the 1996 elections approached, changes in the nature of corporate lobbying, in the availability of electoral information, and in the tactics of campaign finance posed a significant threat to BIPAC's historic role as leader of business electoral mobilization. Corporate lobbying strategies began to change in this period, creating financial demands that led some companies to rethink their commitment to electoral politics. Although corporations have generally relied on professional lobbyists to provide information to Congress and to advocate specific policies, during the health care debate corporations began to use grassroots mobilization, long a tactic of labor and environmental groups. Mass advertising, exemplified by the "Harry and Louise" ads questioning the benefits of national health care programs, was believed to have been instrumental in mobilizing the public opposition that helped defeat Clinton's proposal. Many organizations combine electoral activity with lobbying, but others with limited government relations budgets found that the financial demands of new grassroots lobbying techniques made it more difficult for them to afford electoral activity, including BIPAC membership.

At the same time, political information was becoming more generally available to political professionals through a variety of means. Specialized newsletters, Internet sites focusing on politics, and national party communications disseminated timely information about the viability and issue positions of candidates. As information about competitive elections and the positions of candidates became more widely and easily available, the information provided by BIPAC became less valuable, and the longtime role of BIPAC as information conduit for the business community was threatened.

Finally, the announced efforts at issue advocacy by organized labor, environmental groups, and other organizations that often opposed probusiness candidates led some in the business community to advocate similar tactics. BIPAC's historic role was to direct corporate PAC contributions to probusiness candidates in close elections, but more aggressive elements in the business community argued that corporations should help fund issue advocacy campaigns instead. For the 1996 elections, then, BIPAC had a number of goals, including reelecting a probusiness Congress, reeducating the business community about the linkages between electoral and legislative strategies, and reestablishing itself as the primary leadership PAC in the business community.

Reestablishing Itself as a Lead PAC

BIPAC made an early effort in the 1996 election season to reestablish its image within the business community. Although BIPAC had been actively raising money for probusiness candidates for thirty-three years, younger chief executive officers in many companies were unaware of the group's existence. During 1995, BIPAC sought new ways to make its efforts known to the business community. BIPAC modernized its publications, launched a home page on the Internet, and asked members of Congress to identify business leaders in their states or districts who might be interested in serving on BIPAC's board of directors. Charles Mack, the president of BIPAC, explained, "there is a new generation of political leaders, these new political leaders know the new generation of business leaders and are well suited to identify new business leaders" (Mack 1996). For example, a rising star on BIPAC's board of directors was recommended to BIPAC by a member of Congress, but the C.E.O. had not previously heard of BIPAC. It is interesting that an organization that was a creature of the business community would, over time, turn to elected officials to identify a new generation of business political activists.

Not all of the new initiatives were successful. BIPAC's presence on the Internet, for example, was largely abandoned during 1997. Yet both Charles Mack and Bernadette Budde feel that, overall, BIPAC's efforts to update its image among the business community in 1995 were successful, and 1995 was BIPAC's best year financially. Once it revamped its image, BIPAC sought to reestablish its role in the business community.

Early in the 1996 election cycle, BIPAC officials felt the need to persuade business leaders that electoral politics was important to maintain a probusiness Congress. Following the 1992 elections some people in the business community began to think that political activity was an unnecessary luxury that they could no longer afford, and after the 1994 elections others felt they needed to focus solely on legislation to take advantage of the probusiness

GOP majority. The ability to work closely with members of Congress and the staff of important congressional committees was a new experience for many business lobbyists, who sought to draft and influence as much probusiness legislation as possible in the heady early days of the 104th Congress.

BIPAC worked hard during the 1996 elections to convince the business community that there is an important connection between electoral and legislative activity, and that continued electoral activity was necessary to reelect a Congress sympathetic to the business legislative agenda. BIPAC also worked to enhance the business community's participation in elections, both by increasing the number of companies and people involved and by expanding the range of political activities business engaged in.

During the 1996 cycle, BIPAC encouraged the business community to do more than merely make PAC contributions. In May of 1996, BIPAC published *Rising to the Challenge in 1996: What Business Groups Must Do to Protect Free Enterprise Majorities in Congress.* The publication was sent to one thousand corporations and five hundred trade and business associations, which were encouraged to reproduce the report for their memberships (Mack 1996). The publication set forth five "political tools" available to the business community: direct financial and in-kind contributions, independent expenditures, grassroots political programs, internal corporate communications, and issue advocacy; it explained how each tool might be used during the 1996 elections. The publication was put together in part as a response to the issue advocacy campaigns of the AFL-CIO and environmental groups. Many of these activities were relatively new and untested by business interests.

BIPAC's leaders believe the organization is indispensable to the business community, and they made efforts during the 1996 elections to get more companies and associations to think that way as well. The organization's effectiveness comes not from its direct contributions to candidates, but rather from the impact that a BIPAC endorsement has on other business PACs. A study done by BIPAC following the 1994 elections suggests that BIPAC's support can be formidable. BIPAC supported ninety candidates in the 1994 elections. Between the time of BIPAC's endorsement and election day, the ninety candidates raised $7.3 million from the business community. Only two of the ninety candidates were incumbents, and three-fifths of the candidates were elected (Budde 1996a). Senate candidates endorsed by BIPAC raised an average of $268,000 from the business community, and winning Senate candidates averaged even more, $360,000. House candidates endorsed by BIPAC raised on average $41,000 from business interests, and winning House candidates averaged $50,000 (www.bipac.org/vtl_succ.htm). It is important to remember that since the mid-1980s corporate and other business PACs have overwhelmingly favored incumbents. More than 70 percent of business PAC contributions go to sitting members of Congress. The ability of BIPAC to identify and generate support for challengers and open-seat candidates can be critical to those campaigns.

There were a large number of competitive House candidates in the 1994 elections, and an independent review of their financial condition also demonstrated that BIPAC support is important. The seventy-five House Republican challengers and open-seat candidates who received BIPAC endorsements received over $7.5 million from business PACs during the 1994 elections. The other eighty Republican nonincumbent candidates who received at least 40 percent of the general election vote (and so might be considered competitive) received only about $2.5 million from business PACs. The BIPAC seal of approval was clearly representative of broad business support and proved important to those challengers and open-seat candidates who received it.

The 1996 Elections

For many years BIPAC primarily supported nonincumbents in an effort to build a probusiness majority, but 1996 presented a different challenge and led to a different strategy.[3] With Republican majorities in the House and Senate, but polls showing many GOP freshmen in trouble, BIPAC focused on reelecting the freshmen House members, which it had helped elect in 1994. The decision was inspired in part by the highly publicized efforts sponsored by organized labor to defeat probusiness Republicans.

BIPAC feared the impact of the massive efforts of organized labor on the fortunes of GOP freshmen, and so did the freshmen themselves. When the AFL-CIO announced it was targeting seventy-five House candidates, all the Republican freshmen assumed they were among the seventy-five. Charles Mack said that when he met with the Republican freshmen caucus in the spring of 1996, "There was so much water coming out of the crying towel there were tides" (Mack 1996).

BIPAC promoted a strategy in 1996 that focused first on reelecting Republican freshmen, and then on "holding their [the business community's] own" in the open-seat races (Budde 1997). Early in 1996, BIPAC expected its support to be divided approximately equally between incumbents and nonincumbents, but eventually the organization remained true to its history and supported forty-six incumbents and seventy-three nonincumbents (www.bipac.org/cand-1.htm). Nonincumbents received almost twice as much money from BIPAC ($93,302) as incumbents ($49,088). Not surprisingly, given the heated battle for control of the chamber, House candidates received the bulk of BIPAC's contributions: BIPAC contributed $111,086 to House candidates and $31,304 to Senate candidates.

As Table 3.1 shows, Republican incumbents, all of whom were freshmen, received the most support from BIPAC, followed by Republican open-seat

Table 3.1   BIPAC Contributions to House and Senate Candidates in the 1996 Elections

	House Candidates	
	Democrats	Republicans
Incumbents	$0	$43,705
Challengers	0	22,373
Open Seats	8,745	36,363
Total	8,745	102,441
	Senate Candidates	
	Democrats	Republicans
Incumbents	$0	$5,383
Challengers	0	9,599
Open Seats	0	16,322
Total	0	31,304

Source: Federal Election Commission.

candidates. BIPAC was involved in twenty-three Senate races and ninety-six House races and contributed a total of $142,490 to House and Senate candidates. The 1996 elections included an exceptional number of competitive Senate campaigns that added to the pressure for BIPAC and business support. The historic number of open seats meant that control of the Senate was also in doubt throughout the campaign. BIPAC was somewhat more active in Senate elections in 1996 than in other recent elections. The organization's focus on Senate races was to ensure continued support for the business community's position on the issue of product liability. The growth of lawsuits claiming corporate responsibility for allegedly faulty products and occasional damage awards of very large sums were seen as a major threat to business interests. Five of the retiring Democratic senators—J. Bennett Johnston (D–LA), Sam Nunn (D–GA), Jim Exon (D–NE), David Pryor (D–AR), and Claiborne Pell (D–RI)—had voted with the business community on product liability, and BIPAC officials feared that these Democrats might be replaced by others of their party who would not take a probusiness position on this issue (Budde 1996a).

The focus on product liability issues also led BIPAC to concentrate on campaigns in which trial lawyers were active, including some House races in which these attorneys were Democratic candidates. Trial lawyers and their professional associations were the primary defenders of existing product liability laws, which the business community believed unfairly penalized companies.

Table 3.2 Percentages of BIPAC-Supported Candidates Elected in 1996

	House	Senate
Incumbents	75%	80%
Challengers	69	69
Open Seats	6	0

Source: BIPAC, "1996 Election Results of BIPAC Candidates."
http://www.bipac.org/cand-1.htm

BIPAC officials believed that their efforts in 1996 were successful, at least with respect to incumbent and open-seat candidates. Eighty percent of Senate incumbents supported by BIPAC were reelected, and 75 percent of BIPAC-supported House incumbents won. Sixty-nine percent of both House and Senate open-seat candidates supported by BIPAC were successful, ensuring that the 105th Congress would maintain a probusiness majority.

The Impact of BIPAC on the 1996 Elections

BIPAC made all of its campaign contributions in the 1996 elections by the end of September because it wanted to encourage other business PACs to support candidates BIPAC had endorsed. BIPAC officials believed that their endorsements played a role in the success of the Republican freshmen and business-oriented open-seat candidates. Freshmen who raised money on their own in 1995 and early 1996 got a new wave of money in October, partly because of BIPAC efforts. BIPAC's leverage may have helped keep the candidates they endorsed competitive; BIPAC spent October telling business PACs not to give up on the freshmen, that they could be successful (Budde 1997).

Evidence of BIPAC's effectiveness can be seen in the FEC records of PAC activity during this period. The forty-two Republican freshmen supported by BIPAC received an average of $190,504 during the election cycle from corporate PACs. They received an average of nearly $39,000 from these committees in October of 1996 alone. Meanwhile, the twenty-nine other Republican freshmen who sought reelection received an average of only $106,000 from corporate PACs, receiving only $12,500 on average during October.

There was a Republican resurgence at the end of the campaign: Tracking polls showed significant movement toward the GOP among voters deciding late in the campaign. The controversy over the Democratic National Committee's fund-raising practices may have helped turn the tide, but money was a key in October, and Republicans had enough money to be competitive (Budde 1997).[4]

While BIPAC contributed more money to candidates in 1996 than it had anticipated, BIPAC officials believe that their most important role in 1996 was as an advocate for the candidates the PAC had supported. Prior to 1992 the business community felt familiar and comfortable with congressional incumbents and generally knew which candidates were probusiness. Following the 1992 and 1994 elections, there were many new incumbents who were largely unknown to the business community, and some of these new members were on important committees for the business community. In the 104th Congress, for example, there were eight freshmen on the House Commerce Committee.

BIPAC spent a lot of its time in 1996 trying to educate the business community about both candidate choices and new political techniques. In 1996, Budde felt there was a "multiplicity of choices" among probusiness incumbents and open-seat candidates in the House and Senate. BIPAC found itself with more requests for information about candidates, and also for more contextual information about the larger political situation in the country. Throughout the 1996 cycle BIPAC held seminars to brief the business community on probusiness candidates monthly, instead of every two months as in previous off-year elections.

BIPAC not only contributed to educating the business community about candidates, it also played a role in explaining how the five areas of political involvement discussed in *Rising to the Challenge* could be used. BIPAC itself was not involved in issue advocacy campaigns but urged the business community to think about more varied approaches to political involvement. Budde felt it was difficult to measure the direct impact of varied approaches such as issue advocacy in the 1996 elections, but she felt a base had been built for the 1998 elections and beyond (Budde 1996b).

Keeping a Probusiness Congress

While the strategy for the business community was clear from the outset of the 1996 elections, a strategy for 1998 was much less clear when the dust had settled from the previous race. Most of the freshmen elected in 1994 survived challenges in 1996, and they appear to be reasonably safe going into the 1998 elections. Having come through the challenges of 1996 successfully gives them both renewed understanding of what needs to be done to win and renewed confidence that they can do what is necessary.

Postelection analysis of the campaign commissioned by BIPAC suggested that while issue advocacy campaigns may have had some marginal impact on the outcome, money directly available to candidates was more significant in protecting the Republican Congress. The study argued that the business community would be most effective if it channeled its resources into direct contributions to candidates, particularly in the earliest and last phases of the campaign, rather than mounting issue advocacy campaigns. Of course, such a strategy will coincidentally enhance the influence of BIPAC in coordinating business contributions.

BIPAC will continue to focus on electing a probusiness Congress in the years to come and to adapt to the introduction of new techniques. Budde predicted that issue advocacy and improved targeting may become more important components of public affairs and political activity programs. In the past, the business community has learned how to identify and give PAC contributions to candidates. The challenge in future elections is for BIPAC to help its members use new political techniques to bridge the gap between legislative and political activity.

Budde expects continued Republican control of Congress at least through the year 2000 and the redistricting which will follow, but she also thinks the majorities will be small, whichever party gains control. If, at some point, there is a period of dominant Republican control of one or both branches of Congress, similar to Democratic control of the House for the 1950s through 1994, BIPAC's contribution strategies may change. BIPAC got involved in some primaries in 1996, and it had greater success in Democratic primaries than in Republican primaries because it is easier to isolate the probusiness candidate in a Democratic primary than in a Republican primary. Budde thinks that if there were to be a prolonged period of Republican control, labor, trial lawyers, and environmental groups might decide to get involved in Republican primaries. Their involvement makes it easier for the business community to identify probusiness candidates because they would be themes opposed by the liberal community (Budde 1996b).

While BIPAC is a bipartisan PAC, its strongest allegiances are to the Republican Party. However, there are tensions within the Republican Party between "Wall Street," "Main Street," and "Church Street." Wall Street represents multinational corporations, Main Street represents the small business community, and Church Street represents the Christian Coalition. Budde believes the business community needs to continually examine its role within the Republican Party, given the divisions within the party's coalitions (Budde 1996b).

There is also the issue of the gender gap. Working women are the most hostile to the Republican Party. How can the business community address the gender gap? Is there a way to frame races in terms of economic issues, rather than social issues, that will attract working women to Republican candidates? These are issues that BIPAC and the business community will be addressing in coming elections. A final long-term issue facing the business community is the role of minor party candidates. Budde thinks it is possible that in the not-too-distant future BIPAC will look at minor party candidates, despite the fact that none were the clear choice of the business community in 1996.

Although BIPAC succeeded in helping vulnerable GOP incumbents and many open-seat candidates in 1996, it did so at the expense of helping challengers. Only one challenger supported by BIPAC was successful in 1996. This is not surprising, for in 1996 the economy was robust and Clinton was popular, and challengers of the out-party rarely do well in such elections. Add to this the general dissatisfaction in the electorate for the Republican leadership—especially Speaker Gingrich—and it should not be surprising that Republican challengers had a difficult time. Yet Budde thought that the election was a disaster for probusiness challengers and is considering a variety of options to help challengers in the 1998 elections when the GOP is likely to gain seats in the House.

Conclusions

BIPAC's strategy for the 1996 election was clear on the day following the 1994 elections. BIPAC successfully implemented its strategy and helped to return a probusiness majority coalition to Congress. The need to reelect Republican freshmen in electoral trouble encouraged BIPAC to change its approach. It supported fewer challengers than it had in past elections, and only one of those won, leaving BIPAC to reevaluate the way it supports challengers in future elections. While BIPAC continued its traditional mission of endorsing, contributing to, and advocating support for candidates within the business community, it also launched a major effort to encourage businesses to use new political techniques. The challenge for BIPAC in the years to come is to continue its successes in 1994 and 1996 while adapting to the rapidly changing political landscape.

Notes

[1]In the past the Candidate Review Board had three Democratic and three Republican members, but that practice was changed to reflect the decreasing importance of partisanship for many of BIPAC's board members. Many board members now think of themselves as Independents, not Democrats or Republicans. The Candidate Review Board now has at least one Democrat and one Republican among its members.

[2]For a more detailed description of BIPAC's history, organization, and decision-making process, see Candice J. Nelson 1994.

[3]For an explanation of this pattern of giving, see Candice J. Nelson 1994.

[4]Throughout October there were almost daily press reports chronicling potentially illegal contributions from foreign citizens to the Democratic National Committee. The DNC eventually returned almost $1.5 million in questionable contributions, and the Justice Department formed a task force to look into DNC fund-raising practices. For a more detailed description of the controversy, see Candice J. Nelson 1997.

THE DOCTORS' LOBBY

Michael Gusmano

The American Medical Association (AMA) is the largest physicians' association in the United States. After the 1994 elections, the AMA was poised to establish a healthy relationship with the new GOP majority. The new Republican majority helped the AMA in two important ways. First, the AMA's long support of Republican candidates, including many competitive nonincumbents, assured the group access to key policy makers in the new majority. Second, many public interest groups that had competed with the AMA to shape the new direction of U.S. health care found it much more difficult to gain access to crucial congressional policy makers, thus allowing the AMA to more easily dominate the health care policy arena.

The AMA is an extraordinarily well-financed, politically powerful, and secretive organization.[1] Its political action committee, the American Medical Political Action Committee (AMPAC), was the first PAC established by a trade association, and it has consistently been one of the leading contributors to congressional campaigns. AMPAC has also been extraordinarily innovative, using in-kind contributions and independent expenditures to advance the political interests of the AMA.

AMPAC is a large, institutionalized PAC with a complex structure and decision-making process. This can make it difficult to respond effectively to changes in the environment. However, because AMPAC has long been committed to establishing a conservative majority in Congress, it fared quite well in the 1994 and 1996 elections.

Recent changes in the health care system have put the AMA on the defensive. Fifty years ago, the AMA was clearly the dominant force in U.S. health policy (Starr 1982). At the close of the twentieth century, it must compete with a growing number of health policy interest groups (Peterson 1993). Nevertheless, its formidable resources and close alliance with the Republican majority in Congress make it a major player in health policy.

Evolution of the AMA

The AMA was founded in 1847 to advance medical education and establish a
code of professional ethics for physicians, and until the 1960s it was primarily
a scientific organization (Starr 1982).[2] Following the adoption of Medicare in
1965, a major political defeat for the AMA, a new generation of leaders,
many of whom had experience in AMPAC, assumed the leadership of the
AMA and forced the older generation of "purists," who stressed the scientific
and educational functions of the association, from power (Campion 1984).

   The central function of the contemporary AMA is representing the interests of physicians to the public, the press, and government (American Medical
Association 1996). Providing and evaluating scientific information is clearly a
secondary mission for the AMA, though through its scientific committees and
publications it continues to have an enormous effect on what physicians and
the public know about health and medical care (Wolinsky and Brune 1994, 2).

Organization and Decision Making

The AMA has a federated structure that is similar to the National Association
of Realtors (Bedlington 1994). The national organization, which is governed
by a House of Delegates, has its headquarters in Chicago, Illinois. The
House of Delegates, which meets twice each year, is the policy-making body
of the AMA (Campion 1984, 47). Members of the House of Delegates
include representatives from the fifty state medical associations and the medical associations of the District of Columbia, Guam, Puerto Rico, and the
Virgin Islands. Most AMA delegates have been active and held offices in their
state and local medical societies (Garceau 1941).

   The House of Delegates debates and votes on hundreds of resolutions on
a wide range of medical care and public health issues, and it also elects the
AMA's powerful Board of Trustees, which consists of fifteen members, including the AMA president and chairman. The board meets five to six times a year
and has the authority to make policy decisions between the biannual sessions
of the House. The board is much more closely involved than the full House of
Delegates with day-to-day AMA operations and the association's staff.

   The association's professional staff of twelve hundred, led by the association's executive vice president, who acts as its chief executive officer, has
enormous influence on AMA policy (Campion 1984; Garceau 1941). Although
there is some debate about the autonomy of the professional staff (Garceau
1941, 84; Pressman 1984, 17), there are constraints placed on AMA lobbyists
by its House of Delegates. These constraints help to explain why other
health lobbyists often accuse the AMA of being inflexible and uncooperative
when they participate in coalitions (Gardner 1997).

Membership and Resources

The AMA often presents itself as the "voice of medicine." For years, it was difficult to argue with this rather bold claim. At its peak in the 1940s, nearly 90 percent of U.S. physicians belonged to the AMA (Rayack 1967). However, since the 1960s, that percentage has declined. According to the AMA, just over 40 percent of eligible physicians are members of the organization (Moore 1996). Instead of joining the AMA, many physicians now join associations of specialists like the American College of Surgeons. In addition, many physicians who work in HMOs and other forms of managed care belong to the Group Health Association of America, rather than the AMA (Baumgartner and Talbert 1995).

Responding to the decline in its membership, the AMA is engaged in an aggressive campaign to boost enrollment. The AMA's weekly newspaper has a new section called "AMA for You" that emphasizes the benefits of membership. It also specifically hired ten new staff members in 1996 to sign up new members (Moore 1996).

Despite this decline in membership, AMA officials still try to claim broader representation. When Hillary Rodham Clinton spoke at the group's annual meeting in 1993, they claimed that the AMA represents "Ninety percent of the doctors in the country and a hundred percent of the patients" (Wolinsky and Brune 1994). This claim, however, accounts for the physicians who belong to the various specialty societies that are affiliated with the AMA. It does not reflect those who belong directly to the AMA itself.

While the percentage of physicians who belong to the AMA has declined significantly over the last forty years, it still enjoys an impressive array of resources. Dues for full members are $420, about a quarter of which is used for lobbying efforts (Wolinsky and Brune 1994). Before Congress adopted lobby reform in 1995, information about the total spent by the AMA on political activities was incomplete and difficult to obtain. However, according to one estimate, it spent roughly $100 million on its Washington office and various political education campaigns between 1970 and 1993 (Wolinsky and Brune 1994). According to the first federal disclosure reports required by the new lobby reform law, the AMA spent $8.7 million in lobbying expenses during the first half of 1996, second only to Phillip Morris, and more than any other health care group (Weissenstein 1996). By comparison, the American Hospital Association spent less than $2 million.

The AMA also benefits from the grassroots political activity of its members. Doctors are politically active in virtually every congressional district (Andelman 1997). As one health care lobbyist stated, "Every congressman has a doc or a couple of docs who are on their steering committee" (Gardner 1997). This kind of mobilization gets the attention of members of Congress. Representative Fortney "Pete" Stark (D–CA), a frequent opponent of the

AMA, attributes much of the association's power in Congress to its grassroots activity. According to Stark, "My colleagues listen to folks from home and that's the AMA's strength" (Feder 1993). The association works to mobilize these physicians through the Physicians Grassroots Network, which has over one hundred thousand members. As a result, many congressional staffers claim that individual physicians from the AMA's grassroots network visit their offices more often than the association's professional Washington lobbyists (Gardner 1997).

During the late 1980s and early to middle 1990s, the AMA and AMPAC have facilitated this grassroots activity. As late as the mid-1980s, the AMA did not have an effective grassroots organization (Pressman 1984, 19). Since then, however, the AMA and AMPAC cosponsor political education and grassroots training courses, "designed to assist members of the medical community in their legislative efforts on behalf of patients and organized medicine" (AMA 1997). The AMA also conducts a biennial political grassroots conference in Washington, DC, during which physician activists are briefed on current legislation and given the opportunity to meet with congressional leaders and leading political consultants.

Standing Out in a Growing Crowd

While the AMA may still be the "proverbial eight hundred pound gorilla on Capitol Hill" (Wolinsky and Brune 1994), it is now forced to compete for influence with a growing number of health policy interest groups, including several rival physicians' groups (Peterson 1993). For most of this century, health care policy was dominated by a relatively small coalition of providers and business interests, in which the AMA was clearly the dominant player. During the 1990s, the health care interest community has grown and fragmented in spectacular fashion (Peterson 1993). Between 1979 and 1992, the number of national health interest groups in Washington, DC, grew from 117 to 741 (Pear 1993b). Similarly, the number of health PACs increased by 28 percent between 1989 and 1992 (Weissert and Weissert 1996). Although more than 43 percent of all health PAC contributions in 1980 came from AMPAC, by 1990 this percentage had dropped by half (Wolinsky and Brune 1994). The AMA must compete not only with other provider groups but also with public and private purchasers who want to keep their health costs in line and with managed care organizations that try to assert greater control over the clinical decisions of doctors.

The debate surrounding the Clinton health care reform proposal illustrates the split within the health policy community. Rather than dominating the debate, the AMA faced competition from a number of other physician groups, including the American College of Surgeons and American Academy of Family Physicians, that expressed support for a single payer approach (Pear 1993a). Disagreement over policy among physicians is certainly not a new phenomenon, but the tensions within contemporary medicine are more acute than ever (Garceau 1941; Peterson 1993).

Along with these new challenges from other provider groups, the AMA now finds itself at odds with its longtime ally: the business community. Historically, business supported organized medicine's opposition to government involvement in the health care system, but growing health care costs have damaged this relationship. In 1980, one survey found that corporations were neither concerned nor motivated to do anything about their health care costs (Sapolsky et al. 1981). By the early 1990s, however, businesses were more concerned with health costs and supportive of a government solution (*Business and Health* 1991). In 1991, the Washington Business Group on Health, an association of large corporations, found that 89 percent of their members believed that broad reform was necessary to fix the health care system. Even after the collapse of health care reform at the national level, employers continue to encourage greater use of managed care to hold down health costs.

Indeed, the demise of health care reform in Congress preceded a dramatic transformation of the health care system in the United States (Thorpe 1996). More than 70 percent of Americans with private, employer-paid health insurance are currently enrolled in some form of managed care (Wolf and Gorman 1996). This presents a new challenge for the AMA and its physicians. Managed care organizations (MCOs) often try to lower their costs by reducing the utilization of medical services (Luft 1981). This leads to struggles between MCOs and physicians over which services are actually "medically necessary." In short, the AMA is in a fight with these organizations over physician autonomy.

In response to the pressure created by these competing groups, the AMA's attitude toward the need for health care reform underwent an important shift in the early 1990s. In a striking reversal, the AMA developed its own health reform proposal that called for universal access to health care. When it appeared that national health reform was inevitable, the AMA moved away from an obstructionist position to one of compromise and negotiation (Pear 1993b).

The AMA's support for health care reform was short-lived, however. Pressure from the Republican leadership in Congress led the association to back away from its support for reform. Newt Gingrich and other House Republicans sent a letter to the AMA, which stated, "We are dismayed by the actions of the leadership of the AMA...[who are] out of touch with rank-and-file physicians." In response to this pressure, the AMA made it clear that it did not support the administration's reform proposal (Pear 1994).

The Formation of AMPAC

When the AMA created AMPAC in May 1961, it became the first trade association to establish a political action committee. The election of President

Kennedy in 1960 and his support of Medicare provided the impetus for establishing AMPAC, but it had actually been in the works for years. Near the end of the Depression, the AMA founded the National Physician's Committee for the Extension of Medical Service to finance its political activities and bolster its political power. The committee spent $1 million on advertisements before it was disbanded in 1948 after an embarrassing episode in which they mailed a letter to physicians addressing "fellow Christians" (Wolinsky and Brune 1994, 70). The AMA's interest in creating a PAC was renewed when the AFL-CIO established COPE in 1955 (Campion 1984). After Representative Abe Forand introduced the first version of Medicare in 1957, the AMA set the process for establishing AMPAC in motion (Fein 1986).

In 1958, the Board of Trustees and the Council on Legislative Activities asked AMA lawyers to investigate the legal implications of forming a PAC (Campion 1984, 211). AMA board members were concerned that establishing a PAC would threaten the group's tax-exempt status. They were also concerned that an autonomous PAC might strip power away from the AMA itself. Although at least eight state medical societies had already established their own PACs, the AMA did not move forward until the 1960 election. Once Kennedy defeated Nixon, the Board of Trustees acted quickly to create AMPAC.

Membership in AMPAC is open to physicians and their family members. The governing body is a seven-member Board of Trustees. The AMA's Board of Trustees appoints the directors of AMPAC's board to a one-year term. The AMPAC board appoints the executive director, who is responsible for the PAC's day-to-day operations and has a great deal of influence on spending decisions.

AMPAC has consistently ranked in the top ten in receipts among all PACs, and it is by far the largest health care PAC (Weissert and Weissert 1996). What makes AMPAC even more formidable is the fact that, unlike many PACs, a large percentage of its receipts are used for contributions to candidates. The rest is spent on overhead for the group and information distribution programs for AMA members and the press (Sabato 1984, 16–17).

AMPAC's board decided early to stay out of presidential campaigns because endorsing presidential candidates would effectively prevent them from pursuing a bipartisan strategy. According to Joe Miller, AMPAC's first executive director, "For an organization like AMPAC to be successful...you have to keep your lines of communication open with the leadership of both parties" (Campion 1984, 219).[3] While committed to a bipartisan strategy, AMPAC has an explicit ideological bias. Its primary political goal is to elect a strong conservative, bipartisan coalition in Congress (Campion 1984). In practice, this has usually led AMPAC to contribute more money to Republican congressional candidates.

AMPAC Decision Making

Like other institutionalized committees, AMPAC has a complex process for making contribution decisions (Herrnson and Wilcox 1994, 242). Its Congressional Review Committee, headed by the chairman of AMPAC and three other directors, decides how to target the committee's funds. All final decisions must be approved by the full board of trustees.

The Review Committee first considers the competitiveness of the election. During its early years, AMPAC only contributed to candidates competing in elections likely to be decided by less than 5 percent (Campion 1984). While it has broadened the scope of its contributions considerably, it still provides more support to candidates in close elections.

Along with the competitiveness of the election, ideology and support for the AMA's policy agenda are also important criteria for AMPAC. The committee regularly solicits input from state and local medical societies, not only on these matters, but to learn more about the quality of each candidate's campaign organization. Occasionally, there is some tension between local committees and the Washington office. Local committees tend to focus more on ideology, whereas the Washington office tries to balance ideological considerations with issues important to the AMA's lobbyists, including incumbency and position within the chamber. According to the AMA, disagreements between the local committees and the Washington office are rare (Campion 1984, 228).

In addition to gathering information from its state and local committees, AMPAC regularly consults with leaders from both major parties, particularly for information about incumbents and their support for the AMA's legislative agenda. AMPAC has often enjoyed a particularly close working relationship with the Republican leadership in Congress. In the 1960s, for example, Representative Gerald Ford worked with AMPAC to help identify candidates for the House (Sammons 1991, 23).

AMPAC tries to downplay the conflicts that exist within the organization, but its Washington office is sometimes constrained by the PAC's complicated decision-making structure and the demands of state affiliates (Campion 1984). To counter these problems, it created separate decision-making procedures for contributions and independent expenditures. The decision-making process for independent expenditures gives much "greater latitude to their professional staff" and provides the Washington office with a degree of flexibility (Biersack et al. 1994, 252).

The AMA and AMPAC

The AMA took great pains to establish AMPAC as an independent organization. It even located the offices of AMPAC three blocks away from the AMA headquarters to emphasize the separation. Yet there were and still are strong ties between the two organizations. AMPAC's directors are not only appointed to one-year terms by the AMA board of trustees, AMPAC was also dependent on the AMA for almost all of its nonpolitical operating funds until 1972. In the 1970s several confidential AMA memos that were leaked to the press suggested that AMPAC responded directly to the requests of the AMA's Washington lobbyists by contributing to specific candidates (Wolinsky and Brune 1994, 76).

For the first three years of AMPAC's existence, the AMA also took advantage of its relationship with the pharmaceutical industry and arranged $1 million in "soft" money support from seventeen of the largest pharmaceutical manufacturing companies in the country (Campion 1984, 220).[4] In recent years the AMA and AMPAC have engaged in more overt efforts to coordinate their activities. In the 1980s, Kevin Walker, AMPAC's treasurer (who later became its executive director), established the AMA's physician grassroots program, known as the Division of Political and Legislative Grassroots (POLEGRA). This program is an explicit attempt to coordinate AMPAC's campaign activities with the lobbying efforts of the AMA. As the AMA describes it, "POLEGRA programming is targeted to ensure that contributors get the maximum impact for their dollar" (AMA 1996). Through POLEGRA, the AMA and AMPAC keep members up-to-date on what is happening on the Hill through "blast faxes" and a toll-free hotline that has continually updated information about congressional action on important health issues.

Campaign Activity: Securing Access and Taking Risks

The AMA's involvement in congressional elections predates the formation of AMPAC in 1961. In 1950, the AMA conducted a $3.1 million advertising campaign to elect conservative congressional candidates (Wolinsky and Brune 1994, 70). Throughout the 1950s, the national and state organizations ran campaigns designed to defeat liberal congressional candidates.

The most striking feature of AMPAC's congressional contributions is their scope. Its vast resources permit AMPAC to get involved in most congressional races not only because it has enough money to spread around, but also because it has "the organizational resources to monitor closely a number of races" (Biersack et al. 1994, 242). While the ability to get involved in many races is part of AMPAC's strength, it is a challenging strategy for the organization. According to campaign finance expert Herbert Alexander, "AMPAC has had so much money it has a hard time distributing it" (Wolinsky and Brune 1994).

Large institutionalized PACs tend to direct most of their contributions to incumbents running for reelection, and AMPAC is no exception (Alexander 1992; Biersack et al. 1994). It regularly gives about 70 percent of its House contributions to incumbents and about 50 percent of its Senate contributions to incumbents. Even in 1992, when there were an unusually large number of retirements and vulnerable incumbents, approximately 60 percent of AMPAC's contributions went to incumbents. Furthermore, AMPAC targets incumbents who are members of important health committees, particularly committee chairs (Gusmano and Tennant 1993). When AMPAC was formed, it gave large contributions to conservatives on the Ways and Means Committee in the House (Wolinsky and Brune 1994).

AMPAC officials stress that party affiliation is not a factor in their contribution decisions. Historically, AMPAC has contributed to a roughly equal number of Democratic and Republican candidates, but the amount of money contributed to Republicans has always been significantly higher (Wolinsky and Brune 1994). Support for the AMA's policy agenda is clearly an important factor for AMPAC, but questions remain regarding which policies are most important. A recent analysis by Sharfstein and Sharfstein demonstrated that AMPAC contributed more to members of the 103rd Congress who voted against the AMA on three key public health issues—tobacco export promotion, handgun control, and the "gag rule" prohibiting doctors in federally funded clinics from discussing abortion with their patients—than it gave to members who voted with the AMA on these issues (Wolinsky and Brune 1994). Many of those supported were political conservatives, who tended to oppose AMA positions on public health issues. Conservative members of Congress may be more likely to agree with the AMA on economic or political issues, but there is no direct evidence supporting such a claim. The belief that AMPAC and the AMA put the financial concerns of physicians ahead of public health issues is widespread. As Wolinsky and Brune put it, "If you believe the AMA's claims that your well-being as a patient is its first priority, then you probably believe that Marcus Welby was a real doctor" (Wolinsky and Brune 1994, 3).

AMPAC has been cited as one of the more aggressive "punishment PACs." In 1980 AMPAC gave the maximum contribution to defeat House member Andrew McGuire (D–NJ) after AMA officials found him difficult to work with in committee (Sabato 1984, 129). AMPAC also used votes on President Carter's hospital cost containment proposal as a litmus test in 1980. It contributed an average of $2,500 to incumbents who voted against cost containment compared to an average of $340 to those who voted for the bill (Wright 1983). These differences were significant even after controlling for ideology. These findings also lend support to the notion that AMPAC places an emphasis on the economic concerns of physicians.

AMPAC's use of both punishment and reward strategies is illustrated by its use of independent expenditures. The AMA is well versed on the use of advertising in pursuit of its objectives. In the late 1940s and early 1950s, the AMA spent millions of dollars in magazine, radio, and newspaper advertisements attacking national health insurance as "socialized medicine" (Starr

1982). In 1949, it hired a public relations firm, Whitaker and Baxter, to promote the group's opposition to President Truman's national health insurance proposals (Schlozman and Tierney 1986, 174). However, the AMA did not become involved in specific political advertising in support or opposition of a candidate for office until the 1980s.

The National Conservative Political Action Committee (NCPAC) was the first group to take advantage of independent expenditures when it spent almost $4 million in advertising against six incumbent liberal Democratic senators in 1980 (Malbin 1984). The success of NCPAC and other ideological PACs in the early 1980s encouraged a number of trade association PACs to adopt this strategy by the end of the decade (Biersack et al. 1994).

In 1986, AMPAC engaged in independent expenditure campaigns against Democratic representatives Pete Stark of California and Andrew Jacobs of Indiana, both of whom were members of the Ways and Means Subcommittee on Health. Jacobs was targeted because of his support for limiting payments to physicians under Medicare. Stark angered the AMA when he called physicians rich, greedy troglodytes. AMPAC spent $252,199 on "billboards, benchmark surveys, tracking polls, radio ads, direct mail, flyers, opposition research, and consultants" in its attempt to defeat Stark (Wolinsky and Brune 1994, 88). Stark used the AMPAC campaign to his advantage. He ignored his opponent, made the AMA the focus of his campaign, and was reelected with 70 percent of the vote.

AMPAC set a record for independent expenditures in a single race with its campaign against Andrew Jacobs. It spent $315,838 on advertisements, polls, and consultants to try to defeat Jacobs. Again, its efforts were unsuccessful. Jacobs was reelected with 58 percent of the vote. In 1988, AMPAC's chairman announced that they would no longer engage in independent expenditure campaigns against secure incumbents (Wolinsky and Brune 1994, 90).

The backlash from the Stark and Jacobs campaigns caused AMPAC to become somewhat more risk-averse but did not lead it away from taking strong political stands. The PAC may have backed away from its punishment strategy, but it continues to use independent expenditures to reward members of Congress who support the AMA's policy agenda.

In 1992, in anticipation of the upcoming debate on health care reform, AMPAC spent heavily on behalf of several individuals whom they considered influential members of Congress. For example, AMPAC provided a great deal of support for Republican Senator Bob Packwood who was opposed by Democratic House member Les AuCoin in Oregon. AMPAC spent heavily on behalf of Packwood throughout the election, and, when the polls showed that AuCoin was getting close, it took out a number of advertisements in the last two weeks of the campaign costing $227, 808 (Gusmano and Tennant 1993).

In addition to its efforts on behalf of candidates, AMPAC provides hard and soft money support to the major political parties. It is also one of many committees that carries out "activities that have traditionally been conducted by political parties" (Herrnson 1995, 121). AMPAC provides candidates with a variety of in-kind contributions. It has funded surveys that cost over $380,000, but it uses a depreciation option to minimize the size of the contribution reported to the Federal Election Commission (Sabato 1984, 94). PACs are allowed to depreciate a poll by 50 percent if they do not share it with candidates for sixteen days, and they can depreciate the poll 95 percent if PACs wait more than sixty days. AMPAC also provides candidates with opposition research and occasionally pays the travel costs of congressional staffers who visit their members' district (Pressman 1984; Weissert and Weissert 1996).

The AMA and AMPAC recruit and train congressional candidates and their volunteers. AMPAC's five-day campaign academy is run by some of the nation's leading political consultants. The academy provides physicians with the skills they need to be effective campaign volunteers. The AMA and AMPAC also run a program called "Medicine's Candidate: A Prescription for Political Success," which is designed to encourage physicians and their spouses to run for office. The program teaches these individuals how to raise money, develop a message, and become an effective public speaker. It is important to note that AMPAC is not always supportive of a candidate just because the person is a physician. Again, AMPAC's failure to support some physician candidates can cause tension between the Washington office, the state medical societies, and local PACs that want to back their candidate.

The 1994 Elections

Institutionalized PACs, like AMPAC, do not always respond quickly to changes in the environment, but the Republican victories in the 1994 midterm election did not take the AMA by surprise (Herrnson and Wilcox 1994). Anticipating a Republican takeover, and faced with a number of quality Republican challengers, AMPAC targeted Republican candidates to an even greater degree than in the 1992 election. The proportion of AMPAC contributions to House Republican candidates increased from about 50 percent of its total House contributions in 1992 to 55 percent in 1994 (see Table 4.1). The level of contributions to Senate Republican candidates increased even more dramatically, jumping from about 59 percent of AMPAC's total Senate contributions to over 82 percent (see Table 4.1).

AMPAC backed thirty Republican challengers running for the House in 1994, compared to eighteen in 1992. Furthermore, twenty-six of these thirty were in competitive elections, compared to only six in the previous election.

Table 4.1 AMPAC Contributions to House Candidates in the 1992, 1994, and 1996 Elections

	1992	1994	1996
DEMOCRATS			
Incumbents			
Shoo-Ins	17%	15%	6%
In Jeopardy	21	25	5
Challengers			
Hopefuls	1	0	0
Likely Losers	1	2	1
Open-Seat			
Prospects	4	3	5
Long Shots	6	1	2
REPUBLICANS			
Incumbents			
Shoo-Ins	19	29	32
In Jeopardy	13	6	28
Challengers			
Hopefuls	1	6.5	5
Likely Losers	2	.5	3
Open-Seat			
Prospects	10	10	12
Long Shots	5	3	1
Total Contributions	$2,318,077	$2,080,995	$1,878,453

Source: Compiled from Federal Election Commission data.
Note: Incumbents in jeopardy, hopeful challengers, and open-seat prospects are all defined as those who lost or who won by 20 percent or less of the two-party vote. Shoo-ins are incumbents who won by more than 20 percent of the two-party vote. Likely-loser challengers and long-shot open-seat candidates are those who lost by more than 20 percent of the two-party vote.

On the other hand, AMPAC contributed to fewer House Republican open-seat candidates in 1994. It also increased the number of Republican Senate challengers it supported from three to eight, and the number of Republican Senate open-seat candidates from seven to ten.

While there was a decrease in both the number of Democratic candidates that AMPAC supported and the amount of money they received, more of the PAC's money was targeted to House and Senate Democratic incumbents in jeopardy of losing. Among House candidates, the percentage of

Democratic incumbents in close races who received money from AMPAC increased from 33 to 49 percent between 1992 and 1994. The total number of Senate Democratic incumbents that AMPAC supported fell from sixteen to seven in 1994, but five of those candidates were in close races. AMPAC supported only six Senate Democratic incumbents in close races in 1992.

Despite the greater concentration on close races in 1994, AMPAC supported more winners that year than it had in 1992. In fact, over 79 percent of the candidates who received AMPAC contributions won in the general election, compared to just over 72 percent in the 1992 election. Unlike many PACs, AMPAC did not have to make up for "backing the wrong horses," and scramble to retire the campaign debts of newly elected Republican members following the 1994 election (Weissert and Weissert 1996; Weisskopf 1995).

Access and Lobbying in the 104th Congress

While the AMA has always enjoyed substantial access to members of Congress, the Republican takeover of Congress after the 1994 election improved its relations with key policy makers. The increase in access enjoyed by the AMA can be illustrated by comparing its role in shaping health care reform proposals in the 103rd Congress with its role in developing the Republican plan to reform Medicare. The Clinton White House and its congressional allies did not involve the AMA in the initial health care reform process (Pear 1993a). By comparison, the AMA was invited to negotiate directly with the Speaker about the Medicare changes proposed by the Republican leadership (Gardner 1997; Pear 1994).

At first glance, it appears that the 1994 election may have hurt the fundraising efforts of the AMA. Its total receipts fell from $4,465,815 in 1994 to $3,943,172 in 1996. The Republican majority in Congress represents less of a threat to AMA members and, as a result, the association is having more trouble raising money. Even though AMPAC's receipts decreased between 1994 and 1996, the PAC currently has its highest membership in four years (AMA 1996).

Comprehensive health care reform was no longer on the agenda, but health care issues continued to play an important role after the 1994 election. The 104th Congress worked on a host of issues that were meaningful to the AMA. The association took advantage of public anxiety about managed care and helped to push anti–managed care legislation through Congress, including a ban on "drive through deliveries" and "gag clauses," which are used by managed care plans to restrict medical communications between physicians and their patients. It also supported the Kassebaum–Kennedy health insurance reform law, which extends the portability of employer-paid health insurance, restricts the use of preexisting conditions, and creates a demonstration project to test the effectiveness of Medical Savings Accounts (MSAs). Its efforts were not enough to help enact either the Medicare Preservation Act or the Product Liability Bill, but, in general, the AMA's lobbying efforts in the 104th Congress were quite successful.

Clearly, the most important health care initiative in the 104th Congress was the Republican Medicare reform proposal. The new Republican majority committed itself to a balanced budget by the year 2002, a $245 billion tax cut, and higher defense spending. They quickly discovered that it was impossible to achieve these goals without cutting Medicare and Medicaid. The Republican Medicare proposal called for $270 billion in cuts that would be paid for with higher premiums for upper-income beneficiaries, reduced rates for hospitals and physicians, and incentives to expand the use of managed care and establish medical savings accounts (Clymer 1995).

Initially, the AMA voiced support for the GOP proposal, but it backed away when it became concerned that a large percentage of the $270 billion in Medicare savings would come from reductions in payments to physicians (Clymer 1995). House Speaker Newt Gingrich then began direct negotiations with the AMA. Gingrich wanted the AMA to announce its support for the Republican Medicare proposal and to mobilize its physician grassroots network on its behalf (Gardner 1997). The AMA agreed to support the measure in return for a number of concessions. Not only did the Speaker agree to scale back physician fee cuts, he also agreed to allow physicians to create their own health plans without the financial reserve requirements faced by other managed care plans. In addition, the Republican proposal would promote medical savings accounts without any limits on physician billing (Pear 1995a; Schear 1996). After this meeting with Gingrich, the AMA announced its support for the Republican Medicare plan (Pear 1995b).

The negotiations with Gingrich represented a tremendous victory for the AMA, but its statements to the press following the meeting strained its relationship with the Republican majority. AMA officials told the press that "they cut a great deal that averted billions of dollars in Medicare physician fee cuts" (Gardner 1997). Democrats quickly accused the Republicans of bribing doctors to support their Medicare plan. This put the Republican leadership on the defensive and angered a number of Republican members and their staffs. Representative William Thomas (R–CA) accused the AMA of misrepresenting the meeting, and a number of congressional staffers stopped speaking with AMA lobbyists (Gardner 1997). The AMA, however, claims that it still enjoys a good relationship with the leadership.

Although President Clinton eventually vetoed the Republican Medicare reform bill, the AMA viewed the process of negotiation in the House as an important victory for the association. According to the AMA, "the House GOP plan agrees with AMA positions on many critical issues.... The bill represents an advocacy accomplishment by organized medicine" (AMA 1995).

The AMA clearly enjoyed greater support for its legislative agenda in the 104th Congress and had a much better working relationship with congressional leaders. As one AMA official stated, "throughout this exceptional year the AMA was a significant player" (AMA 1996). These themes were emphasized in the AMA's publications and in its solicitations to contributors during the 1996 campaign.

The 1996 Elections

The AMA continued to follow a bipartisan strategy in the 1996 congressional elections, but it was clearly pleased with the general direction of the Republican-controlled 104th Congress. In the association's newspaper, the AMA encouraged its members to support the efforts of the GOP. In an editorial on Medicare reform published in the *American Medical News*, the AMA praised the Republican Party, not only for supporting much of its legislative agenda but for treating doctors with greater respect.

> It's also important not to lose sight of something else the House GOP [Medicare] proposal represents. It has to do with a matter of trust. The AMA's position consistently has been that when writing the rules that govern health care, "the devil is in the details." Some policymakers clearly had another idea in mind—that the devil is in the doctor. The House GOP's Medicare proposal rejects that notion and helps tug the devil's mask off the medical profession (AMA 1995).

AMPAC's executive director Kevin Walker predicted early in the campaign that the Republicans would maintain their majority in both houses of Congress (*Campaigns & Elections* 1995). Both of these factors were reflected in AMPAC's spending patterns in the 1996 election (see Tables 4.1 and 4.2).

There was a huge increase in money contributed by AMPAC to House Republican candidates. The percentage of AMPAC contributions to House Republican candidates jumped from 55 percent in 1994 to over 81 percent in 1996. Roughly 75 percent of the contributions to House Republican candidates went to incumbents. In general, the distribution of AMPAC's contributions between 1996 House incumbents, challengers, and open-seat candidates did not change significantly. It contributed over 71 percent to incumbents, 20 percent to open-seat candidates, and only about 9 percent to challengers.

The percentage of AMPAC contributions to Senate Republican candidates did not change substantially. As was the case in 1994, over 80 percent of AMPAC's contributions in Senate races went to Republican candidates. There was a dramatic increase, however, in the percentage of contributions to Senate open-seat candidates. More than 42 percent of AMPAC's contributions to Senate Republican candidates were for open-seat candidates, compared to

Table 4.2 AMPAC Contributions to Senate Candidates in the 1992, 1994, and 1996 Elections

	1992	1994	1996
DEMOCRATS			
Incumbents			
Shoo-Ins	15%	4%	0%
In jeopardy	16	12	6
Challengers			
Hopefuls	0	0	0
Likely Losers	0	0	0
Open-Seat			
Prospects	9	0	10
Long Shots	2	3	1
REPUBLICANS			
Incumbents			
Shoo-Ins	8	22	9
In jeopardy	22	18	33
Challengers			
Hopefuls	10	14	4
Likely Losers	2	4	2
Open-Seat			
Prospects	10	22	34
Long Shots	7	2	2
Total Contributions	$228,917	$259,600	$263,230

Source: Compiled from Federal Election Commission data.
Note: Incumbents in jeopardy, hopeful challengers, and open-seat prospects are all defined as those who lost or who won by 20 percent or less of the two-party vote. Shoo-ins are incumbents who won by more than 20 percent of the two-party vote. Likely-loser challengers and long-shot open-seat candidates are those who lost by more than 20 percent of the two-party vote. Some columns do not add to 100 percent due to rounding.

29 percent in 1994. Among Senate Democratic candidates, the shift to open-seat candidates was even more extraordinary, reflecting the unusually large number of open seats. AMPAC gave 65 percent of its contributions to Senate Democratic open-seat candidates in 1996, compared to only 16 percent in 1994. Three of the five Democratic open-seat candidates and ten of the fourteen Republican open-seat candidates running for the Senate in 1996 were in close races.

For the second election in a row, more than 79 percent of the candidates who received contributions from AMPAC won in the general election. The PAC had more success in the House, where 81 percent of the candidates it supported (308 candidates) won in the general election. In the Senate, 56 percent of the candidates AMPAC supported (twenty-two candidates) won in the general election.

After making no independent expenditures in 1994, AMPAC made $388,137 in independent expenditures on behalf of five House candidates and $129,697 on behalf of one Senate candidate in 1996. All of its independent expenditures were made on behalf of candidates in extremely close races, and only one candidate lost. These candidates won or lost by an average of 3 percent of the vote in the general election.

In the House, more than 90 percent of AMPAC's independent expenditures went to Republican candidates, over half of which were spent on incumbents. AMPAC only made independent expenditures on behalf of one Democrat, open-seat candidate Victor Snyder, who was elected to represent Arkansas's second district with 52 percent of the vote. The lone Senate candidate to benefit from AMPAC independent expenditures was also an open-seat candidate.

The shift of AMPAC money to Republican Party candidates is also evident when examining its pattern of in-kind contributions. House Republican candidates received 88 percent of AMPAC's in-kind contributions in 1996, compared to 76 percent in 1994, and only 53 percent in 1992. AMPAC provided $114,866 of in-kind contributions to House Republican candidates, compared to only $15,593 to House Democratic candidates.

Over three-quarters of AMPAC's in-kind contributions to House Republican candidates went to incumbents, most of whom were in close elections. For example, the PAC gave a poll to Representative Fred Heineman, who lost a tight race to former Congressman David Price in North Carolina's fourth district. Ironically, Price was the recipient of a poll purchased by AMPAC when he ran as an incumbent in 1990 (Herrnson 1995). AMPAC also provided a poll to Representative J. C. Watts of Oklahoma, who defeated state representative Ed Crocker in another close contest. Indeed, the vast majority of House Republican candidates who received in-kind contributions from AMPAC won.

AMPAC gave in-kind contributions to only two House Democratic incumbents, Gene Taylor of Mississippi and Frederick Boucher of Virginia, both of whom were reelected. AMPAC contributed polls to three House Democratic open-seat candidates, two of whom were successful. Jim Turner narrowly defeated Brian Babin with 52 percent of the vote in Texas's second district, and Virgil Goode defeated George Landrith with 60 percent of the vote in Virginia's fifth district. Ben Graber, the third Democratic open-seat candidate to receive a poll from AMPAC, lost to state senator Robert Wexler in Florida's Democratic primary. Richard Hill, who lost a primary bid to become the Democratic candidate in Washington state's ninth district, was the only House Democratic challenger to receive an in-kind contribution from AMPAC.

AMPAC usually does not provide a great deal of in-kind support to Senate candidates, and this trend continued in 1996. After giving in-kind contributions worth $4,636 to three Senate Republican incumbents in 1994, AMPAC made in-kind contributions worth $5,705 to two Senate Republican open-seat candidates in 1996. One of these candidates, Wayne Allard, won in an extremely close contest with Tom Strickland for retiring Republican Senator Hank Brown's seat in Colorado. The other, John Barrasso, lost to Michael Enzi in Wyoming's Republican primary. AMPAC did not give any in-kind support to Democratic Senate candidates in 1994 or 1996.

The GOP's new majority status in Congress also encouraged AMPAC to shift its soft money contributions to the Republican Party. In 1992, AMPAC contributed over $32,000 in soft money to the Democratic Party and only about $14,000 to the Republican Party. In 1994, these percentages were reversed with over $41,000 given to the Republican Party and $19,000 given to the Democratic Party. Soft money support for the Republican Party from AMPAC exploded in 1996, however. AMPAC contributed $91,200 to the Republican Party but only $5,250 to the Democratic Party.

Conclusions

The evolution of the U.S. health care system has changed the dynamics of health care policy making. Not only is the AMA unable to claim to be the unchallenged "voice of medicine," it is now forced to compete for influence with insurance companies, managed care organizations, and representatives of businesses interested in reducing health care costs. While the AMA's dominance has clearly been challenged, the group is still a formidable political force on Capitol Hill. The results of the 1994 and 1996 elections helped to reinforce its power.

Historically, AMPAC has tried to balance its goal of creating a conservative, bipartisan coalition in Congress with the need to maintain access to members of Congress for AMA lobbyists. As a result, it gave a large percentage of its contributions to Republican incumbents running for reelection. This strategy served the AMA well in the 1994 elections. After the 1994 general election results were in, AMPAC found that it had backed even more winners than in the previous election. Furthermore, AMA lobbyists enjoyed greater access to congressional leaders and found more support for their legislative agenda. This resulted in an extraordinary shift in resources toward the Republican Party in 1996.

Notes

[1]The AMA refused to participate in this study. According to a spokesperson, "The issue of campaign finance is extremely volatile, so as a matter of policy we do not participate in this type of study."

[2]Before 1982, physicians were required to join their county and state medical societies before they could become members of the AMA.

[3]Although AMPAC does not get involved directly in presidential elections, five former AMA presidents created a separate committee called "Physicians for Reagan-Bush," in 1980. The committee took out a full-page ad to endorse the Republican ticket in the *AMA News* (Wolinsky and Brune 1994).

[4]According to Donald W. Light, the AMA developed a close relationship with the pharmaceutical industry in the United States at the turn of the twentieth century. Despite repeated efforts by the medical profession to maintain control over the pharmaceutical industry, many critics argue that they are now dependent on it for many facets of their professional life (Light 1991).

CHAPTER 5

POLITICAL FIREPOWER:
THE NATIONAL RIFLE ASSOCIATION

Kelly D. Patterson

The National Rifle Association (NRA) is one of the most powerful ideological interest groups. Its stated goal is to promote and protect the rights of gun owners, and it has zeroed in on this goal like few other interest groups. Many organizations as large and complex as the NRA lose their commitment to the rank-and-file members, but the NRA's strategy of seeking the opinions of its members has produced some fairly impressive results. Very few interest groups have such strong reputations for grassroots firepower. Consequently, very few organizations are as active in so many campaigns.

The 1996 elections featured a large number of close races and a significant number of vulnerable freshmen. The NRA strongly desired to retain the pro-gun majority in the House that had voted to repeal the assault weapons ban in 1996. This electoral environment taxed the decision-making and financial resources of the organization and forced it to adopt different strategies for House and Senate races. In the end, the NRA participated in over ten thousand races at the local, state, and national level and claimed to be successful in 84 percent of those races, up from its 82 percent success rate in 1994 (http://www.nra.org/exec.office/tkm1196.html). The NRA can participate in so many races because of its aggressive fund-raising efforts, the loyalty of its membership, leadership at the national office that is willing to listen to its rank-and-file members, and innovative campaign activities that maximize its effectiveness.

History

The NRA was founded in 1871 to improve the marksmanship of the Union Army in the aftermath of the Civil War. Low levels of membership and very little activity characterized the first thirty years of the NRA's existence

(Spitzer 1995).[1] The organization grew slowly until passage of the Militia Act of 1903. This act authorized creation of a National Board for the Promotion of Rifle Practice. One of the first acts of the board was the sale of surplus weapons and ammunition to rifle clubs around the United States. The sale of these weapons created potential members who could sustain the organization and fuel its growth. Through the first half of this century, the NRA grew modestly. It had no more than three hundred thousand members in the 1950s and was concerned primarily with serving the sporting needs of its members.

The NRA has adapted to the changing political times. The assassinations of President Kennedy, Martin Luther King, Jr., and Robert F. Kennedy in the 1960s placed gun control on the national agenda and prompted a slew of gun control efforts in Congress. The NRA committed an ever-increasing amount of its resources to stop efforts to regulate firearms. With the change in political times, more and more of the NRA's activities became political in nature.

The culmination of these political activities came in 1975 with the founding of the Institute for Legislative Action. The Institute formalized the NRA's political activities. It broadened the role of the NRA from education about firearm safety to lobbying and political campaigns. One of the leading proponents of this change was Representative John Dingell (D–MI), who served on the board of directors. The Political Victory Fund (PVF), the NRA's PAC, was formed one year after the Institute. The PAC's purpose was to elect representatives and senators who shared the same views on gun control and the NRA's interpretation of the Second Amendment.

The Second Amendment plays an important role in the NRA's identity and rhetoric. The amendment states: "A well regulated Militia, being necessary to the security of a free State, the right of the people to keep and bear Arms, shall not be infringed." The Supreme Court has consistently interpreted the amendment to mean that it does not afford individuals the simple unconditional right to bear arms; rather, it has asserted that governments can regulate the flow of firearms and munitions (Spitzer 1995, 39). Despite the clarity and consistency of the Court's interpretation of the law, the NRA's magazine, *The American Hunter*, and other literature preach the primacy of gun ownership over gun regulation. The NRA's stylized interpretation of the amendment is designed to suit its lobbying, fund-raising, and publicity interests. The NRA invokes "the defense of the Second Amendment" as a rallying cry to mobilize its members during elections and to influence the legislative process.

At the close of the twentieth century, the NRA had over three million members and an annual budget of approximately $80 million, which was funded primarily through membership dues. This budget supports a staff of over three hundred individuals, 20 percent of whom are involved in lobbying. The NRA has one of the nation's largest PACs, both in terms of the amount of money it contributes and the number of candidates it supports. In 1993, the NRA moved to its new headquarters in Fairfax, Virginia (http://www.nra.org).

Organization

The NRA is governed by a seventy-six-member board of directors, who are elected by voting members of the NRA. The president, Charlton Heston, reports to the board of directors. Kayne Robinson is the vice president and Wayne LaPierre is the executive vice president. These individuals oversee a complex system of thirty-six standing and special committees that work on matters of interest to the NRA membership. Just beneath the vice president on the organizational chart is Tanya Metaksa, who is the executive director of the Institute for Legislative Action (ILA). The ILA contains the lobbying arm and the Political Victory Fund.

The NRA is a national organization with affiliates and club members. Members have influence on the organization and the candidates it supports through a variety of means. The members are encouraged to write, e-mail, and fax their opinions to the national office. The members have influence primarily because they give the money that is disbursed to the candidates. The NRA also makes efforts to learn what its members think. It takes opinion polls of its members and actively solicits their perceptions of candidates. The process by which the organization learns of political candidates was described as "interactive" (Metaksa 1996a).

It is clear that candidates must support the NRA's objectives to receive any NRA electoral support. The NRA has volunteer coordinators in every congressional district who gather information about candidates and pass it along to the national office. The members also lobby on behalf of candidates to see that they get some financial support. There are often disagreements between the national office and the local members over which candidates should receive support, but it is clear that the information-gathering mechanism is a combined effort of the national office and its local members. This combined effort is important for the national office because it makes elected officials understand and respect the members of the organization, not just the power of the national office (Metaksa 1996a).

The combined effort of local members and the national office can be explained partly by the sources of the NRA's funds. Most of the money raised by the Political Victory Fund comes through mail solicitations of members, although some fund-raising is done by telephone and by sponsoring special events. The NRA's dependence on its members for funds helps to explain the solicitous attitude the national organization has toward the rank-and-file membership.

PAC Decision-Making Strategy

Metaksa, as director of the ILA, is in charge of the PVF and all of the lobbying activities. The PAC steering committee, which consists of the individual in charge of federal affairs, the individual in charge of state and local affairs, and the treasurer, helps her decide which candidates should receive PVF contributions. The inclusion of these individuals on the steering committee ensures a close relationship between lobbying and electoral activities. Indeed, it is difficult for NRA leaders to conceptualize how political activities on such a contentious issue as gun control could be separated. There is no legislative success without electoral success first; therefore, the two activities are combined. The PAC steering committee has one overriding guideline for deciding which candidates receive support: the PAC will not give money to candidates who do not support its pro-gun positions. The NRA staff sees itself as a trustee of the members who give money, mostly in small contributions, that finance the NRA's political activities. Metaksa made it clear that the national office is careful not to betray the trust it receives from its members (Metaksa 1996a).

The PAC has a policy of supporting incumbents that it has supported in the past. These tend to be overwhelmingly Republican. In 1994, the NRA contributed almost $200,000 more to Republican incumbents than it did to Democratic incumbents. The gap grew to almost $600,000 in 1996 (see Table 5.1). The gap is even more pronounced with independent expenditures. In 1994, the NRA spent only $9,000 more on behalf of incumbent Republicans than it did for incumbent Democrats. However, in 1996 the gap between independent expenditures for Republican and Democratic incumbents ballooned to over $560,000. The large gap between contributions to and independent expenditures for Democratic and Republican incumbents in 1996 can be accounted for by the NRA's efforts to protect the large number of Republican freshmen. According to the former vice president of the NRA, Neal Knox, the NRA must protect at all costs its majority in Congress (*Mother Jones* 1996, 38). The PAC does contribute to Democrats, but they must exhibit the same kind of zeal and commitment to NRA goals. For example, the PAC donated money to forty-five Democratic incumbents who supported the NRA's position against President Clinton's 1994 crime bill, which contained the ban on assault-style weapons.

The PAC also considers macroelectoral conditions to determine where its money ought to go. The specifics of an election year are particularly important when deciding whether to concentrate giving in House or Senate races. For example, in 1994 the NRA made large independent expenditures and gave more money to Senate candidates in order to make it more Republican. In 1996, the NRA shifted its attention away from Senate races and sought to protect the large freshman class of House Republicans. In the 1996 cycle, efforts in the Senate revolved around open seats and the races of long-time supporters of the NRA.

The PAC relies on numerous sources when determining which races to get involved in. In addition to the information provided by local members, the national office reads reports on the races that are published in national

Table 5.1 NRA Contributions and Independent Expenditures in the 1994 and 1996 House and Senate Elections

	Contributions	Independent Expenditures	
		For	Against
1994 House Elections			
Democrats			
Incumbents	$357,719	$84,402	$39,937
Challengers	11,650	4,145	0
Open-Seat Candidates	25,300	1,397	0
Republicans			
Incumbents	544,327	93,422	17,381
Challengers	355,900	75,743	0
Open-Seat Candidates	312,692	39,686	18,635
1996 House Elections			
Democrats			
Incumbents	$194,700	$42,119	$0
Challengers	19,800	15,856	15,451
Open-Seat Candidates	27,250	20,049	0
Republicans			
Incumbents	764,825	610,782	0
Challengers	174,109	118,756	10,000
Open-Seat Candidates	140,887	158,846	0
1994 Senate Elections			
Democrats			
Incumbents	$6,950	$0	$63,195
Challengers	5,950	62,682	0
Open-Seat Candidates	2,950	0	8,078
Republicans			
Incumbents	58,050	50,989	0
Challengers	84,950	669,923	0
Open-Seat Candidates	86,600	275,426	0
1996 Senate Elections			
Democrats			
Incumbents	$0	$0	$34,493
Challengers	1,000	0	35,512
Open-Seat Candidates	0	1,157	0
Republicans			
Incumbents	94,150	123,175	0
Challengers	33,700	201,252	0
Open-Seat Candidates	72,300	245,933	0

magazines and newsletters. They exchange information with other lobbyists on Capitol Hill. There is very little communication with other PAC directors, but the steering committee listens to the parties' congressional and senatorial campaign committees when making its deliberations and deciding on races in which to get involved.

The NRA usually reserves its involvement to local, state, and congressional campaigns, limiting its involvement in presidential races. Endorsements are an important electoral tool of the NRA. They can energize a membership to work on behalf of the candidate and can attract other resources that can be converted into votes. Most importantly, endorsements signal rather prominently to members of the organization who the candidates are that actively support NRA goals. There is some empirical evidence that suggests that these endorsements actually increase the vote totals of candidates (McBurnett, Kenny, and Bordua 1996). Sometimes the organization will even endorse a candidate with a lower grade than the competitor. In the 1996 elections, a candidate who had the lower grade from the NRA went out of his way to help the organization with some of its activities. This individual received the endorsement over the challenger who had the higher grade.

The race in Idaho is an example of the work done by the NRA on behalf of longtime friends in the Senate. The race was not supposed to be close, but the organization wanted to show its support for a friend. The NRA ran negative radio ads attacking Senator Craig's opponent, Walt Minnick. A controversy arose when Minnick announced that he was pulling his negative ads. Craig's campaign manager supposedly called the NRA and asked it to change the ads. The director of federal affairs for the NRA told the campaign manager that he could not discuss the matter because the expenditures are to remain independent, but the campaign manager had already stated his point. The NRA contributed $4,950 directly to Craig's campaign but made over $20,000 worth of independent expenditures.

In the 1996 House races, the contributions and expenditures were concentrated in the large number of close races. The NRA did not expect the House to change hands, but it did expect the Republicans to lose about six seats. The NRA sought to minimize losses for the Republicans by supporting House Republican freshmen (Metaksa 1996b). The organization presumed that there would be many close races, the bulk of which involved the freshman class. In Indiana, the NRA helped defend freshman John Hostetler. Early in this campaign, Handgun Control, Inc., placed billboards in Hostetler's district urging voters to call the representative and ask him why he voted to repeal the assault weapons ban. Not to be outdone, the NRA had billboards up in a matter of days asking voters to call Hostetler and thank him for his vote (http://www.crp.org/pacanalia/pac30.html).

Ideological groups tend to have decision-making strategies that allow them to take advantage of changing electoral conditions and shifts in a candidate's stands (Herrnson 1998, 112). The NRA is no different; the PVF has a dynamic decision-making process. It relies on media reports, public opinion polls, and interviews with candidates when making its contribution and independent expenditure decisions. A widening or tightening of the contest or controversies that engulf the candidate can lead to changes in NRA support. For example, Al Salvi, a Republican Senate candidate in Illinois, stood to benefit from the strong program of independent expenditures that the NRA conducted in 1996. The NRA planned to spend fifty thousand dollars on Salvi's effort to defeat Democrat Dick Durbin. However, in a midcampaign interview on *NewsHour* with Jim Lehrer, Salvi said that there should not be a repeal of the assault weapons ban. The NRA then stopped spending money in the race. Salvi attempted reconciliation by stating that he would vote for a repeal but would not pressure Congress to consider it. The NRA changed its position and eventually spent the money, but Salvi lost anyway (Jacoby 1996).

Giving money to candidates is only one way the NRA becomes involved in a campaign. The NRA has five distinct levels of participation. The first is simply grading the candidates from an A to an F. The grade appears in *The American Rifleman*, a magazine that is sent to all NRA members. An A is given to candidates who actively participate in protecting gun owners' rights and an F is given to individuals who favor legislating restrictions on gun ownership. Individual candidates who believe in the goals of the NRA, but do not actively work on behalf of those goals, are normally not rated as highly as those who actually do the legislative work for the organization. Key votes can also influence the grade given to a representative. For example, Representative Brian Bilbray (R–CA), whom the NRA helped elect to his first term, received an A grade in 1994. Even with a four out of five record on crucial NRA votes, Bilbray dropped to an F in 1996 because he voted against the repeal of the assault weapons ban and was critical of the NRA in campaign commercials and appearances. The NRA claimed that he was overtly and persistently antagonistic. Bilbray attempted to appease the organization by explaining that he would not vote for the Violence Protection and Handgun Control Act (Brady II), but the NRA was not convinced (Braun 1996).

The second level of support consists of an endorsement for the candidate. An endorsement is better than a grade because it actually helps to activate NRA members on behalf of the candidate. Giving money to the candidate is the third level. In-kind contributions, such as hosting a fundraising or a meet-and-greet event, constitute the fourth level. Independent expenditures make up the NRA's highest level of involvement. The PVF airs television and radio ads and sends out direct mailings, including bumper stickers. It also urges its members to work for the candidate. Candidates understand the differences between these levels of involvement and often petition the members and the national office to move from one level to the next.

The national office uses creative ways to help candidates gain publicity, which is level five. Metaksa travels the district or state with candidates to generate media exposure and to energize local members to work on the candidate's behalf. The national office schedules high-profile events, namely for level-five candidates in close races.

The dynamics of presidential campaigns differ slightly from those of congressional campaigns. The organization does not usually endorse presidential candidates, so the levels of support evident in presidential campaigns are less formal. Only three times in the 126-year history of the organization has it endorsed a presidential candidate. While the NRA was lukewarm in its support of Senator Dole, it was hostile toward President Clinton. Dole did not receive an endorsement from the NRA in his 1996 presidential bid, an omission that some attributed to the senator's decision to hold up repeal of the assault weapons ban in the Senate. Metaksa added that the members of the NRA did not want to endorse Dole. The endorsement process is based on principle (Metaksa 1996a). Despite the public controversy over Dole's failure to secure the NRA's endorsement, the organization did make independent expenditures against President Clinton. The campaign was aimed more at eroding support for President Clinton than generating enthusiasm and votes for Senator Dole. Support for Senator Dole seemed to be predicated on the belief that any candidate would be better than President Clinton, a situation that explains the indirect financial support without a direct endorsement. In an article entitled "The Clinton War on Guns," Metaksa stated that, "if Bill Clinton achieves his goal—another four years in the White House, backed by an anti-Second Amendment Congress—gun owners can expect both vigorous regulatory attacks on the Second Amendment as well as legislation to license, tax, and ban the Second Amendment out of existence" (http://www.nra.org).

1994 and Its Aftermath

The results of 1994 took many longtime observers of politics by surprise. Metaksa said that they saw the election victory coming the weekend before the vote. They were obviously surprised and overjoyed with the outcome. Like most other institutions in Washington, DC, the NRA endured some changes in the wake of the Republican victory in the House. On the positive side for the NRA, longtime friends soon found themselves in positions of power while longtime enemies were no longer in charge. Metaksa referred specifically to Representative Charles E. Schumer, former chair of the Crime and Criminal Justice Subcommittee of the Judiciary Committee. Committee chairs have the power and the means to get certain items into bills. With the sudden reversal in electoral fortune, the lobbyists of the NRA could educate individuals in power who might actually be predisposed to listen to them. Finally, the 1994 elections made it possible for the NRA to worry less about presidential initiatives that might damage the cause. A Congress less susceptible to presidential influence made it easier to block presidential initiatives. Indeed, the NRA could become proactive in legislation such as the efforts to repeal the ban on assault-style weapons.

The 1994 elections, however, hurt NRA fund-raising. Members generally had the feeling that they had won, and when people think they have won, they believe they do not need to continue to give. Metaksa believes that losing is better to preserve the vitality of issue advocacy (Metaksa 1996a).

However, financial problems were compounded by slowdowns in fund-raising efforts in 1995. The organization did not raise money as vigorously in 1995 as it did in 1993. It placed a little more emphasis on raising money for special events, such as the Second Amendment symposium and Waco hearings. It also raised money in 1995 for "right to carry" legislation in state legislatures (Metaksa 1996a).

The electoral victories in 1994 spawned competing activities within the organization for which funds needed to be raised. Members can give to fund programs, the PAC, or both. There do seem to be some financial problems, and the NRA has made efforts to curb its losses. In August of 1996, it announced that it was eliminating about forty staff positions at its national headquarters. The positions affected mainly "hunter service programs and other general operating programs" (Stone 1996b, 1910). The financial problems of the NRA have put pressure on the group to evaluate its goals and activities. The organization seems torn between those who want to spend more money on campaign activities and those who want it to serve the hunting and sporting interests of its members (Seelye 1997, A1).

The NRA continued its efforts to repeal the ban on assault-style weapons in the 105th Congress. Other issues of importance to the NRA involved taggants, which enable law enforcement officials to identify the company that produced gunpowder, and the establishment of a national injury and prevention center. While the NRA pursued much of the same agenda in the 105th Congress that it did in the 104th, it found that representatives and senators acted differently. Metaksa thought the members were much more cautious and less strident because of the close brushes with electoral defeat (Metaksa 1996a). Still, the NRA found the 105th Congress to be more sympathetic to its aims than the Democratic-controlled Congresses of recent years.

Lobbying reforms should not have a significant effect on what the NRA does. Because it relies so much on its members to write letters and to contact members of Congress, Metaksa claims that the influence of the NRA will not diminish much. She argues that the tactics of the lobby are "educational in nature." The lobbyists act more as "educators" to instruct legislators on the effects of such initiatives as the assault weapons ban. She contends that these tactics work much better than sound bites. Education and hard work, not sound bites, convince representatives to vote a particular way. The combined effects of NRA members in the districts and educational efforts of the lobbyists produce results for the NRA lobby (Metaksa 1996a).

While Congress is now more sympathetic to positions of the NRA, the organization and its lobby do not mind settling scores with enemies. David Satcher, head of the Centers for Disease Control and Prevention, made the elimination of death and injury from firearms a top priority. He argued that the loss of life through violence is "a public health problem" (Stevens 1994, 22). When Republicans assumed control of Congress, the NRA used its influence to take funding away from the CDC's injury prevention center and reallocate it to breast cancer research (Montgomery 1996, 6). Clearly, the lobby of the NRA has found new and creative ways to respond to presidential initiatives that it views as hostile toward its mission and enjoys having sympathetic chairs of relevant committees and subcommittees.

Conclusion

The NRA is the epitome of a single-interest organization. Its goal is to elect officials to public office who subscribe to its beliefs about firearms. This goal enables its nationwide membership to participate in thousands of political campaigns. The NRA is like most ideological organizations; it manipulates powerful symbols to mobilize members and pursues most of its policy goals primarily through the electoral arena. Policy goals cannot be easily separated from success in the electoral arena. To achieve policy success, it must put members in Congress who share the same views as the organization. To this end, the NRA merged its lobbying activities with its PAC. The NRA remains one of the largest and most powerful interest groups in U.S. politics because it unifies electoral and policy efforts and pursues flexible campaign strategies that maximize its effectiveness.

The NRA makes most of the major decisions about campaign contributions and independent expenditures in the midst of the campaign season. Overall strategy for 1996 was set early in the election season as the group decided to support Republican freshmen in the House. Individual decisions are made as the campaign season unfolds and races change. This permits the NRA to concentrate the bulk of its resources on races in which it can have the most impact. The ideological cohesiveness of the organization and its members contributes to the success of this flexible strategy. The organization can move resources, such as money and campaign workers, to the races where they will have the most impact. Very few candidates ever receive the maximum allowable contribution. This strategy frees more resources for races in which a well-timed contribution or campaign activity can make a real difference.

The NRA is pleased with the success it has enjoyed electorally and legislatively, but it has found that the new environment contains certain pitfalls. Fund-raising has suffered. Ideological groups need a certain amount of fear and urgency to energize their members. With Republicans in control of the Senate and the House, no such urgency exists. The irony is that the NRA needs gun control initiatives from a president hostile to its cause to raise money. Wayne LaPierre, Jr., admitted as much in an interview on National Public Radio (aired February 10, 1997). But Republican control of Congress makes such initiatives less likely. This means that many of the group's most important goals will not receive much legislative attention. Members in the 105th Congress may worry about going too far, thus complicating their efforts to retain control of the Congress in the next election. The group's electoral success has resulted in new financial challenges and questions about the ultimate aim and mission of the NRA.

Note

[1]This section relies heavily on the history reported in Spitzer's book. I suggest that readers see this excellent book on the NRA if they desire a more detailed discussion of the history and development of the NRA.

BUILDING TO WIN, BUILDING TO LAST: AFL-CIO COPE TAKES ON THE REPUBLICAN CONGRESS

Robin Gerber

It was June 18, 1996, and Republican Speaker of the House, Newt Gingrich, was traveling to Boston for a $1,000-per-plate fund-raising dinner for two GOP Congressmen from Massachusetts. In Boston that same evening, the American Federation of Labor–Congress of Industrial Organizations (AFL-CIO) was holding one of thirty town hall meetings, where rank-and-file members would tell labor's leaders from Washington, DC, about the issues of most concern to working people. Learning of Gingrich's arrival, AFL-CIO Secretary–Treasurer Rich Trumka extended an invitation to Gingrich and company to "give up that dinner" and come listen to the struggle of working families in Boston.

The Republicans went ahead with their fund-raiser, which helped them collect record contributions in the election, and Trumka succeeded in generating free media at the Republicans' expense. The incident juxtaposed labor's member-targeted issues agenda with a high-level Republican fund-raiser. It helps set the stage to examine the methods and motivation for labor's PAC spending and political activities in the 1996 elections.

The elections of 1994 were a major defeat for the AFL-CIO, whose close ties to Democratic lawmakers could no longer help them influence the congressional agenda. As a symbol of labor's reduced access to congressional policy makers, the new Republican majority changed the name of the House and Labor Committee to the Education and Workforce Committee, and the Senate Labor Committee to the Labor and Human Resources Committee to signal a less prolabor focus. House Republican leaders warned their party's rank and file not to meet with representatives of organized labor and effectively froze the AFL-CIO out of the policy process. Thus, the AFL-CIO made restoring a Democratic majority in the House its top political priority in the 1996 elections.

The History of AFL-CIO Political Action

Since the New Deal, labor unions had an ongoing history of political involvement for the labor movement. The CIO was formed in 1935 to organize workers on an industrywide basis in mass production industries such as steel, auto, and rubber. Under the leadership of mine worker John L. Lewis, the CIO was militant and politically active. In 1936 it formed Labor's Nonpartisan League, giving strong support and large contributions to Franklin D. Roosevelt. In 1943, the CIO had created a new entity for "effective action on the political front." By July of that year the Political Action Committee, as it was called, raised $671,214 in voluntary contributions for election activities. Another committee established by the CIO, the National Citizens Political Action Committee, was made up of professionals, artists, writers, and others sympathetic to labor (Taft 1964, 609).

By 1944, the PAC was conducting voter registration drives and issuing a tabloid called *The Political Action News.* The PAC spent $948,351, and more than another $350,000 was spent by the National Citizens PAC. The American Federation of Labor (AFL) had not established a permanent political arm by the 1940s, but it continued its policy of biennially selecting a Nonpartisan Political Campaign Committee to provide information to members and present its demands to both political parties. The AFL expended few resources on political activity prior to the passage of the Taft–Hartley Act in 1947 (Taft 1964, 611).

Labor's League for Political Education (LLPE) was created by the AFL convention in 1948 in response to the Taft–Hartley Act, which severely restricted political activities of unions. AFL President Green told other union presidents that "he had been surprised by the strength of antilabor feeling in the Congress and by the overriding of President Truman's veto of the Taft–Hartley Act." A voluntary assessment of ten cents per member from affiliated unions funded the early operation of LLPE. By 1951, special assessments had been abandoned and the AFL made the LLPE part of its budget (Johnson 1991, 42).

The CIO's PAC and the AFL's LLPE continued to operate along parallel lines during the late 1940s and early 1950s. Both committees believed that labor's agenda must include education, housing, health care, civil rights, and other issues of social concern that affected working people generally. By 1952 the two committees were working closely together and had formed a joint coordinating committee. The PAC reported spending $505,722 and the LLPE $249,258 in the 1952 campaign (Taft 1964, 616).

At the merger of the AFL and CIO in 1955, the Committee on Political Education (COPE) was formed as the nonpartisan political arm of the new organization with broad responsibilities for political action. The AFL-CIO

Constitution states that COPE has the task "of encouraging workers to register and vote, to exercise their full rights and responsibilities of citizenship, and to perform their rightful part in the political life of the city, state, and national communities." COPE was intended to carry forward the work of both PAC and LLPE. In the report of proceedings of the founding convention in 1955, it was resolved that the AFL-CIO would support "worthy candidates regardless of their party affiliation" (Taft 1964, 617).

In practice, support has been weighted heavily toward Democratic candidates and the Democratic Party. This party loyalty did not translate into major legislative gains in the 1960s or 1970s despite a Democratic-controlled Congress and three Democratic presidents. Business PACs began to outstrip the growth of their labor counterparts, and the parties developed more sophisticated approaches for raising political contributions. Ten years after its creation, COPE had the highest budget of any department in the AFL-CIO. The 1966–1967 Financial Report of the AFL-CIO shows COPE had a budget of $897,141 for fiscal year 1967 and spent $375,000 on voter registration activities. By the 1994 elections, COPE's budget had grown to $10,256,337. Attempts at major labor reform were largely abandoned by 1980 with the election of Ronald Reagan, and the subsequent twelve-year presidential reign for Republicans. During the 1980s and up to the Republican takeover of Congress in 1994, labor enjoyed easy access to the Democratic leadership in Congress. Labor lobbyists frequently met with the Senate and House Democratic leadership. Labor enjoyed close relationships with majority committee staff and chairpeople of key committees. Although this access did not translate into major reforms in labor law, individual unions were often able to affect the appropriation process or alter bill language in ways favorable to their membership. While labor was not making great strides in the federal legislative arena, it was also not under direct attack or investigation. Perhaps the most visible sign of labor's integrated presence on Capitol Hill prior to 1994 was a room centrally located in the Capitol, in the suite of offices occupied by the Doorkeeper, Jim Malloy. In this windowless, smoky headquarters union lobbyists were allowed to make telephone calls and wait between meetings with legislators and their staff. It was an enviable outpost in a world where access and information are prime commodities.

It was in the Doorkeeper's offices on the night of November 8, 1994, that labor's representatives to Congress learned that their political world had turned upside down. With several televisions tuned to the returns, horrified Hill staff and union lobbyists learned that for the first time in forty years the House was to be under Republican control. Labor's access to the congressional majority abruptly ended. The Doorkeeper's office was abolished.

This difficult legislative climate put labor in an unfamiliar posture on Capitol Hill. Prior to 1994 labor had a positive agenda on a broad range of issues, including reform of occupational health and safety laws, pension law reform, a minimum wage increase, and universal health care. Labor lobbying was proactive; it involved soliciting members of Congress to sponsor or cosponsor legislation and persuading Democrats and moderate Republicans to support labor bills.

After the Republicans became the majority in Congress, labor was on the defensive. Labor lobbyists felt like they were in a "bunker" because of attacks by the Republican leadership. On March 22, 1996, Speaker of the House Newt Gingrich called a meeting of Republican leaders and moderate members to present a campaign against organized labor. The plan included holding numerous hearings on union activities, soliciting corporate money to run ads against AFL-CIO initiatives, and a series of memorandums called the "Message of the Day" from House Republican Conference Chairman John Boehner. These memos to House Republicans attacked unions on various issues and provided them with talking points and sample press releases.

The Republicans also used their newly won control of congressional committees to directly attack labor organizations. Twenty such memos were sent out in the spring of 1996. The Committee on House Oversight held hearings on March 21, 1996, on the political activities of labor unions. The AFL-CIO leadership refused to testify and committee Democrats walked out of the hearing denouncing it as a "kangaroo court." On May 28, 1996, Jim Bunning (R–KY), chairman of the Social Security Subcommittee of the House Ways and Means Committee, announced that his committee would hold hearings on the use of Social Security trust fund money to finance union activities at the Social Security Administration. On June 6, 1996, Representative Christopher Shays (R–CT), chairman of the Human Resources and Intergovernmental Relations Committee of the House Government Reform and Oversight Committee, announced he would hold hearings on labor union racketeering. Meanwhile, Representative Harris Fawell (R–IL) introduced legislation to require union leaders to get written approval from employees before using union dues for any activity other than collective bargaining. The Republican leadership augmented their congressional activities with a barrage of harsh rhetoric against unions, and the AFL-CIO issued advertisements that attacked GOP positions on Medicare, Medicaid, and the minimum wage.

By May of 1996, the Republican attacks on labor had created a backlash among more moderate Republican members of Congress. Peter T. King, a Republican congressman from Long Island, New York, said, "Instead of going for solid working people, people who work hard, are patriotic and put their kids through school, the people who would be role models for Republican campaign commercials, we're driving them away" (Greenhouse 1996, A9). Republican House members from New York, New Jersey, and other northern states were becoming increasingly concerned that the largely Southern leadership's antiunion attacks would hurt their chances for reelection. Senator Alphonse D'Amato, Republican from New York, contended, "We make a mistake if we just say labor is the enemy.... These are working men and women who are our neighbors.... Do we just want to condemn them all?" (Greenhouse 1996, A9). The split in Republican ranks resulted in enough GOP support for passage of labor's long-sought increase in the minimum wage in May 1996.

The New AFL-CIO

The 1994 Republican takeover of Congress was one of many factors contributing to growing discontent and restlessness by labor leaders with the president of the AFL-CIO, Lane Kirkland. In the year prior to the 1996 elections, the leadership of the AFL-CIO underwent a dramatic transition. In October 1995, the AFL-CIO had its first contested leadership election in decades. Kirkland faced intense pressure as a result of shrinking union membership and a hostile national climate toward unions. Union representation in the private sector had decreased from a high of 34.7 percent in 1954 to 10.4 percent in 1995. The total U.S. workforce represented by unions in the public and private sector is 14.9 percent (Weisman 1996, 3163). Kirkland's opponents criticized him for spending too much time abroad and failing to take strong action to organize workers at home. Kirkland resigned in the summer of 1995.

Factions formed around two candidates in the race to replace Kirkland: Tom Donohue, who had been the longtime second in command at the AFL-CIO, and John Sweeney, who was head of the Service Employees International Union (SEIU), one of the fastest-growing unions in the federation. Sweeney won the election and quickly replaced the head of the department that had been known as COPE with Steve Rosenthal, an experienced political operative who had also spent many years on the Communication Workers of America staff. Under Rosenthal the operation was renamed the Political Department, but the federal PAC retained the name COPE. The Political Department developed a plan for the 1996 elections that emphasized educating and organizing members for political and legislative action over raising and spending PAC dollars. Nevertheless, the AFL-CIO's PAC raised more money than in previous elections, mostly as a result of heightened communication and political action.

Under the former leadership of the AFL-CIO, the federation's political operation was heavily weighted toward distributing COPE PAC funds. This was primarily done through two committees, called the Senate Marginal Committee and House Marginal Committee (Wilcox 1994, 23). Less emphasis was placed on AFL-CIO staff working to organize members politically in congressional districts or on educating rank-and-file members about candidates and issues. These types of political activities were largely left up to the individual unions.

Under new leadership, the AFL-CIO disbanded the "marginal" committees, reframed PAC decision making, and placed most emphasis on building active union member political involvement and education. The program to accomplish the new grassroots approach to politics was called "Labor '96." It was composed of six elements: grassroots education and mobilization, media, voter registration, get-out-the-vote (GOTV), training, and coalition building. PAC contributions were closely tied to the Labor '96 effort, as were the efforts of the Legislative Department as it lobbied for labor legislation on Capitol Hill. PAC contributions were put entirely in the hands of Marta David, assistant director of the AFL-CIO's Political Department, who had spent years analyzing races and recommending contributions for COPE and for the Democratic Congressional Campaign Committee, where she had worked in the early 1980s.

COPE's structure, activities, and influence reflect the larger Labor '96 program and its component parts. The AFL-CIO explained its motivation and methodology for the 1996 campaign by stating, "It is no secret that for many years American working families have had virtually no voice in our political system. That's why the AFL-CIO allocated $35 million in 1996 for an independent issues education campaign to push key issues important to working families and to give voters the records and positions of candidates on working family issues" (AFL-CIO 1996a). The $35 million dollars were collected through a special assessment of fifteen cents per member per month for a twelve-month period from affiliated unions. The plan, in the words of AFL-CIO President John Sweeney was to "take back the Congress and take back our country" (Gruenwald and Wells 1996, 993).

Labor's political strategy for 1996 evolved from the central tenet that business had and would continue to outspend labor in elections. In a May 1960 article, the *American Federationist* had lamented that the political contributions of "a mere dozen families of means" exceeded the total direct political expenditures of workers in the 1956 campaign. By June 1996, the Center for Responsive Politics was reporting that, "business money swamped all other sources. In all, the center tracked $242 million in donations from business groups—nearly seven times more than the $35 million that came from labor." It reported that corporate interests distributed more than three times the direct contributions made by labor PACs and that "the business–labor ratio tilts in favor of business even if the AFL-CIO's much reported $35 million in spending on issues ads is added to direct contributions" (Center for Responsive Politics 1996).

Business money was raised outside of the PAC structure as well. Corporate executives and their spouses may each give $1,000 to an individual candidate, up to a maximum of $25,000 for all candidates receiving contributions.

The watchdog group, Citizen Action, reported that there was an increase in large individual contributions as more attention was focused on money raised from PACs. According to the records reviewed by Citizen Action, "the leading categories of individual contributors mirror the top categories of PAC contributors" (Citizen Action 1996).

Labor '96 was developed in the context of the overwhelming PAC superiority of corporations and trade associations. If labor could not compete dollar for dollar, it could compete "on the ground" by educating, energizing, and organizing its members. Labor's superiority lay in human capital, which could not be matched by any business interest listed in the reports of the Federal Election Commission. As Diane McDaniel, the labor political director for Washington state put it, "Money is important, but if you haven't got your grassroots base, you ain't got it" (McDaniel 1996).

Labor '96

Labor '96 originally targeted seventy-three congressional districts, which received grassroots assistance and television and radio ads. At the request of affiliated unions that participated in Labor '96, an additional thirty-two districts were added during the election year. These districts received only grassroots help from Labor '96 coordinators rather than targeted media. The factors for targeting were based on comparison of Democratic versus Republican voter registration, past performance of registered voters, union membership, and President Clinton's vote share in 1992. Consideration was also given to incumbents' voting records and past margins of victory.

Once these districts were targeted, a staff structure was put in place to organize within the congressional district. The congressional district (CD) coordinator was charged with implementing the Labor '96 Education and Mobilization Political Program and worked with officers of the AFL-CIO state federations, the state COPE director (a parallel position to the national AFL-CIO political director), and Central Labor Council officers. The state federations act as umbrella organizations for the statewide entities of international unions. For example, the International Brotherhood of Electrical Workers (IBEW) has an office in Washington, DC, to coordinate national and Canadian efforts, and statewide IBEW offices in most states to coordinate efforts at that level. Central Labor Councils coordinate the activities of AFL-CIO–affiliated unions within a city, county, or other geographic region of a state.

Specifically, the CD coordinator was to meet with local union officers to develop and implement the plan for that area and to get their commitment to attend the kickoff meeting the CD coordinator organized with a call from AFL-CIO President Sweeney. The CD coordinator assigned the next level of staff assistance, and the local union coordinator provided support for mobilizing members, ran briefing sessions, and oversaw the development and distribution of issue leaflets and action plans. The CD coordinator also mobilized union members around important legislative issues and developed and implemented the fall political mobilization. They were responsible for signing up one hundred to one hundred fifty new activists on pledge cards and reported regularly to the regional director. As of December 12, 1996, the AFL-CIO reported a total of 17,404 pledge cards in Labor '96 districts (AFL-CIO 1996b).

The local union coordinator was charged with recruiting the next level of staff assistance, the work site coordinators, and assisting them with building a one-on-one structure in the workplace. The local union coordinator was to keep records on the number of members participating at each work site, answer questions, and distribute materials. The work site coordinator was the base for building a one-on-one structure at the workplace with a ratio of one coordinator to ten to twenty workers. These coordinators were to work together as a team to talk to union members one on one, distribute materials, and mobilize members to participate in political actions.

Using this congressional district staff structure, Labor '96 moved forward with its six-part program, which was organized around federal issues of concern to working families: the economy and taxes, retirement benefits, health and safety, and education. These issues were selected using polls and focus group interviews of union members. Postelection polling by Hart Research Associates indicated that 77 percent of all union members felt that "government should do a lot more than now" to protect Social Security. An equal percentage felt the same way about pension fund abuse, and 74 percent felt the same way about keeping jobs in the United States and health insurance portability. Sixty-four percent believed the government should do more to extend health coverage for kids, and 61 percent wanted more government action in promoting equal pay for women.

As part of the grassroots education and mobilization effort, flyers were distributed on the four issue groups plus compensatory leave time. These flyers compared candidates in selected congressional districts, listing their positions in a side-by-side comparison format with the heading: "What's at stake for working families in the 1996 elections?" Flyers were distributed in conjunction with 114 congressional elections, 15 Senate contests, and 2 gubernatorial races. Spanish translations were provided in several states. Nine million pieces of direct mail carrying the Labor '96 message were delivered during the general election. Ninety percent of this distribution was done during the critical last month of the election. Local unions and central labor councils mailed another 2.5 million letters.

The effect of the issue-comparative communications was described by Montana State Federation President Don Judge, "We used a new format. We provided side-by-side comparison of candidates on issues our members cared about, and let them decide who to vote for. It was deeply appreciated by them" (Judge 1996). Grassroots education and mobilization also meant involving union members in lobbying, letter writing, phone campaigns, leafleting at work sites, and organizing public events. The AFL-CIO reported 5.5 million phone contacts as a result of the program.

The most reported aspect of the Labor '96 program was the money spent for television and, to a lesser extent, radio advertising. Voter guides were also used to compare candidates on the issues identified as central to the union program. The ads included an 800 number that could be called to receive written voter guides. While innovative in its level of outreach, the AFL had been informing members about legislative matters and chronicling voting records for members of Congress since 1895, and the CIO had done the same since it was formed in 1935 (Taft 1964, 606–607).

In late August 1996, new TV and radio direct-message ads focusing on Medicare and Medicaid cuts were aired in twenty-seven areas represented by Republican members of Congress. The ads demanded that these members change their votes and oppose their party on these issues. In response, Republicans charged the AFL-CIO with violating campaign finance laws and filed complaints with the Federal Election Commission. Federal law (2 USC 441(b)(a)) prohibits unions from making contributions or expenditures in connection with a federal election out of general treasury funds, as opposed to PAC dollars. The unions presented these ads as issue-related, not intended to influence a particular election. Nevertheless, five complaints had been filed by September 12, 1996, by the National Republican Congressional Committee alleging that the ads should have been paid for with PAC funds, which are subject to FEC contribution limits as in-kind contributions to candidates and constituted partisan communications to the general public. Labor '96 also included events designed to attract free media coverage, such as the invitation to Gingrich to join the union town hall meeting. This coverage was part of the effort to educate and mobilize members.

Project '96, an independent coalition that included the National Council of Senior Citizens and Citizen Action, was largely funded by individual unions. Project '96 organized events against Republican members of Congress including press conferences, protests, and press events, such as using the site of a senior center to highlight cuts in benefits to the elderly. The actions were meant to dramatize issues and attract "earned" media coverage. In the words of Executive Director Scott Wolf, Project '96 brought "issue education and grassroots lobbying" to twenty-nine GOP-held districts (Gruenwald and Wells 1996, 998). The AFL-CIO contributed approximately one hundred thousand dollars to Project '96.

Voter registration was the third part of the Labor '96 plan. Union members and their families were registered to vote. Emphasis was placed on using the National Voter Registration Act (commonly known as motor-voter) to attract new registrants. In another coalition strategy, the AFL-CIO gave money to nonpartisan voter registration projects. A special AFL-CIO coordinator spent approximately $2 million dollars to administer and fund nonpartisan voter registration drives. Priority was given to efforts in AFL-CIO–targeted states. Additional consideration was given to registering racial minorities.

Get-out-the-vote drives were the fourth part of Labor '96. The AFL-CIO vote coordinator worked with state federations of labor and central labor councils to get registered union members and their families to the polls. Nonpartisan GOTV was conducted in forty-eight locations, with 108 staff assigned from eleven international unions and the AFL-CIO. There were 22.08 million union votes cast, an increase of 2.32 million over 1992, compared to a decrease of 8 million votes among all voters nationwide.

Another key part of the Labor '96 program was training. All Labor '96 staff were trained in the organizational, motivational, and mobilization techniques for use in an issue education campaign. The newly established National Labor Political Training Center trained 175 CD coordinators in four sessions. Another 1,750 union activists were trained in Labor '96 congressional district "kickoff" economic education sessions held in fifty-four congressional districts. "Project GOTV" trained fifteen hundred staff for its late-election activities. In addition, a candidate issue seminar was held on July 17, 1996, for fifty U.S. Senate and House challengers and twenty-five of their campaign managers. Campaign skills training was provided for union member candidates for state and local office. These programs were successful in three states. In New Jersey, two of the three members of the Ironworkers' union and AFSCME who ran for the office of freeholder—a post similar to county commissioner in other states—were elected. In Colorado, two of the three members of the Teamsters and International Brotherhood of Electrical Workers who ran for state representative were successful. In West Virginia, thirteen of the twenty members of the mine workers', laborers', teachers', locomotive engineers', carpenters', and electrical workers' unions who ran for state representative were victorious, including six incumbents and seven nonincumbents.

Coalition building was the last element of the Labor '96 campaign. The AFL-CIO worked with Citizen Action, the Interfaith Alliance, the A. Phillip Randolph Institute, the Coalition of Labor Union Women, Labor Committee for Latin American Advancement, Asian Pacific American Labor Association, the National Baptist Convention, the National Rainbow Coalition, Rock the Vote, and the Women's Vote Project to boost voter registration and turnout. Working Women Vote was organized by the new Working Women's Department of the AFL-CIO. Labor '96 organized three hundred events, including rallies, conferences, bus tours, precinct walks, leafleting, mailings, registration drives, and phone banks in forty-six states. They coordinated their efforts with thirty international unions and twenty nonprofit groups to get a total of thirty-five thousand activists involved in the election.

COPE's Role in the Elections

COPE, the AFL-CIO's PAC, collected money from union members and distributed it to federal candidates. COPE collected funds in three ways: through voluntary checkoff from salaried staff of the AFL-CIO (including field staff), from individual voluntary contributions of union members directly collected at COPE meetings in a state, and through joint fund-raising with affiliated unions. Union members make joint voluntary contributions to their union and the AFL-CIO, with the international union serving as collecting agent for the AFL-CIO.

COPE's contribution decisions are influenced by the AFL-CIO's federated structure. Candidates for federal office can receive COPE funds only if they have received the endorsement of the AFL-CIO state or local political committee in their area. Endorsements are given through a committee process and usually involve interviewing candidates or having them fill out a COPE questionnaire to determine the likelihood of their support for union-supported issues. A candidate must receive two-thirds of the vote to be endorsed.

The endorsement procedure can be a mini-political battleground. Affiliated unions hotly contest support for a challenger or open-seat candidate or a rubber stamp for a longtime union-friendly incumbent. Often the local labor bodies will make endorsements in primaries. If the union-backed candidate loses, the state federation will have to decide whether to make an endorsement in the general election. North Carolina's seventh congressional district was an example of this scenario in 1996. The North Carolina AFL-CIO state federation endorsed Rose-Marie Lowry-Townsend, who was a member of the National Education Association, the nation's largest teachers' union.[1] She lost in the runoff that followed a close primary.[2] The winner of the runoff, Mike McIntyre, was endorsed by COPE and ultimately won the election.

Occasionally the endorsement process at the local level becomes a fight between unions that support different candidates. In the 1996 race in the thirtieth congressional district of New York, for example, Democrat Francis Pordum, who was challenging Republican incumbent Jack Quinn, had received an endorsement in May by the Buffalo Central Labor Council with a vote of 150 to 3. The endorsement was based on both candidates' voting records. In Quinn's race in 1994, the Central Labor Council had stayed neutral, but the state federation had endorsed Republican Quinn, angering many local union leaders. In 1996 the New York State Federation of Labor accepted the recommendation of the Central Labor Council and gave Pordum the state endorsement in mid-July. This angered Quinn's supporters in the Transit Workers Union and several other union locals from the downstate New York area. They felt that the early Central Labor Council endorsement was unfairly made since Quinn had not been interviewed. Quinn had

cast several prolabor votes, although he had only a 33 percent prolabor voting record. At a state labor convention in September, the pro-Quinn unions
tried to force a vote of the delegates to overturn the Pordum endorsement.
The state federation leadership would not allow the vote and the endorsement
stood, but the controversy over the endorsement left bitter feelings. The
Quinn–Pordum endorsement battle demonstrates the challenges and limita-
tions of developing a highly democratic process for political decision making.
While COPE based its contribution to Pordum on the endorsement, the controversy hurt Pordum's fund-raising from other affiliated unions that also look
to their local bodies for direction.

A number of criteria are used to determine whether to give a contribution,
and how much to give. The process for giving to incumbents is less dependent
on local endorsements than that for giving to nonincumbent challengers or
open-seat candidates. For incumbents, the voting record on union issues is the
major predictor for contributions and is normally in concert with endorsements. David occasionally consulted with Peggy Taylor, director of the AFL-
CIO Legislative Department, when deciding which incumbents would receive
contributions. The vote to increase the minimum wage in 1996, for example,
was a key vote that was considered when determining contributions to an
incumbent. For nonincumbent endorsed candidates, David would consider
viability or being "in places where we think we can win."

COPE relied more on polls to determine the relative strength of candidates in 1996 than in other years. The polls were used to determine whether
the incumbent was vulnerable and whether the unions had a strong candidate. Many of the polls were done prior to filing deadlines and primaries to
enable labor to back the candidate who would be strongest in the general
election. This strategy was only partially successful because many other candidates would not step aside for the candidate determined by the unions to be
the most viable. It was, nevertheless, considered worthwhile to do the polling
to determine the vulnerability of incumbents. COPE also collected information about political campaigns from its field staff, state and local labor bodies,
and professional publications such as the *Hotline* and *Cook Political Report*.

Senate candidates were funded as fully and as early as possible because
their budgets are bigger. In the 1996 elections, House races that promised to
be competitive were funded as early as possible. An example of this was the
open seat in Illinois 20 (vacated by Richard Durbin, who ran successfully for
the Senate). The COPE committee endorsed state representative Jay Hoff-
man and gave the maximum five-thousand-dollar contribution in early summer. Another part of the PAC strategy was to hold as much money as possible
until after Labor Day so that money would be available for the closest races
that had the most need. The PAC does not have any written guidelines. No
members of Congress automatically receive support, with the possible exception of Democratic minority leader, Richard Gephardt of Missouri.

The Political Department also kept affiliated unions informed of endorsements. Each affiliate acted as an autonomous body when deciding which candidates to support and the amount to contribute. AFL-CIO affiliates have independent contribution limits under FEC law, meaning that each can contribute the maximum to a federal candidate. This is not the case for the Building and Construction Trades Department and the Transportation Trades Department of the AFL-CIO, which maintain their own PACs but are tied to the contribution limits of the AFL-CIO. For example, if the Building and Construction Trades Department were to give $4,000 to John Kerry for his general election campaign in the Senate race in Massachusetts, the AFL-CIO would be limited to an additional $1,000 for that race. This reflects the law's $5,000 PAC contribution limit per candidate in the general election.[3]

State union federations occasionally endorse both candidates in a race. The COPE philosophy is to avoid working "against our own money," which means that if there is a dual endorsement, neither candidate receives PAC funds from COPE. Challenges to local decision making by the AFL-CIO national office are rare.

The Republican takeover had an impact on COPE's willingness to give to incumbents. In 1996 the PAC required them to show why they needed PAC funds, instead of automatically contributing them. Nonincumbent House candidates were considered very carefully because of the large number of open-seat races. FEC reports for the 1994 and 1996 elections reflect this change in emphasis. Democratic House incumbents received $445,499 in 1994, compared to the $313,020 they received in 1996. Democratic House challengers and open-seat candidates received $358,710 in 1994, as compared to $657,353 in 1996.

The vulnerability of the incumbent was important in determining challenger support. Challengers who held elective office or had some other significant political experience received some preference. A nonincumbent's ability to put together a campaign organization, raise money, and make a good rationale for his or her candidacy was also considered.

In the Senate, where there was an historic number of open seats, some races received no COPE endorsement. This was true in the Idaho Senate race, in which a business-oriented Democrat, Walter Minnick, ran against incumbent Larry Craig. Even though Craig had a poor record on labor issues, the state federation refused to endorse Minnick and, consequently, COPE made no contribution to the race.

COPE gives more total money to House than Senate candidates simply because there are more House races to fund. The PAC made no independent expenditures or in-kind contributions. COPE has had a tradition of contributing to moderate House Republicans. The PAC gave them a total of $6,850 in 1994 and $9,000 in 1996. No money was given to Republican challengers or candidates for open-seat races. The PAC gave no money to Republican Senate candidates.

A Comprehensive Approach

The Republicans' victory in the 1994 elections of Congress took labor by surprise. No one at COPE anticipated the outcome early enough to make a change in the PAC's decision making. Tracking polls in September and October showed that many Democrats were in trouble, but no one believed that the House or Senate would change hands. Thus, COPE did not change its strategy immediately before the election.

The lessons of 1994 were reflected in labor's 1996 strategy, which focused on educating union members about candidates' stands on issues and maximizing COPE contributions in races that would most likely determine the balance of power in the Congress. The new AFL-CIO leadership made an early endorsement of President Clinton in March 1996 and built a list of Republican "targets" in the House and Senate.

> Aggressive grassroots and/or media campaigns were run in 102 Congressional districts, 14 Senate races, two gubernatorial races and state legislative districts to assure that working families get the representation they deserve from the State House to the White House (AFL-CIO 1996c).

Labor broadcast ads in forty of the most competitive races to criticize incumbent Republicans' records on health care and other issues. These issue ads were run as much as eighteen months prior to the election and "softened the ground" for the field operation. Voter guides that compared the records of Democratic and Republican candidates on labor's priority issues were distributed eight weeks prior to the election. Labor soft money contributions to the Democratic Party that amounted to more than $9.9 million further helped Democratic candidates for Congress. It gave a mere $622,335 to the Republican Party (Center for Responsive Politics 1996).

The concentration of television ads, field operations, and voter guides in targeted districts was matched by a concentration of PAC funds from COPE and other union PACs. Labor '96 targets received more COPE dollars and more labor PAC dollars than the nontargeted races (see Table 6.1). This combination of efforts played an important role in many races, including the contest between Maine Republican incumbent James Longley, Jr., and Democratic challenger Tom Allen. A labor-led effort, which included the National Council on Senior Citizens, publicized the slogan, "Longley votes wrongly" early in the race. Once the slogan was picked up in the press, Longley's electoral support began to crumble, enabling Allen to win the race by a 10 percent vote margin.

The Impact of the AFL-CIO Efforts in 1996

Labor's activities in the 1996 congressional elections had a significant impact on their outcome (see Table 6.1). Of the 175 candidates who appeared on the

Table 6.1 COPE and Labor Support for Democratic Candidates in the 1996 House Elections

	Challengers		Incumbents		Open Seats	
	To Republican Freshmen	Other Republicans	Freshmen	Other	Formerly Democratic	Formerly Republican
Untargeted Races						
Avg. COPE contributions	$4,000	$2,289	$2,213	$2,690	$3,636	$4,875
Avg. contributions from labor PACs	$94,763	$46,104	$154,226	$128,997	$103,998	$72,731
(N)	(4)	(21)	(8)	(66)	(11)	(8)
Targeted Races						
Avg. COPE contributions	$5,400	$5,500	$7,167	$5,186	$6,063	$7,429
Avg. contributions from labor PACs	$123,480	$98,951	$261,562	$187,082	$143,644	$128,645
(N)	(5)	(5)	(3)	(18)	(16)	(7)
Targeted Races That Featured Issue Ads						
Avg. COPE contributions	$5,718	$5,700				
Avg. contributions from labor PACs	$153,617	$141,634				
(N)	(20)	(3)	(0)	(0)	(0)	(0)
Targeted Races That Featured Issue Ads and Video Guides						
Avg. COPE contributions	$7,621	$7,917				
Avg. contributions from labor PACs	$149,717	$187,632				
(N)	(20)	(3)	(0)	(0)	(0)	(0)

Note: COPE made no contributions in five targeted races, and it contributed to Representative Bernard Sanders (I–VT) and five Republican House members.

AFL-CIO's final target list, 45 won. COPE-endorsed challengers defeated Republican incumbents in eighteen races and lost in only thirty-nine. This 31.2 percent success record is remarkable given that incumbent reelection rates are typically well above 90 percent. Defeated incumbent Republican Congressman Martin Hoke of Ohio gave credence to the muscle that organized labor flexed in the 1996 elections when he told a National Public Radio interviewer, "This should've been a big victory for me, but labor made it impossible." House Speaker Newt Gingrich concurred, maintaining that "the truth is without the union bosses we'd be gaining at least thirty seats" (Associated Press 1996).

AFL-CIO postelection analysis primarily blamed negative media coverage for the Democrats' failure to regain control of the House. Revelations about fund-raising scandals involving the White House and the Democratic National Committee saturated the media in the month prior to the election. Polls showed that voters who made up their minds more than one month prior to the election were split, 51 percent Democrat and 47 percent Republican. In the wake of Democratic fund-raising scandals, these numbers shifted dramatically. Voters who made up their minds in the last three days prior to the election voted 55 percent Republican and 41 percent Democratic (AFL-CIO 1996b).

Several other factors were also central to Republicans' ability to hold on to over forty of the most competitive races. First, the change in GOP legislators' positions on and support for the minimum wage increase, the Kennedy–Kassebaum health care bill, the Safe Drinking Water Act, and education made it difficult for Democratic challengers to attack GOP candidates on these issues. Second, the Republicans' fund-raising advantages were too large to overcome in many races. Few, if any, challengers can defeat an incumbent who outspends them by more than $1 million, as Republican incumbent John Ensign did against Democratic challenger Bob Coffin in Nevada's first congressional district. Despite AFL-CIO television ads that ran eighteen months prior to the election, and a district with seventy thousand union members, Ensign won the election with 50 percent of the vote to Coffin's 44 percent.

Third, some Democratic challengers were not experienced or articulate enough to wage a competitive campaign. Many of Coffin's difficulties, for example, stemmed from his inability to articulate a message. There is little labor or any other organization can do to overcome a lackluster candidate. Other factors that prevented the Democrats from regaining control of the House were that many of the open seats were located in heavily Republican southern states and the Democratic Party's failure to articulate its stands to voters clearly.

The AFL-CIO Plans for the New Millennium

As the result of its success in the 1996 elections, the AFL-CIO intends to continue its issue-oriented approach to politics. It also plans to involve more union members at the grassroots level by expanding the base of activists who work on its legislative, political, and organizing campaigns. Additional plans include better organizing communities where union members work and live, increasing the union's get-out-the-vote apparatus, and creating a permanent labor center to train political activists as campaign professionals and candidates. The Political Department intends to maintain a continual presence among labor activists, expand its work with coalitions, and get its affiliates to commit their staff to organizing districts earlier in the election season. The AFL-CIO's challenge will be to find ways to keep its corps of nearly eighteen thousand volunteer activists involved in politics.

Although labor lost its battle to defeat the Republican Party in 1996, it won back much of its political power. In the rugged political terrain of the Montana mountains, state federation President Don Judge said he witnessed a "rebirth of trust" among union members in 1996. That is a victory that politicians in both parties should envy (Judge 1996).

Notes

[1] The National Education Association is not affiliated with the AFL-CIO.

[2] In North Carolina, when a primary winner garners less than a majority of the vote, a runoff election is held between the two top finishers.

[3] PACs can give an additional $5,000 in the primary and another $5,000 in the runoff, if one is held.

STILL BRINGING HOME THE BACON: THE UNITED FOOD AND COMMERCIAL WORKERS INTERNATIONAL UNION

Marni Ezra

The United Food and Commercial Workers Union (UFCW) is the largest private sector union in North America, representing 1.4 million members. Like most unions, the UFCW has strong ties to the Democratic Party and had to adjust to the new GOP congressional majority. The union was forced to adopt a defensive legislative strategy of blocking Republican measures. Its PAC did not drastically overhaul its contribution strategy, but it did distribute more of its funds to Democratic challengers in an attempt to change the party control of Congress. The UFCW's fund-raising and voter turnout efforts also increased during the 1996 elections.

The union was founded in 1979 as a result of a merger between the unions of two sectors of supermarket workers, the Amalgamated Meat Cutters and the Retail Clerks. The merger united workers in the rear of most supermarkets, the meat cutters, and those in the front, the retail clerks. It was a logical marriage of convenience reflecting the unification of unions representing these two sets of supermarket workers around the country. Since the early 1980s, the UFCW joined with other unions and includes members of many other industries.[1]

The goals of the UFCW are simply stated by its president, Doug Dority: "We want to make government work more for working families, and to bring the benefits of union membership to low-wage and minority workers" (UFCW 1996, 2). The union seeks to bargain for better wages and benefits for its workers and attempts to influence legislation at all levels of government. The most important issues concerning the UFCW are those that concern the working middle class, including living wages, affordable health care, a pension for retirement, a safe workplace, and job security (*Active Ballot Club Handbook*).

Organizational Structure

The UFCW has a two-tiered external organizational structure. Externally, the UFCW operates both as an independent union and as a member of the AFL-CIO's Executive Council. The relationship between the AFL-CIO and the UFCW can be characterized as one of loose coordination, similar to other unions in the federation. The UFCW works within the guidelines provided by the AFL-CIO but is not bound to them, and they have minimal impact on the day-to-day operation of the UFCW (Landers 1996a). However, when it comes to political decision making, the UFCW frequently acts in concert with the federation and contributes to its coordinated activities.

The UFCW also has a two-tiered internal structure. The upper tier, the International Union, acts to coordinate the union's political and nonpolitical activities. It is the governing body that sets down the union's bylaws, issues and revokes charters, and organizes the union's activities by region (United States, Canada, and Puerto Rico). The lower tier, the 733 local unions, serve as the backbone of the union's grassroots organization. The locals conduct membership drives, resolve grievances, and bargain on behalf of their employees. The relationship between the two tiers is one of mutual respect, combining autonomy and coordination to further the organization's goals.

The Active Ballot Club

The UFCW's PAC, the Active Ballot Club, was created at the time that the unions merged. It was formed from the Amalgamated Meat Cutters' and the Retail Clerks' existing political action committees. The goal of the UFCW, working through the Active Ballot Club, is to elect "pro-working people candidates." Through contributions to candidates and lobbying members of Congress, the Active Ballot Club attempts to elect candidates and pass laws that promote their political agenda.

The UFCW's PAC also has an internal two-tiered structure. The Active Ballot Club is the PAC of the International Union and is a federal, nonfederated PAC. It is the only International Union organization that contributes to federal candidates. A few of the local unions have PACs, but they participate in state, not federal, races.

When it comes to political decision making, the two tiers work together; one does not typically act without the advice and consent of the other. Though contribution decision-making power is centralized in the International's PAC director, the International will not support a candidate without the approval of the local. In addition, many of the local unions look to the International for political information and financial assistance.

Fund-Raising

The Active Ballot Club is a formidable fund-raising organization. It contributed approximately $1.5 million to hundreds of candidates during the 1994 elections, and in 1996 it contributed approximately $2 million to 382 candidates. The money the Active Ballot Club uses to make political contributions comes from four main sources: Leadership 21, checkoffs, silver cards, and special fund-raising events. Leadership 21 is coordinated by the International Union and is the UFCW's only source of high dollar contributions. Staff and officers of the UFCW are strongly encouraged to contribute $240 annually to Leadership 21, and 80 percent of them do so. In contrast, checkoffs are small dollar donations from union members that allow the membership to give throughout the year directly from their paychecks. The recommended contribution is one quarter per week or thirteen dollars a year. Approximately 20 percent of the membership contributes through the checkoff system. Silver cards, used when a company will not allow a checkoff or for additional contributions, range from two to ten dollars. Finally, small contributions are made through special events such as raffles conducted by the local unions. The money raised from checkoffs, silver cards, and special fund-raising events is divided evenly between the local and the International PAC, whereas fund-raising from Leadership 21 goes entirely to the International PAC.

Though all locals are encouraged to raise money, less than half actually do. A local's only source of hard money is its membership and if it does not solicit funds from its members, it cannot make political contributions. However, if a local strongly supports a candidate but does not have the money to do so, it frequently appeals to the International for support. The International often encourages the local to show its investment in the candidate by raising money and mounting grassroots activities. In return, the International will match the local's contribution.

Contribution Decisions

The PAC director decides which candidates receive International Union PAC contributions using four criteria: local union support for the candidate in the district or state, and the candidate's record on labor issues, viability, and need. First, in order to receive a contribution from the UFCW, the candidate must be endorsed by the local union. If the local has not taken a position in the race, the International will ask the local if it would object to the union's involvement in the race. If there is no local chapter, the International will make the decision. When the International and the local disagree, the International may attempt to persuade the local by providing information about a candidate, but in the end, the International defers to the local's decision.

When soliciting contributions, many candidates attempt to bypass the local union and go directly to the International. These candidates are told to seek the endorsement of the local first. Those who do not are less likely to convince the International to receive the PAC's support. As Assistant PAC Director George Landers explains:

> Candidates apply both to the local and International, but the smart ones go through the local—active ground support must go hand in hand with contributions. It is a no go without local support (Landers 1996a).

The PAC director of International makes the final contribution decisions, but the locals work as an informal committee to the director.

The second criterion the PAC uses when deciding to give financial support is the candidate's record on labor issues. The union does not use any one specific issue or vote as a litmus test but looks at a candidate's overall record on issues of concern to the union. The PAC director and lobbyist work closely to determine which members are the most and which are the least supportive of the union's agenda. The PAC obtains information on members' voting histories, retirement possibilities, and interest group scores.

The third and fourth criteria the PAC director uses are the viability of the candidate and the candidate's need. The UFCW will not typically contribute to candidates who have little chance of winning or are so secure that they are not in need of immediate assistance. The PAC director works with the Democratic Party, the AFL-CIO, and other sources to determine which candidates have the highest viability.

The union does not make its contribution decisions based on the candidate's party, chamber, or incumbent status. However, certain candidates are more likely to receive contributions than others because they better fit the above four criteria. Officially, the union is nonpartisan and it contributes to members of both major political parties. As Landers explains, "we give to folks who support working people; unfortunately, the majority of that legislation is supported by Democrats" (Landers 1996b). In the 1994 elections, only 2 percent of the UFCW's contributions went to Republican candidates and, in 1996, 1 percent, or a total of $23,050, went to eleven Republicans. The partisan pattern of financial support did not change with the Republican takeover, for the UFCW believed that a Democratic majority would better address union concerns and that they were unlikely to gain significant access to GOP lawmakers by contributing to them.

The UFCW gave a slightly larger percent of its funds to House than Senate candidates in 1996, but the average contributions given to House and Senate candidates are indistinguishable. The UFCW gave two-thirds of its House contributions to incumbents in 1994, 22 percent to open-seat candidates, and only 12 percent to challengers. Senate contributions in 1994 were divided almost equally between incumbents, open seats, and challengers.

These patterns reflect the fact that Democrats were trying to defend their majority and the union supported many vulnerable incumbents.

In 1996, however, the UFCW switched its contribution pattern because it recognized that the Democrats could only take back Congress by defeating Republican incumbents (see Table 7.1). The PAC made 50 percent of its House contributions to incumbents, 34 percent to challengers, and only 16 percent to candidates for open seats. The UFCW realized that the Democrats were not likely to take control of the Senate. It contributed 57 percent of its Senate resources to open-seat candidates, 23 percent to challengers, and 20 percent to incumbents, a clear change from the previous election cycle in which incumbents received 41 percent.

The Impact of the Revolution on Lobbying

The 1994 elections forced the UFCW to modify its lobbying activities. The union sought to court Republicans, especially those who typically support organized labor, but it did not change its issue positions or lobbying techniques in order to gain their support.

The greatest change for the union was its shift from a "proposing" to a "blocking" organization. Instead of attempting to get legislation passed, the union attempted to obstruct Republican bills (Hutter 1997). The union's lobbying efforts in the 104th Congress concentrated predominantly on four pieces of legislation: the creation of employer–employee teams (the TEAM Act), an increase in the minimum wage, the revision of OSHA reforms, and allowing workers to substitute compensatory time for overtime pay. On all but the minimum wage increase, labor attempted to block the measures put forth by the Republicans.

The UFCW did not wield as much clout as it had in the past. What made lobbying more difficult for the UFCW in the 104th Congress was the party discipline enforced by the Republican leadership, especially when it was voting on the provisions of the Contract with America. Due to the pressure put on the

Table 7.1 UFCW Contributions by Percentages to U.S. House and Senate Candidates

	House		Senate	
	1994	1996	1994	1996
Incumbents	67%	50%	41%	20%
Challengers	12	34	26	23
Open-Seat Candidates	22	16	33	57

Republicans to support the leadership's agenda, it was difficult for the union's lobbyists to have relationships with the Republican members. Though toward the end of the 104th Congress the Republicans' discipline began to loosen, it was still difficult for the union to make inroads among Republicans.

Organized labor suffered numerous temporary setbacks on a series of close votes on issues such as employer unions and compensatory time. After the TEAM Act passed in both the House and Senate, President Clinton vetoed it on July 30, 1996. The law would have allowed companies to create worker–employer unions, which were made illegal under the National Labor Relations Act of 1935. A "comp time" bill that would give employees the option of receiving time off instead of overtime pay also passed in the House but was stalled in the Senate. The UFCW opposed the comp time legislation because it did not adequately protect workers from employers who might force them to use the time off option. Neither bill ultimately became law, but both were passed in the House despite labor's lobbying effort. The outcome for labor was favorable, but the passage of both bills in the House signals a weakness in labor's blocking strategy.

The UFCW and organized labor also enjoyed some victories in the 104th Congress, including the enactment of the minimum wage increase. Though opposed by the Republican leadership in both Houses and the business community, the minimum wage increase was passed with bipartisan support. The UFCW's lobbying strategy was not the only aspect of the organization to change after the Republican Revolution. The UFCW used the Republican takeover to strengthen its ties and reconnect with its membership (Hutter 1997). Through a series of retraining sessions with regional and local leaders, the UFCW increased its coordination and communication with its membership. The regional leaders reviewed present and future issues of importance to the UFCW and developed a strategy to communicate those issues to the grassroots.

The Republican Revolution greatly influenced the UFCW's fund-raising capabilities. Because most of its money is raised through payroll deductions resulting from face-to-face solicitation, the Republican takeover provided the UFCW with the perfect fund-raising pitch. Congress's big business agenda went from "being the theoretical bogeyman to the real thing," which enabled the union to increase its fund-raising (Landers 1996). In addition, after the UFCW's education initiative, its members were better informed of the importance of pending legislation in Congress and in turn were more likely to contribute.

Labor Strategy in 1996

The elections of 1996 were both a relief and a disappointment to organized labor and the UFCW. Although the Democrats did not retake either branch of Congress, the UFCW and other labor organizations played a role in assisting Democrats and prolabor candidates in several key races across the country. The PAC director compiled a list of "closely watched" House races that included twenty incumbents with unfriendly records toward labor, seventeen of whom were targeted by the AFL-CIO, and concentrated most of the PAC's resources in their districts. This was the first time the union focused its resources on a limited number of races.

The UFCW used three specific rules to choose its closely watched districts in 1996 (Landers 1996). First, the district had to have an unfriendly incumbent who won with less than 55 percent of the vote in 1994. Second, the district had to have a UFCW membership base of at least one thousand. Finally, the district had to be in a key battleground state. In all twenty races, the UFCW supported Democrats, many of whom ran against targeted Republican freshmen in marginal seats.

The Democrats in these twenty races received the maximum five-thousand-dollar contribution from the PAC. These districts were also targeted for voter education programs, voter registration drives, and political communications. The union put its organizers on the ground in those districts to help the locals mobilize their membership and made a few independent expenditures consisting of direct mailings on labor issues in districts that had many union members that were represented by antilabor representatives. The UFCW also used soft money, collected as dues, to finance direct mail highlighting the antiunion votes cast by representative members of Congress without advocating the candidate's defeat. Finally, it joined other unions in contributing to the AFL-CIO's voter education campaign, which spent money to defeat Republican incumbents who had poor records on labor issues, especially vulnerable Republican freshmen.

Though the Democrats were not able to recover the House of Representatives as the union had hoped, the UFCW had an impressive success rate, defeating half of the Republicans it targeted. Moreover, the ten Republicans who won despite UFCW opposition were in extremely close races. The UFCW's success rate was significantly higher than that of the AFL-CIO, perhaps because the UFCW targeted fewer races.

Conclusion

The UFCW modified both its lobbying and contribution strategies after the Republican Revolution, but it continued to lobby for labor issues and worked with coalitions of proworker organizations to pass or block legislation. It also continued to try to work with Republican members with prolabor positions. The major shift in the union's activities under a Democratic and Republican Congress is that in the former it mostly worked to pass legislation and in the latter it usually strove to block it. Thanks to occasional presidential vetoes, the union's legislative success rate remained high.

The PAC also made some tactical adjustments. Its biggest change was to provide more support for nonincumbent Democrats, specifically House challengers and open-seat Senate candidates. The PAC did not attempt to win the support of Republican incumbents. It continued to contribute to Republicans with good records on labor issues, but it did not give to powerful, unfriendly Republicans in order to gain access.

The UFCW and organized labor fell short of their goal of electing a Democratic Congress in 1996, but their efforts seemed to pay off at the grassroots. Union membership was key to Democratic victories in many areas. Unions were clearly able to involve their membership, get out the vote in the 1996 elections, and capitalize on the Republican takeover in their fund-raising. Voter turnout among union members in 1996 increased by approximately 1.5 million from 1992. Moreover, union voters made up a bigger portion of voters than in prior elections, increasing from 19 percent in 1992 and 14 percent in 1994 to 23 percent in 1996.

The UFCW and the rest of organized labor are beginning to understand what it is like to be on the outside looking in. To say that they have lost their ability to influence legislation in a Republican-controlled Congress is overstated. Labor had not completed its shopping list of preferred legislation under the Democratic-controlled Congress, and some of the benefits wanted became unavailable as a result of the Republican takeover. Based on labor's victory on minimum wage legislation and the potential for Republican members to defect on popular labor issues, the UFCW will continue its strategy of obstruction and savor its victories when they come.

Note

[1]The UFCW's membership consists of local supermarkets (900,000), meatpacking and food processing (250,000), nursing homes and hospitals (35,000), insurance agents, barbers, and beauticians.

THE SIERRA CLUB
POLITICAL COMMITTEE

David Cantor

The Sierra Club is the leading advocate for environmental protection in the United States. After the Republicans took control of Congress in 1994, Sierra Club lobbyists found themselves denied access to lawmakers (Gimpel 1998) and watched helplessly as industry representatives helped draft antienvironmental legislation. This experience led the Sierra Club to attempt to mobilize its members to put grassroots pressure on Congress.

The 1994 elections also forced the Sierra Club to consider new electoral strategies. As public awareness of the threats to environmental protection spread, contributions to the Sierra Club Political Committee increased, allowing the Club to expand its electoral activities. In 1996, the Sierra Club would, for the first time, undertake issue advocacy campaigns, independent expenditure campaigns, and a large voter education project. The Sierra Club also adopted a new strategy, holding more of its resources until the final weeks of the campaign. With this strategy, the Sierra Club was able to target extremely close races, enhancing the Sierra Club's impact on the 1996 elections.

Organizational Development

The Sierra Club is now a national organization, but its roots are far more parochial. It was founded by Scottish immigrant John Muir in 1892. Muir had been active in lobbying the state of California and the federal government for the creation of Yosemite National Park. The new organization was to act as a watchdog, protecting the park from business interests that wanted to encroach on its protected resources (Turner 1991, 23–24).

From the start, the Sierra Club had two purposes. It was a political organization, actively promoting conservation of the environment. It was also an educational organization, planning lectures and outings to promote public awareness. The original articles of incorporation expressed this dual role. The Sierra Club was to:

> explore, enjoy, and render accessible the mountain regions of the Pacific coast; to publish authentic information concerning them; and to enlist the support and cooperation of the people and government in preserving the forests and other natural features of the Sierra Nevada Mountains (Turner 1991, 48–49).

By its third meeting the Sierra Club found itself entering the arena of national politics. The Club sent a petition to Congress, calling for the defeat of a bill to reduce the size of Yosemite and open the park to the timber, mining, and livestock industries. Early Sierra Club Bulletins informed members of "onerous natural resource laws" then on the books and called on them to pressure Congress to repeal them (Turner 1991, 49–50). It was not until 1963, however, that the Sierra Club established a permanent office in Washington, DC, which allowed the organization to play a more active role in national politics and to maintain a more consistent lobbying presence in Congress.

Campaign Activity

The Sierra Club did not mount a serious effort to influence national elections until after the 1980 elections, which brought to Washington a new group of politicians who were hostile to environmental conservation, personified by Ronald Reagan's Secretary of the Interior, James Watt. The Club had issued no endorsements in national elections before or during the 1980 elections. Reagan's victory, coupled with the defeat of several proenvironment senators, including John Culver (D–IA), Frank Church (D–ID), George McGovern (D–SD), and Birch Bayh (D–IN), led to a new strategy.

In the 1980s, the Sierra Club "dipped [its] toes in the treacherous waters of electoral politics (finding it easier to be persuasive with someone they had helped elect)" (Turner 1991, 22). The Sierra Club had long tried to persuade lawmakers to support environmental protection, but the new electoral strategy was intended to make it easier for Club lobbyists to find allies in Congress.

The Sierra Club's PAC, the Sierra Club Political Committee (SCPC), was formed in 1982 so that the organization could play an active role in helping its allies during elections. In that year, the Sierra Club endorsed 140 House and Senate candidates and spent approximately $250,000 in campaign contributions. Club members worked on the campaigns of endorsed candidates across the country. Three-quarters of Club-endorsed candidates won.

In 1984, the Sierra Club expanded its role in electoral politics, endorsing Walter Mondale for president. In 1988, the Sierra Club did not endorse a presidential candidate, in part because neither had strong environmental credentials, but in 1992 the Club endorsed Bill Clinton. The Sierra Club Political Committee has never contributed to presidential candidates.

Political Activities

The Sierra Club has two goals for its electoral activities: to elect better environmental candidates and to foster the most environmentally friendly Congress possible. These goals shape all decisions for the allocation of the Club's two most precious resources: the Sierra Club endorsement and campaign contributions and expenditures. In both cases, decisions are made to facilitate lobbying efforts by Club officials.

Endorsements

The Sierra Club offers endorsements of candidates and uses these endorsements both as an electoral tool to help proenvironment candidates and as a political tool to help in future lobbying efforts. As Political Director Dan Weiss put it, "the Sierra Club is unique in that the endorsement is meaningful because the name means something. There is a noneconomic benefit to a Sierra Club endorsement. In effect, we offer the environmental version of the Good Housekeeping Seal of Approval" (Weiss 1996).[1]

The local chapters generally begin the endorsement process. Their recommendations for endorsements are usually approved by state and regional chapters and then passed on to the national committee, which ratifies 90 percent of the state chapters' recommendations. Endorsement requires two-thirds support of both the local Sierra Club chapter and the national political committee (Sierra Club Political Committee Compliance Guidelines 1995, 10). The chapters usually initiate the endorsement process. The political staff gives input, but all decisions are made by Club members.

In making an endorsement, the Sierra Club considers the candidates' environmental records and the political characteristics of the race. The Club's rules require the endorsement process to begin with an evaluation of each candidate's record on environmental issues: "Clearly, the most important consideration when looking at candidates is their environmental records and pronouncements" (Sierra Club Political Committee Compliance Guidelines 1995, 6).

Yet, the Sierra Club endorsement does not automatically go to the "greener" candidate. Any incumbents with a good environmental record must receive a Club endorsement, regardless of the environmental policy views of their challenger. Although this strategy sometimes means that the

Club endorses the "less-green candidate," it is meant to help the Club's lobbyists work in Congress.

> We must send a consistent signal to members of Congress…that if they are good to us we will be good to them.… If we abandon our incumbent friends to support their opponents, other good incumbents may doubt whether the Sierra Club will support them, making them less likely to carry our banner on legislation when we need them (Sierra Club Political Committee Compliance Guidelines 1995, 7).

The viability of each candidate is also an important factor in deciding what role the Sierra Club should play in a particular campaign. Again, the Sierra Club's Compliance Guidelines make clear that this policy is meant to help when it comes to lobbying Congress. In deciding whether to endorse a candidate, the closeness of the race is important because "at all times we must be concerned with our ability to lobby effectively and with preserving the Club's political credibility" (Sierra Club Political Committee Compliance Guidelines 1995, 8). A challenger may be great on environmental issues, but if the race is a lost cause, he or she will not be endorsed in order to avoid unnecessarily antagonizing an opponent. Close votes in Congress come down to a few key members. Having endorsed a member's opponent makes the job of Sierra Club lobbyists more difficult.

The Sierra Club also makes an effort to endorse candidates in all regions and in both parties, and this leads the Club to apply different standards in some situations. Club decision makers recognize that what passes for a strong environmental record differs by region. A member of Congress with a 60 percent voting record on environmental issues would be viewed as an opponent of the environment in New England, but an ally if from the South (Sierra Club Political Committee Compliance Guidelines 1995, 8).

The Sierra Club is a bipartisan organization, and the Club makes an effort to identify Republicans that it can endorse. The Club's compliance guidelines instruct decision makers to keep an open mind:

> It is no secret that, on average, Democrats score higher than Republicans on most environmental ratings, and that the club has endorsed more Democrats than Republicans. But we cannot let this general record distort our assessment of individual Republican and Democratic candidates who are committed to our issues (Sierra Club Political Committee Compliance Guidelines 1995, 7).

This policy has real implications on endorsement decisions. Political Director Weiss claims to "bend over backwards for Republicans. We have affirmative action for Republicans" (Weiss 1996).

Bipartisanship leads the Sierra Club to endorse Republicans with mediocre environmental records. Democrats with the same record are unlikely to receive an endorsement. This policy is meant to help the Sierra Club's lobbying efforts.

By allying with Republicans who are at least moderately proenvironment, the Club creates a group of legislators it can turn to on the closest votes. If the Sierra Club were not bipartisan, it would be unable to build coalitions and get its agenda passed.

Campaign Contributions and Expenditures

The Sierra Club's endorsement costs the organization nothing and is used by candidates to garner support. Contributions and expenditures require the use of the Club's limited resources. Although the Sierra Club Political Committee is not a small PAC, its resources are finite. As a membership PAC, the SCPC may only solicit funds from its members. The PAC uses direct mail and telephone drives to raise money from members. The average donation is thirty-four dollars per contributor.

Local chapters take the lead in requesting funds to support candidates and recommend the type of support that will be of the most use to the campaign, but it is the national Political Committee that has the final say on distribution of PAC money. Club guidelines instruct the Political Committee to base decisions on the importance of the race, the campaign activities proposed by the chapter, and the effect Sierra Club action will have on the race. The guidelines instruct the Political Committee to target close races: "The goal is to spend money where it has the greatest chance of having an impact, so more money will go to close races than to 'sure winners' or 'sure losers'" (Sierra Club Political Committee Compliance Guidelines 1995, 20).

The closeness of the race is the most important factor when making contribution decisions. Contributions and expenditures are meant to create a Congress that will be friendly to environmental issues. By targeting the closest races, the Sierra Club hopes to gain the appreciation of legislators who owe their seat to Club assistance. Such friends become key allies when it comes time to lobby Congress. While the electoral program helps Sierra Club lobbying, contributions are not given to powerful safe incumbents merely for access. "We never gave to Rostenkowski," says Weiss[1] (Weiss 1996).

To determine which races are close, the Sierra Club relies on a variety of information sources. The Club considers polling data, Federal Election Commission (FEC) financial reports, the Cook Political Report and the Rothenberg Political Report, the House and Senate Democratic campaign committees, and local chapters and field organizers.[2] The SCPC also exchanges information with like-minded PACs. The Progressive Network is an alliance of liberal groups that meets regularly to share insights. Weiss described the Network as a "progressive political coffee klatch where we exchange information, gossip, hearsay, and innuendo" (Edsall 1996, A1).

The SCPC works with limited resources and tries to target contributions to places where they can have the most impact. House races, in general, have smaller budgets, and a single contribution is more likely to have an impact on electoral outcomes. The Sierra Club therefore contributes significantly more money to House than to Senate races.

In addition to cash contributions, the Sierra Club also makes in-kind contributions. Permanent employees of the Sierra Club are shifted to campaign work during the election season, and assigned to work on specific campaigns. In some cases they merely provide another body, but frequently they deliver key services to the campaign, such as serving as press secretaries and field organizers.

The Impact of the 1994 Elections

Since the 1980 election results motivated the Sierra Club to get involved in electoral politics, no single event has so fundamentally changed the political activity of the organization as the 1994 Republican Revolution. In 1994, the Sierra Club Political Committee spent over $600,000, mostly in direct contributions to candidates. There were no independent expenditures, no voter education campaigns, and very little issue advocacy. A lot of money was given early in the election in the hope of assisting friends and providing seed money for challengers. On election night, the Sierra Club realized it had supported a number of candidates who won or lost by large margins.

By September, it was clear to the members of the Political Committee that the Republicans would capture the Senate and that they had a good shot at winning the House. However, it did not change its strategy, partly because the Club is officially bipartisan, and partly because the PAC had already committed much of its resources early in the election cycle.

The effect of Republican control of Congress on Sierra Club lobbying was immediate. According to Weiss, the Sierra Club went from "offense to defense immediately." In most sessions, bills relevant to the Sierra Club do not begin to percolate until March, but the 104th Congress was considering the Unfunded Mandates bill in January. Unfunded Mandates had the potential to prevent the implementation of federal environmental regulation by state and local governments. On March 3, Regulatory Reform passed the House. This bill would prevent new environmental regulations and bring into question most existing statutes.

The Sierra Club quickly found that its access had been severely diminished. Press reports told of the close working relationship between business lobbyists and Republican committee chairs. While business was rewriting environmental policy, Weiss found "we had almost zero access to the committee structure and the people who set environmental policy" (Weiss 1996).

Lobby reform legislation had little impact on Sierra Club strategy; it mainly prevented Sierra Club lobbyists from passing out the popular Sierra Club calendars to members and their staff. Of much larger significance was the closing off to lobbyists of the area on the second floor outside the House Chamber. This reform made it difficult for groups with limited resources to reach swing members on close votes. Businesses have the resources to reach all members in their offices. With its limited political budget, the Sierra Club relied on catching people on their way to and from the floor. With this no longer possible, its ability to lobby members in Washington has been hampered.

The 1996 Campaign

The antienvironmental tone of congressional debate in the 104th Congress received much publicity and made fund-raising easier for the Political Committee. Direct-mail efforts garnered twice as much money as they had prior to the Republican takeover. More money allowed the Sierra Club to conduct a much more aggressive electoral program. During the 1996 elections, the organization would conduct independent expenditure campaigns and large voter education projects for the first time.

Facing a hostile congressional majority with little access to key policy makers, the Sierra Club decided to radically change its programs for electoral involvement. In 1996, the PAC would hold its cash contributions until late in the election cycle, hoping to better identify races where its money might make a difference. In addition, the PAC used independent expenditures for the first time, and the Sierra Club engaged in issue advocacy and launched a large voter contact.

Direct and In-Kind Contributions

The GOP Congress proved a good foil for SCPC fund-raising, and the increased resources allowed the SCPC to maintain its traditional electoral activity while funding the independent expenditures and voter education campaigns. What changed was the targeting of contributions. Club officials believed that they had wasted many of their contributions in the 1994 GOP landslide and planned to target their contributions more carefully in 1996. Weiss explained:

> We are not giving to people we love who have no chance of winning. In 1994, we gave to too many people who ended up with less than forty percent of the vote. The goal is to only give to races that are within ten points at the end (Weiss 1996).

The Sierra Club chose to hold its money until late in the campaign season to enable it to allocate more of its resources to the closest races.

The Sierra Club adopted its late contribution strategy mindful of the fact that early contributions to nonincumbents can provide crucial seed money for their campaigns. For challengers, the ability to raise early money makes them appear viable. Viability fosters more money (Biersack, Herrnson, and Wilcox 1993). In 1994, the SCPC had pursued a strategy of contributing early money to candidates with strong proenvironment credentials, with the hope that these donations would act as a cue to other groups, encouraging them to give to these candidates as well. In retrospect, the SCPC leadership felt that this strategy had failed. In 1996, most money was held until at least September, even though requests for contributions from allies came earlier than in the past.

Because it made later donations, the Sierra Club was able to do a better job of targeting. Although the SCPC still gave a few contributions to sure losers (largely for sentimental reasons), Sierra Club contributions were far more likely to go to candidates in close races. Table 8.1 shows Sierra Club contributions and expenditures for all candidates, and for those who received between 40 and 60 percent of the vote. In 1996, 83 percent of contributions went to candidates in close races, compared with only 58 percent in 1994. Moreover, all independent expenditures were made in close races. Making

Table 8.1   Sierra Club Contributions and Expenditures

1994 Elections			
	Contributions	Expenditures For	Expenditures Against
All candidates	$406,631	$0	$0
Competitive candidates[a]	239,390	0	0
1996 Elections			
	Contributions	Expenditures For	Expenditures Against
All candidates	$370,058	$74,521	$90,061
Competitive candidates[a]	307,249	74,521	90,061

[a]"Competitive" refers to candidates who received between 41 and 59 percent of the vote.

decisions later in the campaign also allowed the Sierra Club to shift to close races staff members who were being employed as in-kind contributions.

By holding on to its money, the SCPC was able to give to candidates in races that only emerged as close near the end. An example is California's 46th district, where Democrat Loretta Sanchez defeated incumbent Republican Bob Dornan. The Sierra Club did not come to view Sanchez as viable until the last weeks of the campaign. While Dornan was high on its list of "environmental bad guys," the race was seen as a sure loser. In October, when it became apparent that it was going to be a very close race, the SCPC sent the Sanchez campaign a contribution and shifted a staff member onto the campaign as an in-kind contribution. When Sanchez won by fewer than one thousand votes, the Sierra Club (along with everyone else who helped the campaign) could reasonably claim that it had provided the margin of victory. If the SCPC had committed all of its resources early in the cycle, as it had in the past, it would not have been able to contribute to Sanchez and might not have gained a congressional ally.

Giving contributions later allowed the Sierra Club to make more informed decisions. The SCPC relied on the same sources as in the past but found that information was more accurate closer to the election. Two sources were of particular help. At the end of the campaign, the Sierra Club found the information it was getting from the Democratic Congressional Campaign Committee (DCCC) to be very useful. The DCCC was able to point to swing races and identify top priorities. The DCCC also provided campaign polling numbers that showed which were the closest races. Late FEC financial reports also were of use. In becoming a late donor, the Sierra Club shifted from being a cue giver to a cue taker. Only challengers who had raised at least $500,000 were deemed truly viable. Late FEC reports helped the Sierra Club channel its money to challengers with a real chance or incumbents facing a well-funded threat. With money on hand until the final weeks, the Sierra Club was able to react to the DCCC and FEC data.

The aggressive campaign strategies employed by the Sierra Club and like-minded groups limited their ability to work together in 1996. For example, the League of Conservation Voters (LCV) was involved in twelve independent expenditure campaigns, targeting what it called the "Dirty Dozen" members of Congress. For the independent expenditure campaigns to be independent, the LCV could have no interaction with the campaigns it was helping. The Sierra Club was not bound by this constraint (except for its own independent expenditure campaigns) and could work closely with many candidates, even placing staffers in thirty campaigns as in-kind contributions. The Sierra Club and LCV could not coordinate their efforts in these thirty races because the high level of involvement of the Sierra Club's staffers in them meant that any interaction between the two organizations would compromise the independence of the LCV's independent expenditures. This limited the ability of the environmental community to work together and share information. Although covered in the press as a prototypical political party, Weiss found the Progressive Network of liberal PACs to be of limited help in targeting.

The Sierra Club continued to be a bipartisan organization in 1996, even as it relied on the DCCC for last-minute information. The Sierra Club only endorsed Democratic candidates for the Senate, but it did endorse thirteen Republicans for the House. The SCPC gave over $15,000 to Republican candidates (more than twice as much as in 1994). However, the reality of the 1996 election was that the Sierra Club continued to find itself more closely allied with the Democratic Party. The Republican 104th Congress had a very poor record on environmental issues. Members of the Republican freshman class had among the worst environmental records in Congress, and many of these new members represented the most marginal districts. These factors led the SCPC to contribute overwhelmingly to Democrats, especially assisting Democrats challenging Republican House freshmen.

Consequently, the proportion of Sierra Club contributions going to challengers was much higher in 1996 than it had been in past elections. Of the sixty races the Sierra Club was most involved in during the 1996 campaign, only about 30 percent involved incumbents with good environmental records, and another 20 percent were open seats. Fully half were challengers facing incumbents with bad environmental records. The Sierra Club turned to challengers as a way to reverse the course Congress was taking on environmental issues. The Sierra Club also continued its policy of focusing on House races. During the 104th Congress, the House took the lead in scaling back environmental regulations. Members of the House had worse records than senators. This made House members even more appealing targets than in past elections.[3]

Independent Expenditures

In addition to cash contributions, the SCPC engaged in independent expenditures for the first time in the 1996 elections. Almost a year before the 1996 elections, the retirement of Republican Senator Bob Packwood set up a special election in Oregon. The Sierra Club endorsed Ron Wyden, the Democrat, and contributed to his campaign. In addition, the SCPC for the first time undertook an independent expenditure campaign. The group's fundraising success made the roughly $150,000 campaign in Oregon possible.

The Oregon independent expenditure campaign was undertaken for two reasons. Wyden was clearly the "greener" candidate in this very close race. His victory could help Club lobbyists in the Senate. The Sierra Club also hoped to use the Oregon Senate race to make "the environment what

Pennsylvania made health care in 1991," Weiss said. In 1991, Harris Wofford won the Pennsylvania Senate race largely by calling for health care reform. In 1992, health care became a dominant campaign theme across the country. By making the environment the swing issue in the Oregon Senate race, the Sierra Club hoped to propel environmental issues to the front of the 1996 campaign.

Much of the SCPC's independent expenditure campaign consisted of attacks on Wyden's Republican opponent, Gordon Smith. The Sierra Club, which did not have any staff working in Wyden's campaign, joined with the League of Conservation Voters in airing television and radio advertisements attacking the environmental record of Smith's frozen foods business. Spots were also run attacking Smith's record in the Oregon state legislature (Kriz 1996, 74). Additionally, environmental groups worked together to identify 100,000 voters in suburban Portland with environmental sympathies and then deluged them with mail and phone calls to motivate them to vote (Murphy 1996, A12).

The environmental effort in Oregon earned a great deal of press attention. After his victory, Wyden credited environmental issues and environmental groups with providing his small margin of victory (Murphy 1996, A12). The press attention coupled with Wyden's statements had the effect the Sierra Club had hoped for. People outside of Oregon saw that elections could turn on environmental issues. Republican attacks on the environment in the 104th Congress helped create an atmosphere in which voters were receptive to environmental pleas. "The Oregon Senate race made this clear," said Weiss (Weiss 1997). This atmosphere gave proenvironment candidates an advantage even before the Sierra Club contributed to their campaign.

The experience in Oregon convinced the Sierra Club to try independent expenditures during the 1996 campaigns. During the general election, the Sierra Club conducted two more successful independent expenditure campaigns. In California's district twenty-two, the SCPC conducted an approximately $75,000 campaign on behalf of Democrat Walter Capps in his campaign against Andrea Seastrand. In Michigan's eighth district, a similar campaign was conducted on behalf of Democrat Debbie Stabenow against Dick Chrysler. In both cases, the target was a Republican freshman from a swing district with a poor environmental record. The Club used direct mail, television, and radio to criticize Seastrand and Chrysler for failing to protect the local environment, and to tie them to big business groups with a vested interest in lax environmental regulation. The advertisements linked campaign contributions from "polluters" with votes cast by these incumbents to cut funding for the Environmental Protection Agency and limit its ability to enforce environmental standards. In contrast, the Sierra Club campaigns stressed that Capps and Stabenow had pledged to block attempts to weaken the nation's environmental laws and had received the Club's endorsement. The spots specifically called on people to vote for Capps and Stabenow. Both won tight races.

The Voter Education Project

Another aggressive new strategy was a $3.5 million voter education project, with the distribution of voter guides in twenty-eight House campaigns and seven Senate races. Although the Sierra Club had engaged in voter education in past campaigns, the organization dramatically expanded the scope of this activity in 1996. Voter education projects must be done without coordinating with the campaigns, so the Sierra Club ran its voter education project out of its San Francisco office, physically separating the project from the rest of the organization's electoral efforts.

In addition, voter education projects cannot openly advocate the election of any candidate. In the past, interest groups have quite openly skirted the boundaries of advocacy, and the FEC has filed suit against the Christian Coalition for its "nonpartisan" voter guides. While more groups used voter guides in 1996 than in the past, the FEC suit has led to less overt support of particular candidates on these guides (Berke 1996, A1; Birnbaum 1996, 32; Marcus 1996b, A9).

The main part of the Sierra Club voter education project consisted of mailing voter guides to individuals identified as having environmental sympathies. Voter guides displayed candidate positions on the issues without explicitly advocating the election of any one candidate. Each guide presented voters with a chart showing candidate stands on environmental issues. By identifying voters with environmental sympathies and targeting races in which one of the candidates had a poor environmental record, the Club allowed voters to draw their own conclusions, knowing full well what they would be. This contrasts with the independent expenditure campaigns in which the Sierra Club openly advocated its support for Wyden, Capps, and Stabenow while attacking their opponents for poor environmental records. The Club mailed three voter guides that presented the same chart of candidate records in the final three weeks of the campaign. Guides were also distributed door-to-door by Sierra Club volunteers in the weeks before the election.

The voter guides compared candidate stands on environmental issues. Because the voter education project had to be independent of any campaign, the Sierra Club had to rely on the public record to identify candidate positions on environmental issues. For incumbents, this was easy: Roll call voting provided a detailed history of their positions. For challengers, finding a public record was more difficult, especially for those who had not held public office before. The Sierra Club was forced to rely on campaign literature and public statements by candidates. Challengers rarely are forthcoming in making antienvironmental views public. If they are not supporters, candidates are usually silent on environmental issues. This made incumbents with bad environmental records prime, but not exclusive, targets for voter guides. The Club mounted these voter education projects in districts where they could find useful information about candidate positions, where the race was close, and where voters were sympathetic with environmental issues.

The preparation of voter guides was very labor-intensive, requiring a great deal of research and weeks of time for production. According to John DeCock, the coordinator of the Sierra Club's voter education project in 1996, this forced the selection of races as early as June. Assessing the voter guide program, DeCock concluded that the early targeting had led to some wasted resources and some missed opportunities. Some races that seemed close in June were landslides by the time the guides reached voters. Such resources could have been better deployed in other races that were not on the radar screen in June. Some flexibility was maintained, and new districts were added to the voter guide program in September, but significant resources had already been expended on one-sided races.

The Club's more aggressive tactics had a large effect on the 1996 elections. The independent expenditure campaigns were very successful. The Oregon race set the debate for the rest of the election season. The California and Michigan efforts resulted in the defeat of members with the worst environmental records in Congress. Proenvironment candidates won in eighteen out of twenty-eight House races included in the voter education campaign (including five proenvironment challengers and two proenvironment candidates in open seats). Proenvironment Senate candidates won in three of the seven races (including one proenvironment challenger), and the grassroots lobbying issue campaigns helped set the early tone of debate that carried through election day.

As the campaign drew to a close, and control of the House remained somewhat in doubt, the Sierra Club was able to use hostility toward the Republican Congress to energize its members. As part of the voter education campaign, the Sierra Club used volunteers to distribute literature door-to-door. When it issued a call for volunteers, the response was overwhelming. In Kansas, 150 people showed up for a final weekend door-to-door literature drop, an unprecedented turnout (Weiss 1997).

For the first time in its history, the Sierra Club was active in presidential politics beyond endorsing a particular candidate. The presidential race was included in the voter education project. Over 150,000 voter guides were distributed in twenty-three states. The guides contrasted Bill Clinton's actions to protect the environment while in the White House with Bob Dole's antienvironmental Senate record. This new activity had limited, if any, impact on the presidential election. The Club did not endorse Clinton until September. "By then, it was already over," Weiss observed (Weiss 1997).

Issue Advocacy

The Sierra Club also waged issue advocacy campaigns in targeted districts. In previous years the Sierra Club had found the environment to be an issue that worked best when used negatively as a weapon. Voters expect their representatives to be "green." Finding out that legislators support Sierra Club positions has limited positive effect. But when voters learn that their member of Congress is not protecting the environment, they become angry. "We have found that we can make the biggest difference in attacking people with bad records," Weiss said.

The 104th Congress provided the Sierra Club with a negative agenda that energized its members and supporters. It turned to grassroots issue advocacy campaigns, using radio ads, letters to local newspapers, and town meetings to put pressure on members of Congress to support Club positions. Issue advocacy campaigns were run in swing districts because these members were expected to be the most responsive to grassroots lobbying. Again, the Club targeted primarily freshman Republicans.

Grassroots lobbying efforts had the added effect of helping the Sierra Club electoral program. Speaking after the 1996 elections, Weiss concluded that where grassroots issue advocacy was employed, the Sierra Club was able to shape the debate for the rest of the campaign. He cited campaigns in North Carolina's fourth district against Fred Heineman and in Maine's first district against James Longley as successful in setting the agenda for the rest of the debate. "We were able to knock them down so far they were never able to get up" (Weiss 1997). Both were defeated in the November elections.

Assessment of the 1996 Campaign and Implications for the Future

It is doubtful that the Sierra Club will be able to duplicate its 1996 campaign efforts. The use of more aggressive tactics in this election was a reaction to the antienvironment agenda of the 104th Congress. Independent expenditure campaigns, a voter education project, issue advocacy campaigns, and traditional campaign contributions were made possible by member response to congressional action. Early antienvironment legislation in the House motivated Club members to get involved. The new, aggressive tactics were only possible because of increased contributions from members to the PAC. The

Sierra Club message would not have resonated so clearly if the 104th Congress had not galvanized support for environmental protection.

The Sierra Club had a large impact on the nature of many campaigns and influenced the outcome of more than a few close races. The record of the 104th Congress gave the Sierra Club an agenda it could use to shape races around the country. After proving that the environment could work as an effective issue in Oregon, the Sierra Club was able to help proenvironment candidates capitalize on heightened voter awareness in other races. By hoarding its money until the end of the election cycle, the Sierra Club was able to more effectively target its assistance to races where it could have an impact.

The Sierra Club's decision-making guidelines only moderately hampered flexibility at the end of the election. The most difficult part of the Club's decision-making process comes at the beginning of the campaign season, when the national Political Committee and the local chapters work together to make endorsements. This process can be cumbersome, but it allows the Sierra Club's PAC the ability to make quick decisions. The only limitation this process places on last-minute decisions comes in places where the local chapter and the national committee are unable to agree on an endorsement. In such cases, the Sierra Club is unable to play a role in potentially close races. For example, in 1996, the Sierra Club endorsed neither candidate in Pennsylvania's thirteenth district. Incumbent Republican John Fox won in one of the closest races of the year. Without an endorsement in the race, the Sierra Club could not play a part in the race, even though it could have had an impact.

Sierra Club candidates won two-thirds of the group's targeted races. Club strategy was also useful in shaping the agenda for the 1996 elections. Citing an internal poll, Weiss claimed that in the sixty or so races in which the Sierra Club was active, "the environment was always the first or second reason why people voted against the incumbent. We were successful in making our issues the ones that decided the elections" (Weiss 1997). Voters held Republicans responsible for the antienvironment record of the 104th Congress.

It is too early to tell if the success of the Sierra Club electoral program in 1996 will lead to a more hospitable Congress. Early actions by the Republican leadership gave indications that they had learned from the backlash. After the November election, Republicans were far less public about their plans to tackle environmental issues. While they did not necessarily change their agenda, they did seem to have changed tactics.

Notes

[1]During the 1980s, the Sierra Club used PAC money to go to Washington fund-raisers as a means to gain access to certain committees. This process was stopped because,

according to Weiss (1997), Club leaders concluded they were not getting much for the money they were spending.

[2]Although the Sierra Club is a bipartisan organization, Weiss (1997) claimed that there were not enough Republicans being supported to warrant regular contact with Republican committees.

[3]Overall totals on SCPC spending on 1996 House and Senate races are a bit misleading because of the large effort the Club undertook in the Oregon Senate race.

LEAGUE OF CONSERVATION VOTERS

Philip A. Mundo

The League of Conservation Voters (LCV) is among the most politically active and effective environmental groups in U.S. politics today. The LCV has historically engaged in a two-pronged political strategy: one that publicized information on the environmental records of members of Congress and one that involved contributing to proenvironment candidates in congressional elections. After the 1994 midterm congressional elections, the LCV changed course dramatically from its long-standing strategy of making campaign contributions to proenvironment congressional candidates. Cutting the level of such contributions dramatically, the group poured the bulk of its resources into a no-holds-barred negative advertising campaign funded by independent expenditures against antienvironment congressional candidates. The 1996 congressional elections represent a major shift in the LCV's political strategy, a risky gamble fostered by equally significant changes in the group's political environment.

History and Structure

The LCV was founded in 1970 to provide an electoral arm to the environmental movement. While attempting to influence members of Congress through lobbying is certainly important, the logic underlying the creation of the LCV was that it is equally effective, if not more so, to try to get proenvironment candidates elected to Congress in the first place. The LCV has concentrated much of its political activity on campaigns throughout its history. The group underwent a major overhaul in 1988 and became more professionalized in order to be more effective in influencing elections (Loyless 1996a). The Board of Directors determines the LCV's goals and strategies and the political director carries out the board's decisions with general responsibility for all political programs of the 25,000-member group, regardless of where they are formally located in the organization. This includes the Education Fund, the Action Fund, and the LCV parent organization (Loyless 1996a).

The LCV's Board of Directors determines the group's goals and strategies. Its president, a volunteer, makes the group's major public statements—such as the endorsement of presidential and vice presidential candidates. The political director has general responsibility for the day-to-day operation of the LCV's parent organization, its Education Fund, Action Fund, and other political programs. The political director is also the LCV's spokesperson on most routine matters. The LCV's professional staff carries out programmatic activities, such as overseeing the group's finances, membership drives, media relations, and communications. The LCV keeps its administrative costs to a minimum by relying on interns to help carry out many activities, enabling it to devote most of its resources to political activities.

The LCV relies primarily on member dues and individual contributions for its funding (Bosso 1995, 108–109). The group receives modest contributions from other PACs. Other PACs rarely solicit funds from the LCV (Loyless 1996a).

Political Education

The LCV has concentrated on two sets of political activities. The first is political education, a function carried out by the League of Conservation Voters Education Fund (LCVEF), the 501(c)(3), or Education Fund, component of the LCV. As dictated by this tax-exempt status, the LCVEF distributes information about environmental issues and the environmental records of members of Congress. The LCVEF publishes the *Green Guide*, which profiles members of Congress according to their views on environmental issues.[1] The *Green Guide* is based on a questionnaire the LCVEF sends to each member of the new Congress before it goes into session. The *Green Guide* on the 105th Congress, for example, was published in early January 1997. The information presented in this document is used by the media, the public, and the environmental community.

Political Activities

The League of Conservation Voters, Inc., is a 501(c)(4) organization, which means that it actively participates in politics. The LCV carries out a number of activities intended to draw attention to the records of members of Congress on environmental issues. Chief among these is the National Environmental Scorecard, "an annual report card on how Congress votes on the environment" (http://www.lcv.org). The evaluation is based on how the legislator voted on key environmental bills that were selected by a policy advisory committee, a panel of environmentalists drawn from other environmental groups and the environmental community in general. This information can be used by the media, the public, other groups, and the LCV Action Fund for a variety of direct political purposes.

In addition to its trademark Scorecard, the LCV composes two lists of the best and the worst congressional candidates on environmental issues. The older and better known of these two lists is the "Dirty Dozen." Originated by Environmental Action, which gave LCV permission to use the name and the concept, the Dirty Dozen lists twelve congressional candidates with the worst records on environmental issues. The more recent list has been dubbed the "Earth List," which contains the names of ten members of Congress with the most proenvironment voting records (http://www.lcv.org). The lists provide information about the environmental records of members of Congress to the media and the public, making it possible for them to hold legislators accountable for their actions. The lists also provide potential candidates with valuable information about their opponents. Just as important, the research used to formulate the lists is used when the LCV Action Fund allocates its resources. Members of the Dirty Dozen make logical targets for an environmental PAC, and legislators on the Earth List are likely to benefit from some form of LCV support.

The LCV endorses challengers, incumbents, and green-seat candidates for Congress. These endorsements do not necessarily cover all the candidates who have acceptable views on the environment, nor do they mean that the LCV PAC will necessarily contribute to their campaigns. However, they do provide an important cue to those with strong interest in environmental issues.

Campaign Activities

Congressional elections are the main event for the LCV, although the PAC contributes to presidential candidates and the LCV endorses them. The LCV Board of Directors determines the LCV Action Fund's general strategy in any given election cycle, and the political advisory board, consisting of environmental activists, representatives of other environment groups, and others, selects the candidates whom the LCV will support (Loyless 1996a). The specific candidates, central issues, targeted campaigns, and the political environment change from election to election, but the basic parameters for deciding to which candidates to contribute remain constant and clear; the LCV Action Fund gives only to proenvironment congressional candidates.

The LCV PAC does not make contributions to congressional candidates with poor environmental records in order to gain access.

The PAC contributes to incumbents based on their voting records on environmental issues, an evaluation the LCV routinely carries out in the creation of the National Environmental Scorecard. The LCV assesses challengers based on public records they may have acquired while holding another office. Evaluating an incumbent's voting record first requires selection of legislation that meaningfully reflects a legislator's views on environmental issues. A political advisory committee handles this task. The LCV's use of the viewpoints of a wide range of individuals helps to connect its political activities to the environmental movement as a whole, thus fulfilling one of its central missions: to be the political arm of the environmental movement.

The LCV is bipartisan; it supports candidates regardless of party as long as their views on environmental issues meet the group's criteria. While the Action Fund has supported Democrats more than Republicans, it has nevertheless contributed to Republican candidates for office if their environmental positions are more in line with the LCV's than those of their Democratic opponents.

Until the 1996 election, the LCV concentrated its efforts on campaign contributions, although it was among the first liberal PACs to make independent expenditures. In the early 1980s, the LCV "mounted extensive door-to-door canvasses and literature drops independent of the campaign organizations of the favored candidates; some contenders have credited the LCV efforts with providing their margins of victory" (Sabato 1984, 106). The PAC ranked tenth in independent expenditures in the 1982 elections, all of which was spent for candidates rather than in negative campaigns against them. The LCV PAC also made in-kind contributions. In 1982, for example, the LCV, along with other environmental PACs, helped candidates by supplying volunteers for canvassing and telephone banks (Sabato 1984, 95). The LCV has been a prominent player in congressional campaigns, ranking among the top ten fund-raisers in the 1982 elections.

In recent years, the LCV has attempted to develop a grassroots component. In 1993, the group established field staff in five states under the auspices of the LCV Education Fund. These staff members encourage environmental groups to work together on state issues; provide computer hardware and software to help state groups create, merge, and organize membership lists; develop demographic profiles of state residents that state environmental groups can use to target new members[2]; and, in general, coordinate the activities of environmental groups in the state (Loyless 1996a). The LCV initiated this grassroots drive to compensate for what group officials believe has been a lack of support for state-based environmental groups by national ones.[3] Along with this grassroots initiative, the LCV has trained young people to do fieldwork during elections. The group placed as many as eighty individuals around the country, twenty of whom were paid, to work on the campaigns of proenvironment candidates (Loyless 1996a).

State Organizations

The LCV has made an effort to encourage and support environmental activism at the state level. The group does not, however, maintain a formal network of state affiliates. Several state leagues of conservation voters have formed on their own without the formal support of the national organization. These groups are directly involved in campaigns for state offices, primarily gubernatorial and state legislative campaigns. They may also endorse candidates for Congress and offer some measure of support for their campaigns, but these activities are secondary to those focused on state offices. For example, they publish voting records of state legislators on environmental issues. Some state organizations also lobby, although the LCV does little formal lobbying (Loyless 1996a).

The state organizations vary in their resources, professional staff, and extent of political activities. The main concern of the national LCV is that it and the state organizations do not operate at cross-purposes. For example, the national organization wants to be sure that state groups endorse the same congressional candidates it supports. League of Conservation Voters representatives meet with state organizations to discuss environmental issues, political strategies, fund-raising, scorecards, and the like. The goal of the meetings is to coordinate state and national activities. The level of coordination may have recently improved, but there is still no formal or legal relationship between these state groups and the LCV (Loyless 1996a).

League of Conservation Voters in 1996

Political Context

The 1996 elections were unusual for the LCV. The congressional Republican majority installed by the 1994 elections was blatantly hostile to environmental laws, and an ostensibly proenvironment president was reeling from the overwhelmingly negative referendum on his administration. This turn of events encouraged the LCV to overhaul its political strategy.

During the first session of the 104th Congress, Republican legislators, especially in the House, attacked environmental laws. GOP lawmakers decided if they could not reduce their effect by directly amending or even eliminating the laws, then they could undermine their usefulness through such measures as requiring strict cost–benefit analysis of every new regulation and, more directly, "defunding" the Environmental Protection Agency (EPA). The second session of the 104th Congress saw somewhat chastened Republicans take a more environment-friendly approach to legislation. Congressional Republicans heard their constituents' opposition to the dismantling of environmental laws, and these legislators subsequently agreed to several environmental bills and the full funding of the EPA.

The LCV and other environmental groups concluded from the GOP change of heart that the public still supported environmentalism and that legislators who had voted against environmental legislation could be attacked for their actions and possibly defeated. That prospect energized the LCV, giving it a strong incentive to attack antienvironment members of Congress. This development was one of the main reasons for the LCV's dramatic rethinking of its central campaign strategy.

Attack, Attack, Attack

Before the 1996 election cycle, the LCV's PAC had routinely contributed money to the campaigns of proenvironment congressional candidates and made independent expenditures in support of individual candidates. All of that changed in 1996. The LCV Board of Directors chose to embark on an entirely new course, using independent expenditures to attack antienvironment congressional candidates. The targets of this campaign were mostly incumbent Republicans. More important than party or incumbency was the candidate's position on the environment. If the LCV determined that the candidate was near the bottom—membership in the Dirty Dozen would be a good indicator—then the PAC would attack him or her.

The LCV made $580,742 in independent expenditures during the 1996 elections, all of it on negative television and radio ads (http://www.tray.com/FECInfo). This represents a dramatic shift from the PAC's spending pattern in prior elections. As promised by the LCV political director in early summer 1996, the LCV PAC spent very little on direct contributions to candidates (see Table 9.1). It contributed a total of $15,961 to Senate candidates and a total of $38,118 to House candidates. Most of the contributions in Senate races went to incumbent Democrats. Most of the money spent on House campaigns went to incumbents. More Democrats received funds than Republicans, but the total amount of contributions was roughly split between candidates of the two parties. In House races, many more Democrats benefited from the LCV contributions than Republicans.

The LCV selected candidates to attack based mainly on their environmental records. In addition, the LCV considered the opponent's chances for election, how much money he or she had raised, and the general interest in the

Table 9.1 LCV Expenditures in the 1996 Elections

Independent Expenditures	$580,742

Contributions to Senate Candidates	
Democrats	$15,173
Republicans	788
Others	0
Incumbents	8,528
Challengers	128
Open Seats	7,305

Contributions to House Candidates	
Democrats	$16,094
Republicans	17,369
Others	4,655
Incumbents	20,199
Challengers	8,109
Open Seats	9,810

Source: Federal Election Commission.

campaign (Loyless 1996b). The targets collectively comprised the Dirty Dozen. The LCV attack ads, both television and radio, generally tried to portray targeted candidates as extreme antienvironmentalists. The goal was to make voters believe that the politicians' views were considerably outside the mainstream and that they were threats to the environment.

The LCV PAC carefully chose the segment of the electorate with which its advertising messages would most likely resonate. One common tactic was to appeal to young married women who had not attended college. Public opinion surveys had indicated that members of this group of voters were particularly concerned with the future of their families (http://www.lcv.org). The substance of the LCV ads focused mostly on two major environmental issues: clean water and notification of toxic waste releases. A second, smaller wave of ads, usually aired two weeks before the election, typically documented the targeted candidate's receipt of contributions from antienvironment PACs. The number and frequency of ads varied from race to race. In some elections, moreover, the LCV PAC concentrated on television at the expense of radio, and in others, the opposite was true. A brief review of the content of some of the campaigns directed against antienvironment congressional candidates illustrates how the LCV's tactics varied according to the circumstances surrounding each race.

The 860 television ads against Senator Larry Pressler (R–SD), all in the last month of the campaign, initially focused on the incumbent's voting to weaken clean water protections. They were broadcast in a state that had 24 percent of its drinking water systems fall short of health and safety standards in 1994 and 1995. This early attack was followed by ads questioning whether the senator's values were consistent with those of ordinary South Dakotans, "pointing out that he has taken more than $400,000 from special interest PACs that lobbied to weaken environmental protections" (http://www.lcv.org). More than 690 radio ads broadcast in major South Dakota cities augmented the television onslaught against Senator Pressler.

The LCV campaign against Representative Jim Longley (R–ME) targeted younger, noncollege-educated women and York County residents— two groups of voters that were concerned that Longley's views on the environment threatened Maine's rivers and way of life. Over 960 television ads focused on Longley's votes that allegedly jeopardized Maine's rivers and Casco Bay. Another wave of ads connected Longley to antienvironment PACs. The LCV also sent out 33,000 pieces of mail driving home the same themes (http://www.lcv.org).

The LCV attack on Representative Fred Heineman (R–NC) pointed to one of the worst environmental voting records in Congress. Over a thousand radio ads calling attention to Heineman's voting record were reinforced with 33,000 pieces of mail. Directed by a full-time organizer, the campaign appealed to younger women, who were especially concerned about safe drinking water (http://www.lcv.org).

Unable to shake the Dirty Dozen label, Representative Randy Tate (R–WA) was attacked by his opponent for his strong antienvironmentalism. Under the direction of a full-time campaign manager in Seattle, the LCV targeted environmentally concerned voters between the ages of twenty-five and forty-nine. The campaign consisted of 66 television ads aired immediately after the Washington State primary that were designed to generate free media coverage. More than 775 radio ads spread out over a month focused on Tate's votes to weaken the Clean Water Act. Thirty thousand pieces of mail bolstered the electronic attack on Tate's record (http://www.lcv.org).

Representative Michael Flanagan's (R–IL) votes to undermine the cleanup of toxics in the Great Lakes and to weaken the Clean Water Act damaged his chances for reelection. The LCV's media campaigns capitalized on Flanagan's positions with 770 television ads broadcast over cable stations during the Democratic National Convention (http://www.lcv.org). The attack ad on Flanagan claimed that he was the only Chicago congressman who voted to put Abraham Lincoln's home, along with 315 other national park sites, up for closure. The text drives the point home by claiming that

"Last year Flanagan voted against our heritage and against our environment ten out of twelve times, even voting to weaken the Clean Water Act that protects Lake Michigan from sewage pollution" (LCV 1996a).

The Oregon Senate race between Republican Gordon Smith and Democrat Tom Bruggere drew a great deal of LCV's attention. Smith established his antienvironment credentials in his failed effort to win a Senate seat in a special election earlier in the year. At issue was Smith's factory's pollution violations. Directed by a full-time organizer, the LCV Action Fund targeted its ads mainly at younger women in the Portland area. Over 550 television ads focused on Smith's factory's pollution record and his antienvironment record as an Oregon State senator. The ads were broadcast in two waves: immediately following Labor Day and two weeks before the election, the latter of the two focusing on Smith's accepting $500,000 in campaign contributions from antienvironment PACs (LCV 1996b). The anti-Smith ad could not rely on the candidate's congressional voting record because he had not served in Congress. So, the audio claimed, "Gordon Smith…he's back," while the text appearing on the screen pointed out that "Gordon Smith's factory was cited twice last year for illegally polluting Oregon's water. Violations at Smith's factory have continued now for more than a decade. One illegal discharge into an Oregon stream killed fish and other life for 23 miles." The ad concludes with what was surely intended to be a memorable line, "Don't send Mr. Smith to Washington" (LCV 1996a).

In Texas, Steve Stockman felt the wrath of the LCV Action Fund. Targeting women voters from twenty-five to fifty years old, the group highlighted Stockman's votes against current environmental protections. The LCV Action Fund sponsored 450 television ads that told the story of Stockman's votes against clean air and the public's right to know about toxic releases. In the last two weeks of the campaign, TV ads detailed Stockman's receipt of $68,000 from antienvironment PACs (LCV 1996b). The anti-Stockman ad picked on a different environmental hazard. The text explains: "47,244,050 pounds of toxic chemicals released into Jefferson County's air, land and water in just one year. But Congressman Stockman voted four times in just five months to weaken the laws that protect our families from toxic wastes and cancer-causing pollution." The text concludes, "He even voted to limit our right to know about new toxic chemicals released into our air and water" (LCV 1996a).

Among the most colorful incumbents targeted by the LCV was Representative Helen Chenoweth (R–ID). Chenoweth, an extreme conservative on most issues, compiled a strong antienvironment record during her first term in the House, making her a prime LCV target. With a full-time organizer based in Boise, the LCV Action Fund aired over 460 television ads and 860 radio spots characterizing Chenoweth as an antienvironment extremist. In keeping with the group's pattern, a second wave of ads focused on Chenoweth's receipt of $93,500 from antienvironment PACs. Finally, 48,000 pieces of mail underscored the LCV Action Fund's central themes (LCV 1996b).

Representative Frank Riggs (R–CA) attracted LCV attention in California. Representing the California North Coast, Riggs proudly proclaimed Newt Gingrich "greener" than himself. The LCV Action Fund's campaign against Riggs was directed by a full-time organizer in Napa. The campaign was designed to appeal to independent, noncollege-educated women voters. The focus of the television ads was Riggs's antienvironmental voting record in the House, especially his vote to weaken clean water protection and regulations surrounding distribution of information about toxic chemical releases. The LCV Action Fund sponsored 472 television ads on Riggs's amendment to allow more sewage wastewater to be dumped in the Russian River, while 592 radio ads focused on antienvironment PAC contributions to the Riggs campaign. Sixty-seven thousand pieces of mail rounded out the attack on Riggs (LCV 1996b).

In California's central valley, Democratic Representative Gary Condit fought to establish his environmentalist credentials in the face of making it to the LCV Dirty Dozen list. In 466 television ads, the LCV Action Fund attacked Condit's votes to weaken clean air and water protections (LCV 1996b).

Iowa Republican Senate challenger Jim Ross Lightfoot's poor environmental record in the House of Representatives made him a likely LCV target. The LCV portrayed Lightfoot as an extremist and an enemy of established environmental protection. Because of limited resources, the LCV converted the independent expenditure campaign against Lightfoot to a coordinated campaign for Harkin (Loyless 1997a). Thus, unlike other races, the LCV worked directly with Lightfoot's opponent, Senator Tom Harkin (D–IA), in a vigorous attack on Lightfoot's antienvironmentalism (LCV 1996b).

Rounding out the Dirty Dozen was Colorado Republican Senate candidate Wayne Allard. As a member of the House of Representatives, Allard compiled a voting record on environmental issues sufficiently poor to place him on the Dirty Dozen list. As in the Iowa Senate race, the LCV chose to run a coordinated campaign in this race, directly helping the campaign of Tom Strickland, Allard's opponent (Loyless 1997a). The LCV Action Fund provided a full-time organizer to Strickland's campaign. In addition, actor Robert Redford, who frequently works with LCV endorsements, accompanied Strickland during the campaign (LCV 1996b).

Although the negative ad campaign was the centerpiece of the LCV 1996 campaign strategy, it was not the only piece. The LCV also coordinated its activities with state organizations, arranged for grassroots activists to work on key elections, endorsed congressional candidates and a presidential ticket, and contributed a limited amount of money to the campaigns of proenvironment congressional candidates. Each activity merits some brief comments.

Coordination with State Groups

As noted earlier, one of the more important goals of the LCV is to coordinate activities, with state groups for example, making sure that state organizations and the LCV support the same congressional candidates. While the extent of interaction between LCV officials and state group officials varies from state to state, the record for the 1996 elections indicates consistency in campaign strategies. State groups participated in congressional and presidential elections independently of the LCV. The California League of Conservation Voters, for example, contributed $36,550 to candidates in House races. The Oregon League of Conservation Voters contributed $500 to House candidates and $500 to Senate campaigns. The New York League of Conservation Voters and the Montana Conservation Voters were also modestly involved in congressional elections. The actions of state groups as reported to the Federal Election Commission are in line with the broad political goals of the LCV. For example, the Oregon League of Conservation Voters contributed $500 to Democrat Tom Bruggere's Senate campaign. In no instance did state groups engage in political actions that ran counter to those of the LCV. In addition to consistent endorsements of candidates, the California League of Voters PAC made a direct contribution to the LCV, suggesting an additional measure of coordinated activity (http://www.tray.com/FECInfo).

Endorsements

The LCV endorsed a large number of proenvironment congressional candidates who did not receive LCV PAC contributions. The group noted that not winning the endorsement of the LCV did not necessarily mean a candidate was antienvironment, however. The decision to endorse these candidates, as others, was made on the basis of their records on environmental issues. In 1996, the LCV endorsed candidates in 104 congressional races, 15 of which were open seats. In the remaining 89 contests, the LCV backed 65 incumbents and 24 challengers. The partisan mix was weighted heavily in the Democrats' favor: The LCV supported 89 Democrats, 14 Republicans, and 1 independent (http://www.lcv.org). In addition to endorsing congressional candidates, the LCV endorsed Bill Clinton and Al Gore for president and vice president (http://www.lcv.org).

Administrative Stress and Strain

The decision to launch a negative ad campaign put new stress on the LCV administrative system. Making campaign contributions to proenvironment congressional candidates is a fairly straightforward exercise compared with devising and implementing negative ads. The former strategy involves a decision based mainly on a candidate's record on environmental issues. The latter, on the other hand, requires creating the ads themselves and more intensive research about each individual race. The greater demands placed on the LCV by the ad campaign, both in terms of resources and staff, strain the organization (Loyless 1996b). Whether the additional demands placed on the LCV by this strategy result in changes in future elections remains to be seen.

Assessment

The LCV's change of strategy for the 1996 elections was genuinely dramatic. The group virtually dropped direct contributions to candidates in favor of a vigorous negative ad campaign funded by independent expenditures. Several questions remain to be answered. First, did the negative ad strategy work? Second, is this the best way for the LCV to use its resources in every election? Third, does the use of this strategy in 1996 mean that it will be used indefinitely, or was it a one-shot gambit?

The LCV's negative ad campaign enjoyed a measure of success. In House races, four members of the Dirty Dozen lost and four won. In the four Senate elections involving Dirty Dozen members, two won and two lost. In the House, the Senate, and overall, the LCV's 1996 win–loss record is .500. The question, of course, is whether the results would have been the same had the LCV used its traditional strategy of making direct contributions to proenvironment candidates.[4] Beyond the Dirty Dozen, all ten members of the LCV Earth List won election, and the candidates whom the LCV endorsed enjoyed considerable success as well. The LCV bundled contributions from its members and channeled these funds to members of the Earth List (Loyless 1997a).

Political Director Betsy Loyless expressed general satisfaction with the LCV's performance in 1996. Through its negative ad campaign, the LCV successfully inserted environmental issues into the public debate. Doing so established the salience of environmental issues in congressional elections. Polls done for the LCV indicate that voters were concerned with the environment. Clean water was the most important issue, followed by the public's right to know about toxic wastes. From a strategic perspective, this outcome demonstrates to future congressional candidates that it is unwise to ignore these environmental issues or to run as an antienvironmentalist. The National Environmental Scorecard

Table 9.2 Results of Dirty Dozen Elections

Dirty Dozen[a]	Vote %	Opponent	Vote %	State	Election
Larry Pressler	48	Tim Johnson	52	SD	Senate
Gordon Smith	50	Tom Bruggere	46	OR	Senate
Wayne Allard	51	Tom Strickland	46	CO	Senate
Jim Ross Lightfoot	47	Tom Harkin	52	IA	Senate
Jim Longley	44	Tom Allen	56	ME	House
Fred Heineman	44	David Price	54	NC	House
Randy Tate	46	Adam Smith	51	WA	House
Michael Flanagan	36	Rod Blagojevich	64	IL	House
Steve Stockman	47	Nick Lampson	53	TX	House
Helen Chenoweth	50	Dan Williams	48	ID	House
Frank Riggs	49	Michaela Alioto	44	CA	House
Gary Condit	66	Bill Conrad	32	CA	House

Sources: League of Conservation Voters, "Dirty Dozen Campaigns at a Glance," November 6, 1996. http://www.lcv.org (December 16, 1996); and "1996 Election Results," November 6, 1996. http://www.results96.politicsnow.com (February 28, 1997).
[a]All Dirty Dozen candidates are Republicans with the exception of Gary Condit, who is a Democrat.

also appears to have been well received, adding to the extent to which the LCV was able to gain credibility for itself and to place the environment in the middle of political debate (Loyless 1997a).

Several campaigns stand out in terms of the lessons they taught to the LCV, to congressional candidates, and to the environmental community as a whole. The LCV failed in its campaign against California representatives Riggs and Condit, and in the Oregon Senate race in which Gordon Smith won the open seat. The LCV was unable to win the advantage in terms of making the environment an issue, especially in the Riggs and Smith races. On the other hand, even in defeat, the LCV considered its campaigns against Idaho Representative Chenoweth and Texas House candidate Tate successful. In Idaho, Chenoweth won by a slim margin, far smaller than that by the GOP Senate and presidential candidates in her district. In Texas, the LCV succeeded in making the environment an issue. The LCV's election victories reflect the inherent strength of the candidates who opposed the LCV targets and the importance of the environment to the electorate. For example, Democrat David Price of North Carolina won back his seat in the House by defeating the decidedly antienvironment incumbent Heineman, and Tom Harkin, an otherwise formidable Democratic Senate incumbent in Iowa, turned back his opponent, probably in part because of his opponent's antienvironment positions (Loyless 1997a).

Political Director Loyless is proud of the fact that the LCV negative ads did not engage in personal or partisan attacks. For example, the ads did not feature negative images of Speaker Newt Gingrich, nor did they attack the Republican Party. Instead, they focused nearly exclusively on environmental issues, mainly clean water, the public's right to know, and the receipt by the targeted candidate of funds from antienvironment PACs.

Although the LCV received requests to contribute to the debt retirement of the campaigns of several 1996 congressional candidates, it did not make any contributions. The LCV made such contributions in past elections, but at a relatively low level, around $2,000 to $3,000. The LCV encountered problems in its negative ad campaign, however. The timing of the ads could have been moved up. In most cases, ads did not appear until around Labor Day. An earlier start of the negative ad campaign could improve its effectiveness. The principal difficulty was the lack of adequate resources, both money and staff, to run all twelve campaigns. In fact, the LCV found it necessary to substitute in-kind campaign assistance for independent expenditures in the Iowa and Colorado Senate elections. LCV President Deb Callahan traveled with the Democratic candidates in these races to give them credibility on environmental issues. At some points during the election, Loyless found it impossible to find enough time to recruit staff for LCV campaign efforts. The shortage of resources is something the LCV will need to address should it choose to launch a negative ad campaign again (Loyless 1997a).

Targeting the candidates of the Dirty Dozen turned out to be a difficult task. Deciding exactly whom to focus on is the province of the political advisory committee, in conjunction with the political director and other members of the LCV staff. The LCV found this a time-consuming effort, as disagreements among the participants in the decision-making process had to be reconciled. Shortly after the election, the LCV conducted an internal review of its procedures and structures. Some modest changes are likely to come out of this assessment (Loyless 1997a).

The Next Election

The LCV's strategy for the 1998 elections will, in part, be determined by the tone of the 105th Congress. If this Congress is less stridently antienvironment, as seems likely, the political context in the 1998 election will be less charged than it was in 1996. A calmer political mood makes it more difficult for the LCV to contrast the antienvironment views of congressional candidates with the environmental concerns of the electorate. Thus, what happens in the 105th Congress will have a great deal to do with the strategy adopted by the LCV.

The LCV might try an independent expenditure campaign featuring negative ads in 1998. It is also considering the possibility of positive ads. In both cases, the LCV would be involved in an independent expenditure campaign. As the 1996 experience indicates, this type of strategy forces the group to concentrate its resources on relatively few races. Thus, LCV officials must evaluate the trade-offs between a narrow, intense strategy and one that distributes resources more broadly across more campaigns. In addition, the group is looking into using a multielection strategy, targeting the same congressional candidates in consecutive elections with the goal of building a cumulative case against them. Eventually, this effort could pay off in the candidates' defeat (Loyless 1997b).[5]

Summary and Conclusion

Since 1970, the LCV has been a major voice for environmentalists in congressional campaigns. The group has sought to influence environmental policy by publishing information on congressional candidates' positions on environmental issues and contributing to proenvironment candidates. Following the successes of the 1992 elections, the 1994 congressional elections were a shock to the LCV. The group saw the environmental agenda swing sharply to the right, as members of Congress openly declared their intent to gut environmental laws. The LCV responded to this change with a sweeping shift in its strategy. Cutting its contributions dramatically, the LCV poured the bulk of its resources into negative ad campaigns funded by independent expenditures against antienvironmental congressional candidates. Moved to action by a radical change in the political environment, the LCV chose to adopt a strategy that promised better results than the traditional practice of contributing to the campaigns of favorable candidates.

The LCV enjoyed some success in its 1996 effort. Whether it will continue the strategy of running negative ads against candidates it finds most undesirable depends, of course, on the group's evaluation of its effectiveness. It will also depend, in part, on the capacity of the group to sustain such a campaign. The 1996 elections strained the organization's funding and staff. Whether the LCV can address those problems successfully is likely to play a significant part in determining its strategy for 1998.

Notes

[1]Until 1996, this document was called the *Green Book*.

[2]This refers to environmental groups other than the LCV. The LCV does not maintain state affiliates as such.

[3]It is worth noting that Loyless began her work in environmental politics at the state level in Tennessee.

[4]This would require analysis beyond the scope of this paper.

[5]Loyless cited the National Rifle Association's targeting of Representative Mike Synar (D–OK) in successive elections, culminating in his defeat.

NARAL PAC: BATTLING FOR WOMEN'S REPRODUCTIVE RIGHTS

Sue Thomas

The National Abortion Rights Action League (NARAL) was founded in 1969 to advocate making abortion safe, legal, and accessible for all women.[1] In 1993, NARAL expanded its mission "to encompass a range of reproductive health needs from prevention to healthy childbearing," and changed its name to the National Abortion and Reproductive Rights Action League. NARAL is the largest national organization working primarily for reproductive rights; the group has thirty-five state affiliates and five hundred thousand members nationwide. NARAL, Inc., is the political arm of the organization, and NARAL PAC is the mechanism for contributing money to pro-choice candidates for local, state, and federal office, and the NARAL Foundation funds policy development, legal and issues research, public education, and leadership training for grassroots activists.

Although NARAL's goals have remained relatively constant, its political tactics have changed in response to political events. The *Webster* decision in 1989 provided the opportunity for the organization to mobilize new members, especially among younger Americans. More importantly, the GOP takeover of Congress in 1994 was a major defeat for NARAL and forced the organization to change its lobbying tactics. When Democrats controlled Congress, NARAL sought to pass the Freedom of Choice Act to ensure abortion rights, but Republican efforts to restrict abortion access have left NARAL primarily trying to block GOP legislation.

PAC Organization

NARAL PAC was formed on August 5, 1977, to elect a pro-choice majority in Congress. NARAL's leaders were concerned that abortion rights, guaranteed by the 1973 U.S. Supreme Court case, *Roe v. Wade*, could be eroded by legislative action in Congress or the states. While the Court had, up to that point, struck down most legislative restrictions subsequent to *Roe*, NARAL's leadership realized that this might someday change. To protect against legislative restrictions on abortion, the PAC would make contributions to candidates for public office who supported reproductive choice.[2]

NARAL PAC is affiliated with NARAL, Inc., and thus may only solicit funds from members of NARAL. Although only a minority of NARAL members give to the PAC (e.g., 18 percent gave in 1990), it nonetheless raises a substantial amount of money, and in 1996 it raised almost $549,000. This makes NARAL a serious player in congressional campaign finance.

Because NARAL PAC was established for the sole purpose of protecting women's reproductive freedom, there has been little controversy over the standards that govern contribution decisions. PAC officials have always considered the viability of the candidate, the extent to which choice is an issue in the race, and the candidate's position on abortion rights (Thomas 1994). When NARAL expanded its mission in 1993, the PAC began to also consider candidate positions on age-appropriate sex education, contraceptive research and development, and RU 486—a pill that induces abortion. In some elections, candidate positions on specific bills become critical: In 1992 NARAL considered candidates' position on the Freedom of Choice Act, which would have codified *Roe*, and in 1996 the PAC focused on candidate positions on late-term abortions. The goal of NARAL's PAC is to maximize the number of pro-choice legislators, so the PAC does not consider candidates' partisanship, race, gender, or region (Thomas 1994).

Contribution decisions are made by the PAC's board of directors. The twelve-member board is headed by a chair and vice chair who are appointed by the elected board. The officers are required to be of opposite parties and the full board is evenly divided in partisanship. The PAC director meets with congressional candidates and makes initial decisions about who should receive contributions. These recommendations are reviewed by NARAL's president and political director before they are forwarded to the PAC board. Staff recommendations are rarely overridden by the board of directors, although occasional disagreements arise because the lobbying staff is more pragmatic than the NARAL membership. Yet controversy over decision making has been fairly low, in part because of the clear purpose of the organization and its PAC.

When the Democrats controlled Congress, the PAC primarily supported incumbents, especially those who held positions of power, such as committee chairs, party leaders, and those with assignments on the appropriations and judiciary committees. But because the PAC seeks to maximize pro-choice votes on bills or amendments considered in committee or on the floor, the PAC has also supported incumbents who lack institutional power and nonincumbents. When the GOP seized control of Congress in 1994, NARAL PAC shifted much of its money to pro-choice challengers and open-seat candidates.

The PAC makes direct cash contributions to candidates, and in-kind contributions are done through the thirty-five affiliates. In-kind contributions include public education efforts, grassroots organizing, candidate recruitment and training, and get-out-the-vote events. NARAL uses these noncash contributions in high-profile, competitive races in places where its affiliates are strong (such as California). NARAL PAC relies on an extensive array of sources including questionnaires sent to candidates, published information in *Roll Call* and *Congressional Quarterly Weekly Report*, meetings with candidates, information from affiliates, board members, and Washington-based advocacy groups to help inform its contribution decisions.

History

When NARAL PAC was formed, some congressional candidates were reluctant to accept endorsements and contributions because they feared that the abortion issue would cost them votes. In the 1992 election, a number of non-incumbents backed by NARAL won election, and after that election incumbents were more willing to accept NARAL PAC contributions.

From 1982 until mid-1989, NARAL and its PAC worked steadily on the goal of electing a pro-choice Congress and president. They had some success in Congress, but antiabortion rights Republican presidents controlled the presidency throughout this period. The U.S. Supreme Court decision in *Webster v. Reproductive Health Services* helped to mobilize pro-choice forces. For the first time, the Court allowed states to enact restrictions on the right to abortion, and the decision appeared to invite states to experiment with new restrictions. Apart from public funding of abortions, this was the first Supreme Court decision that limited the right to reproductive choice.

The *Webster* decision made it clear that the Court was no longer a guarantor of reproductive freedom, and this had a galvanizing effect on the pro-choice movement. Grassroots activism increased dramatically as did NARAL's membership and contributions to its PAC. Pro-choice candidates won key gubernatorial races in Virginia and New Jersey in 1989, which signaled a new electoral dynamic. Candidates began to actively seek NARAL's endorsement and contributions from its PAC. NARAL worked hard to make the public aware of the future danger women might face. Its efforts included mass media campaigns in seven states, 2 million pieces of election-related mail, 500,000 pieces of door-to-door literature drops, 6,000 campaign workers, and student mobilization on more than 300 college campuses. NARAL claims to have contacted 1.5 million voters through these efforts.[3] As a result, in 1990, pro-choice forces won many important congressional, gubernatorial, and state legislative victories as well as several ballot measures.

The 1990 victories by the pro-choice plurality became increasingly important as the personnel on the Supreme Court changed. The retirements of U.S. Supreme Court justices who supported *Roe* as well as the acceptance of a new case, *Planned Parenthood of Southeastern Pennsylvania v. Casey*, led many, including NARAL's directors, to believe that *Roe* itself would be overturned. Thus, the 1992 presidential election became an important battle for NARAL and its allies.

The 1992 Elections

NARAL's leaders believed that 1992 presented special challenges and opportunities for the pro-choice movement. In the wake of *Webster* and in anticipation of *Casey*, only a pro-choice Congress and a pro-choice president would ensure continued national protection of women's reproductive rights. Further, to codify *Roe* in case the Court overturned its own precedent, NARAL sought to pass the Freedom of Choice Act (FOCA). This would require both a pro-choice Congress and either a pro-choice president or a veto-proof Congress. Due to redistricting and a record number of congressional retirements, as many as one hundred open seats were anticipated, and this created the opportunity to dramatically increase the number of pro-choice legislators.

To raise the money for these efforts, NARAL needed to increase its membership because the PAC can only solicit the organization's members. NARAL launched its most extensive membership drive ever and solicited the wider political community with telemarketing, direct-mail appeals, telephone banks, and major donor events. As a result of the threat to the *Roe* decision, as well as NARAL's efforts to expand its base, membership grew and record contributions flooded into the PAC. This pace continued until June 29, when the Court in *Casey* upheld the right to abortion while permitting states to enact restrictions on that right. Because the threat to reproductive rights had decreased, fund-raising leveled off from June through the end of the election.

NARAL used its extra funds for an unprecedented grassroots program to identify more than a million pro-choice voters in key districts and states across the nation. In October, the PAC launched a campaign called "Thirty Days To Save Choice," which argued that an anti-choice president would make Court appointments who would overturn *Roe*. NARAL organized phone banks, leaflet drops, neighborhood canvasses, targeted mailings, distribution of voter guides, and get-out-the-vote rallies in all fifty states. The Choice Action Leader Program trained more than five thousand activists to coordinate these activities and recruit additional volunteers. The goal was to prove to politicians that when reproductive freedom faced a fundamental threat, a candidate's position on abortion would weigh heavily in voters' ballot decisions.

Money raised from these efforts was also used for direct contributions to candidates. NARAL PAC contributed to every candidate endorsed by NARAL, but incumbents received the lion's share of the funds. Combined with independent expenditures and assistance to state affiliates, NARAL PAC spent more than $3 million in the elections of 1992 and endorsed over two hundred candidates.

NARAL was pleased with the results: Pro-choice presidential challenger Bill Clinton beat pro-life incumbent George Bush, and pro-choice forces enjoyed a net gain of eleven seats in the U.S. House of Representatives and one in the U.S. Senate. In addition, pro-choice forces could count on thirty of fifty supportive governors for a net gain of one, and two abortion-related ballot measures, one in Maryland and one in Arizona, were decided in favor of reproductive freedom.

NARAL enjoyed some real successes in the early Clinton administration. On January 22, 1993, the twentieth anniversary of *Roe v. Wade*, President Clinton issued five executive orders overturning policies on abortion. In 1993, Congress passed and Clinton signed the Freedom of Clinic Access (FACE) bill, which holds blockade participants and organizers responsible for monetary damage they cause, including awards for pain and suffering, and allows courts to fine and jail perpetrators.[4] Yet NARAL's top priority, passage of the Freedom of Choice Act, was not accomplished because some legislators sought restrictive amendments to the bill and deadlock halted its progress.

The Midterm Elections of 1994:
A Big Loss for Pro-Choice Forces

Although the election of a pro-choice president and a pro-choice Congress helped NARAL achieve some of its policy goals, it hurt NARAL's fund-raising because pro-choice citizens believed that their reproductive rights were secure. Some state affiliates closed, membership declined, and PAC contributions decreased.

The results of the 1994 elections were alarming for NARAL's leadership and members. Not only did the Republicans control both branches of Congress for the first time in forty years, the pro-choice plurality that NARAL counted on since 1989 was gone. Opponents of choice gained 5 seats in the Senate for a total of 45, and 39 seats in the House, for a total of 218. Not surprisingly, GOP control led NARAL to change its lobbying and electoral strategies. NARAL sought to minimize legislative losses, and to launch a public education campaign focused on what the Republican control of Congress would mean for the issue of choice.

The new GOP majority meant that many senior pro-choice congressional staff who had expertise on reproductive freedom were gone. NARAL representatives were no longer allowed to stand outside the House chamber door to buttonhole lawmakers as they entered. NARAL lacked access to committee chairs and majority party leadership. Most importantly, they could not count on a majority of votes. During the first session of the 104th Congress, a record number of antiabortion bills were enacted, including some that denied funds to protect women's health clinics, ended access to abortion for U.S. servicewomen overseas, prohibited federal employees from choosing health insurance plans with abortion coverage, and prohibited Medicaid coverage for abortion for low-income women who became pregnant due to rape or incest. Other GOP legislation denied access to abortion for women in federal prisons, ended U.S. support for international family planning programs, prohibited the District of Columbia from using its own taxpayer-generated revenues to pay for Medicaid-funded abortions, banned federal funds for human embryo research, and cut abortion training for obstetrics and gynecology residents.

The most difficult issue for NARAL was congressional action on the "partial birth" abortion bill, which outlawed certain late-term abortion procedures and imposed jail sentences on doctors who performed them. The debate was framed by pro-life activists who rendered long, detailed descriptions of the procedure. Media accounts similarly focused on the procedure itself, not on the woman, her family, or the choice.

NARAL fought to refocus the debate on women's reproductive choices. NARAL and Planned Parenthood developed a brochure and did other public education efforts that included personal accounts by women who had needed this abortion procedure. An example of the stories was that of Claudia Ades, who was told in the sixth month of pregnancy that her expected third child had a fatal chromosomal disorder that caused extensive brain damage and serious heart complications, and that the fetus had no chance of surviving. Ades and her husband decided, for the sake of their family and future children, to end the pregnancy. Under the late-term abortion bill, the procedure used by the Ades would have been illegal. Despite efforts to reframe the debate, the "partial birth" abortion ban passed both chambers of Congress but was subsequently vetoed by President Clinton.

NARAL in the 1996 Elections

NARAL officials hoped that the late-term abortion bill might serve as a wake-up call to its membership and to other pro-choice citizens. In an effort to convince Americans that their right to choose was in danger, NARAL spearheaded or participated in several public education efforts in preparation for the 1996 elections. The model for this activity was an earlier effort in a January 1993 special election, in which NARAL helped elect pro-choice Ron

Wyden of Oregon to the U.S. Senate in an election in which reproductive choice was a key campaign issue. In that race, "NARAL and our Oregon affiliate conducted a public education and membership mobilization program targeting nearly 50,000 voters which paid off handsomely; 12,000 Republican and Independent women told NARAL–PAC that they would cross party lines to support Wyden" (*NARAL News*, 1–2).

In 1996, NARAL launched a Who Decides? campaign intended to "reclaim political institutions from right-wing control." It sought to "mobilize America's pro-choice majority for the 1996 elections and defend reproductive rights in the years to come."[5] James Wagoner, NARAL executive vice president, called it "the most intensive public education effort on abortion that we've ever undertaken" (Clines 1996, 18). Who Decides? is and was a comprehensive, long-term political and public education program that concentrated in 1996 on issue advocacy in key races in which members of Congress were out of step with their pro-choice constituents. Another aspect of NARAL's public education campaign was the design and setup of a web site with up-to-date information about legislative events, research information, on-line organizing, and more. The final major public education effort in which NARAL participated was a coalition of forty pro-choice groups that formed a two-year information campaign called the "Pro-Choice Education Project." Together, these groups ran a TV ad titled "Generation" on CNN. This project also had a $2 million media campaign with TV spots highlighting clinic violence, declining access, and the banning of late-term abortions.

NARAL concentrated its Who Decides? campaign in states and districts where voters were especially receptive to pro-choice messages, in most cases where there were anti-choice incumbents. NARAL targeted twenty-two House races and seven Senate contests in the Who Decides? campaign. NARAL's pollsters, Hickman–Brown, found that 84 percent of Americans were unsure of their representative's position about abortion.[6] NARAL hoped that, by informing voters of the positions their members had taken on reproductive choice, they could influence key elections.

Although NARAL sought to convince pro-choice citizens that reproductive freedom was in danger, PAC fund-raising did not increase. Many of the abortion-related battles in the 104th Congress were complex, long-running, and difficult to explain quickly or easily, and pro-choice citizens did not perceive a direct threat to abortion rights. NARAL made endorsements in 135 national races and made contributions to all endorsed candidates. Table 10.1 shows that, in marked contrast to previous election cycles, in 1996 NARAL PAC gave heavily to challengers and open-seat candidates. In 1994 nearly two-thirds of NARAL contributions went to incumbents, whereas in 1996 approximately 60 percent went to challengers and open-seat candidates. In 1994 NARAL was protecting a pro-choice majority; in 1996 it was seeking to re-create one. NARAL also directed significantly fewer resources into direct

Table 10.1   NARAL PAC Campaign Activity in the 1994 and 1996
Congressional Elections

	1994		1996
	Contributions	Independent Expenditures for Candidates	Contributions
House			
Democrats			
Incumbents	$225,164	$11,411	$94,318
Challengers	35,087	0	92,287
Open seats	71,166	0	39,014
Republicans			
Incumbents	$14,000	$0	$8,250
Challengers	5,000	0	0
Open seats	4,000	0	0
Senate			
Democrats			
Incumbents	$38,148	$11,564	$21,696
Challengers	19,961	5,396	10,792
Open Seats	36,994	0	32,065
Republicans			
Incumbents	$10,921	$0	$0
Challengers	0	0	0
Open seats	1,000	0	0

Source: Federal Election Commission.
Note: NARAL made no independent expenditures against candidates in 1994 and no
independent expenditures for or against candidates in 1996.

candidate contributions in 1996, preferring instead to spend money on its
voter education program.

State Efforts

Through its thirty-five state affiliates, NARAL used media contacts, rallies,
phone banks, door-to-door canvassing, town meetings, protests outside campaign events, direct mail to pro-choice voters, and letters to the editors of
newspapers and magazines to communicate with voters. It also carried out
Internet advocacy, get-out-the-vote drives, and other grassroots efforts in an

attempt to influence elections. Throughout these efforts, NARAL sounded a consistent message: "Women and their families—not government and politicians—should decide the personal issue of abortion."

Some examples of state-level organizing include:

- NARAL affiliates held press conferences and rallies highlighting Senator Dole's anti-choice record in competitive states such as Iowa, Montana, Pennsylvania, Oregon, Texas, and Washington (*NARAL News* 1996, 5).
- Colorado NARAL developed an advanced electoral training program in June of 1996 for pro-choice candidates and mounted an extensive phone-bank effort in the primaries. Activists in Colorado also conducted public education activities highlighting the House of Representatives race between anti-choice Republican Wayne Allard and pro-choice Democrat Tom Strickland (*NARAL News* 1996, 5).

Conclusion

In November 1996, the electorate returned Bill Clinton to the presidency and the Republicans to the Congress, with a GOP majority that was diminished in the House but increased in the Senate. Candidates supported by NARAL were successful in seventeen out of twenty-two targeted House races and in four of seven targeted Senate races. How important were NARAL's efforts in the 1996 elections? It is true that the abortion issue has had a higher profile in some elections, as was the case in 1992, and a lower one in others, such as in 1994. Yet abortion was salient in many House and Senate races in 1996 because of the efforts of NARAL and other pro-choice organizations. Their concerted effort to educate the public about candidate positions on issues of reproductive freedom doubtlessly influenced some close races, and their PAC contributions helped as well. NARAL president Jane Michelman claimed that election results did not confirm Christian Coalition director Ralph Reed's prediction that those who voted against the ban on late-term abortions would pay at the polls. NARAL monitored thirty-two House races in which the issue was used in television ads and other ways and found that the pro-choice candidates won twenty-five of them. In the Senate, all seven races in which the issue was used resulted in pro-choice victories.[7]

Nevertheless, the 1996 results were a disappointment for NARAL because the 105th Congress contains solid antiabortion rights majorities in both chambers. In 1998 NARAL faces the daunting task of trying to increase the number of pro-choice members in an off-year election. The president's party routinely loses seats in off-year elections, and a strong GOP year could lead to a filibuster-proof Senate and perhaps even to veto-proof majorities in both chambers on the abortion issue. NARAL and other pro-choice groups are now gearing up to try to minimize their losses in 1998.

Notes

[1]When it was founded, the name of the organization was the National Association for the Repeal of Abortion Laws. After the U.S. Supreme Court decision, *Roe v. Wade*, the name of the organization was changed to the National Abortion Rights Action League. The mission was to protect the *Roe* decision.

[2]Unless otherwise noted, all information for this chapter derives from interviews with NARAL's PAC directors and lobbyist. The interviews took place between 1991 and 1997.

[3]This information comes from a January 11, 1991, memo from NARAL Political Director James Wagoner to the NARAL Board of Directors.

[4]There were 1,700 acts of violence against U.S. abortion providers between 1977 and 1994, including 4 deaths. After FACE, violent protests at abortion clinics dropped to fewer than 400 by November 1996 from 1,800 in all of 1995 (*Ms.* Jan./Feb. 1997, 15). That being said, there have been high-profile incidents such as the January 17, 1997, bombing of an abortion clinic in Atlanta (Sverdlk 1977).

[5]Information from NARAL's web site (www.naral.org).

[6]Poll done July 29–August 4, 1996 (www.naral.org).

[7]Information from www.naral.org.

THE GAY AND LESBIAN VICTORY FUND
COMES OF AGE: REFLECTIONS
ON THE 1996 ELECTIONS

Craig A. Rimmerman

The 1996 elections can be viewed as the first major referendum on the 1994 Republican takeover of Congress and the Contract with America, but for gay and lesbian voters the 1996 elections may have signaled something else. Early analyses of gay and lesbian voting behavior reveal that voter turnout declined significantly in the 1996 elections and that as many as 23 percent of those who bothered to vote cast their ballots for Republican candidate Bob Dole (Keen 1996).[1] One possible explanation for the decline in turnout and surprising support for candidate Dole is that gays and lesbians were dissatisfied with President Clinton's record on gay and lesbian concerns. A second explanation for the decline in voter turnout is that gay and lesbian voters mirrored the larger electorate's dissatisfaction with the quality of candidates in the 1996 presidential election.

For the Gay and Lesbian Victory Fund, the 1996 presidential election signaled an important opportunity to elect openly gay and lesbian officials to local, state, and national office. Going into the 1996 election cycle, the Victory Fund had endorsed more candidates and raised more money on their behalf than at any time in the organization's brief five-year history. The Victory Fund had reason to be optimistic. Slowly but surely, gays and lesbians were moving from the margins and into the mainstream of U.S. society. From Hollywood to television, gays and lesbians appeared to be breaking a stranglehold on the dominant "straight" paradigm of American society. There is now greater tolerance and acceptance of gays and lesbians than ever before, and urban gay enclaves had thrived with their own sense of community for decades.

Yet "many gays and lesbians were cut off from mainstream society with virtually no political representation locally or nationally" (Bull and Gallagher

1996, 4). Moreover, the Christian Right and other conservative groups continued their vociferous opposition to extending basic rights and liberties. The Right mobilized successfully against Bill Clinton's 1993 attempt to overturn the ban on gays and lesbians in the military (Rimmerman 1996) and against local attempts to extend basic rights to gays and lesbians in housing, employment, and freedom from discrimination.

Against this broader political, cultural, and electoral landscape, the Gay and Lesbian Victory Fund hoped to elect an array of openly gay and lesbian officials at all levels of government. Some in the gay and lesbian community argued that the need was particularly acute given the retirement of two of the most visible openly gay elected officials, House members Gerry Studds (D–MA) and Steve Gunderson (R–WI). The issue of whether straight elected officials can adequately represent the interests of the gay and lesbian community is an important one, and one that the Gay and Lesbian Victory Fund addresses by its very existence.

Organizational History

The central goal of the Victory Fund since its creation in 1991 has been to elect openly gay and lesbian candidates to all levels of government. In a book published by the organization in 1994, the Victory Fund argued that "gay men and lesbians are the most underrepresented group in electoral politics" (DeBold 1994, xiii). The organization asks: "If we don't support our own, who will be there for us?" Reflecting on Clinton's failed promise to overturn the ban on gays and lesbians in the military, the Victory Fund concludes that "the events of the past year have proven to the rest of our community what Victory Fund members have known all along—that the inclusion and empowerment of gay men and lesbians in the political process can only happen when we are represented by our own" (DeBold 1994, xiii).

William Waybourn, the founder and first director of the Gay and Lesbian Victory Fund, was influenced by the efforts of EMILY's List in helping Ann Richards defeat Clayton Williams in the 1990 Texas gubernatorial election. Waybourn concluded that there was a need for a similar organization to help openly gay and lesbian candidates seeking election to all levels of government. He contacted Vic Basile, former executive director of the Human Rights Campaign Fund (now Human Rights Campaign), an important Washington, DC, gay and lesbian political action committee. Basile responded enthusiastically and assisted Waybourn in securing the support of gay and lesbian donors throughout the United States. In doing so, they created the organization's first board of directors, individuals who had considerable fund-raising and political experience, and who were each committed to giving or raising ten thousand dollars to launch the newly created organization (Rimmerman 1994, 215).

Organizational Development

With its formation in May 1991, the Victory Fund joined the Human Rights Campaign (HRC) and the National Gay and Lesbian Task Force (NGLTF), a policy institute, as important Washington-based political organizations representing the interests of gays and lesbians nationally. Although the HRC and NGLTF are vital elements in gay and lesbian political mobilization, the Victory Fund fills an important niche. HRC supports only federal candidates and mostly endorses candidates who are not gay or lesbian but who have demonstrated fine records in promoting gay and lesbian rights. NGLTF's central responsibilities are to lobby Congress, advocate, organize at the grassroots level, and engage in policy research of relevance to the gay and lesbian community; it does little work in the electoral arena (Rimmerman 1994, 216). The Victory Fund is therefore the only group that exists solely to recruit and elect openly gay and lesbian candidates to public office at all levels of government.

Over the years, the Victory Fund has received enthusiastic support from both organizations, but HRC was particularly helpful in assisting the Victory Fund in its early years. William Waybourn said: "We [the Victory Fund] wouldn't be here without HRCF [HRC]. They have given us advice, support, and assistance in every way" (Waybourn 1993).

Organization and Decision Making

The executive director of the Victory Fund is responsible for the day-to-day running of the Washington-based organization and coordinates its political and fund-raising strategies. Since the Victory Fund's creation in 1992, William Waybourn (who resigned to head GLAAD, Gay And Lesbian Alliance Against Discrimination in 1995) and David Clarenbach have served as executive directors. The Victory Fund attempts to limit operating costs by maintaining a small office staff. The Victory Fund has an administrative assistant, a staff person responsible for membership services, and a financial service coordinator who all work out of the Washington, DC, office.

From May 1995 through the November 1996 elections, the Victory Fund received $407,039 from 1,295 full-time members and 725 associate members. All full-time members contribute at least a $100 yearly organizational fee as well as pledge another $200 over a one-year period to any two candidates recommended by the Victory Fund. Associate members contribute $35 yearly. Since its inception in 1992, the average member contribution to candidates has been approximately $287. There are several possible reasons for this high figure. The 1992 Republican National Convention displayed several speakers, notably Pat Buchanan and Pat Robertson, who singled out gays and lesbians as targets for hatred, retribution, and scorn. The AIDS crisis is viewed by many as a constant reminder of the importance of electing openly gay and lesbian officials at all levels of government. President Bill Clinton's lofty 1992 campaign promises on gay and lesbian issues, most notably his pledge to overturn the military ban, led to serious disappointment when such promises were not translated into concrete public policy. These developments have all helped the Victory Fund recruit new members.

The Victory Fund spent $19,417 on contributions to candidates running for Congress in the 1996 election. The organization spent $649,967 in "soft money" on contributions to state and local candidates and overhead expenses (Chibbaro 1997, 16). How does the Victory Fund determine who will receive Victory Fund support in a given election? The board of directors, which meets quarterly, plays the central role. Generally comprised of wealthy members who have political connections, the board is responsible for hiring the executive director and for serving as the organization's eyes and ears on the political world. Board members reside in all areas of the United States and generally have contributed significant financial support to the organization over the years.

The Victory Fund has retained the same rigorous process for choosing candidates throughout its history. The Victory Fund hires a private consulting firm to make an independent analysis of races and then its staff makes a recommendation about particular candidates to the board of directors. The firm evaluates the viability of the candidate and recommends the best way for the Victory Fund to become involved in the contest if the board chooses to do so. After often spirited and lengthy discussions, the board then votes to decide which candidates have earned the Victory Fund's support.

Some 180 candidates contacted the Victory Fund asking for its support in the 1996 elections, and the Fund decided to support forty-nine candidates at all levels of government. These numbers represent a significant increase from 1992, when the Fund supported thirteen out of the seventy-two candidates who asked for help.

Candidates who hope to receive Victory Fund support must be openly gay or lesbian and strongly pro-choice. They must publicly endorse the Federal Gay/Lesbian Civil Rights Bill and similar state and local antidiscrimination laws or legislation and advocate aggressive public policies and positions relevant to AIDS research, education, and treatment. The candidate must also have a strong base of support outside of the gay and lesbian community, demonstrate the ability to raise money, and have a viable candidacy (Waybourn 1993).

Unlike many other political action committees, the Victory Fund does not require that a candidate be a member of a particular party. The Victory Fund does, however, prefer to contribute money to candidates who are running for open seats, especially at the congressional level. Such races afford the Victory Fund a greater opportunity to have a positive electoral impact (Rimmerman 1994, 239).

In what ways has the organization encouraged gay and lesbian candidates to seek Victory Fund support and to run for office? First, publicity regarding the organization has been so favorable that potential candidates have sought the endorsement of the organization. In addition, board members have encouraged candidates in their communities to seek Victory Fund support and approval. The Victory Fund's remarkable success in supporting competitive candidates during the course of its existence bodes well for its ability to recruit potentially viable future candidates.

The organization earmarks and bundles funds in order to have the maximum possible impact on the outcome of races. Nonconnected ideological PACs are able to avoid the five-thousand-dollar contribution limit by requiring their members to earmark their contributions to specific candidates. Victory Fund members write their checks, for example, to "Barney Frank for Congress," and the checks are then bundled every two days so that the candidate's campaign has a constant flow of cash at every stage of the electoral season (Rimmerman 1994, 219).

Direct mail is the Victory Fund's most successful means of fund-raising. One of its officers estimated that 90 percent of the organization's funds have come through direct-mail efforts. The Victory Fund works closely with HRC and NGLTF by sharing lists of potential contributors. HRC's and NGLTF's supporters' lists have been particularly helpful to the Victory Fund in its efforts to recruit new members. The organization has also received connections to potential members by belonging to Pro-Net, a Washington, DC-based coalition that runs fund-raising seminars for progressive PACs and provides a forum for exchanging information about candidates. Additional groups belonging to Pro-Net include Clean Water Action, EMILY's List, the Human Rights Campaign, the National Abortion and Reproductive Rights Action League, Handgun Control, Planned Parenthood, the Sierra Club, the National Organization for Women, and SANE/FREEZE. A New York City–based consulting firm, Eidolon Communications, has helped the Victory Fund design its direct-mail fund–raising strategy. Eidolon Communications has also assisted HRC and EMILY's List in their fund-raising efforts (Rimmerman 1994, 220).

As a part of its fund-raising strategy, the Victory Fund also conducts an aggressive mail campaign in an effort to recruit new members. It requests that all those who join the organization send in a list of people who might be interested in contributing. The more a member contributes financially, the more the Victory Fund contacts that individual with direct-mail requests at various points in its fund-raising cycle.

Victory Fund officials estimate that telephone solicitation is the second most successful fund-raising method, accounting for some 10 to 15 percent of the Fund's overall contributions. Major donors often have been initially contacted through telephone solicitation. Receptions are a third type of fund-raising. They account for roughly 5 to 10 percent of the Victory Fund's overall contributions and are generally held in major cities where there are large numbers of gays and lesbians. Advertising in local gay and lesbian newspapers enables the Fund to advertise fund-raising receptions to potential contributors. Board members also send letters to community members, inviting them to attend Victory Fund receptions in their areas.

Once a candidate receives Victory Fund support, he or she must sign a written contract. The contract requires candidates to make several concessions after a campaign: provide the Victory Fund with access to their mailing lists; sign Victory Fund fund-raising appeals; and make appearances on behalf of the Victory Fund. In this way, the Victory Fund secures the support of openly gay and lesbian candidates in fund-raising and adds to its list of possible direct-mail contributors (Rimmerman 1994, 220).

Ultimately, what do Victory Fund endorsements offer candidates? First and foremost, candidates are afforded important resources that should enable them to run competitive races. The Fund also gives financial support and technical assistance, including advice on how a candidate can market himself or herself to the electorate, hands-on campaign management assistance, suggestions on how to raise money from potential contributors, advice on dealing with the media, and help with crisis management. As a part of its technical assistance, the Victory Fund offers a campaign skills consultation program for the openly gay and lesbian candidates it endorses. This program requires that candidates come together for several days to discuss the day-to-day running of campaigns and specific strategies for openly gay and lesbian candidates.

The 1996 Elections

The 1994 midterm elections did not alter the Victory Fund's strategy. Victory Fund officials worried that the Republican successes in 1994 might encourage more candidates to embrace a gay-baiting strategy, but it appears that the use of this ugly tactic did not increase in 1996. Gay-baiting occurred in a number of races within three weeks of election day.[2]

How did the Victory Fund receive its information regarding how its candidates were faring in the months leading up to the election? As in previous years, the organization turned to the local press, local gay and lesbian clubs in various communities, HRC, Log Cabin Republicans, Victory Fund organization members (especially board members), and PACs belonging to the progressive PAC network, which include EMILY's List, the AFL-CIO, the Sierra Club, and the League of Conservation Voters.

One significant difference from previous election cycles is that the Victory Fund gave out more direct PAC contributions than ever before. The reason for this is that there were many candidates who did not apply for Victory Fund money early in the process, so the organization gave them a quick infusion of funds close to the election in order to boost their candidacies. Several of these candidates actually won their elections. This development suggests that the Victory Fund may well follow a similar funding strategy in the 1998 midterm elections.

Of the forty-nine openly gay or lesbian candidates supported by the Victory Fund in the 1996 election, twenty-eight were elected to office, a better than 50 percent record of supporting winners. This is an impressive record, especially for a relatively young organization.

The Victory Fund has raised more money in the first six years of its existence than did EMILY's List in its first six years. The Victory Fund has raised and distributed $1.4 million to candidates since its creation in May 1991, another remarkable record for a young organization. Yet, as the organization heads into the next election, it faces a number of important issues. The possibility of campaign finance reform looms in the background. Many reform proposals include an elimination of bundling, which would have dramatic consequences for how the Victory Fund distributes its members' money to various candidates.

The problem of gay-baiting will probably continue unabated for the foreseeable future. By providing candidate training and technical support, the Victory Fund plays an important role in advising candidates on how to respond to gay-baiters. The Fund will need to refine and develop techniques for candidates who are targeted by homophobic campaigns.

Yet another challenge facing the Victory Fund is ensuring that it raises enough money to support its day-to-day activities and participate in elections. Regardless of how these issues are resolved, the Victory Fund will continue to play an integral role in advancing the cause of gays and lesbians in the electoral arena. This cause is nothing less than the importance of ensuring that openly gay and lesbian individuals have a seat at the table as crucial decisions are made regarding U.S. public policy.

Notes

The author would like to thank Kathleen DeBold and David Clarenbach for agreeing to be interviewed and for supplying important materials pertaining to the Victory Fund's efforts in the 1996 election. This essay also incorporates material from interviews with William Waybourn in 1992 and 1993.

[1]National exit polls revealed that 5 percent of voters identified themselves as gay, lesbian, or bisexual. Conclusions are based on a *Washington Blade* survey of precincts in

heavily lesbian and gay neighborhoods and on a national exit poll that was conducted for the major television networks. The *Washington Blade* survey reports that voter turnout in the "gay precincts" during the 1984 and 1988 presidential elections was roughly 67 percent and in 1992 it was 72 percent, but it reached only 62 percent in 1996 (no figure was available for 1994). Curtis Gans, head of the Committee for the Study of the American Electorate, concluded after examining exit polls that "the decline in the Gay community [turnout] was substantially greater than that [of the overall turnout]." Murray Edelman of Voter News Service said that "it's a substantial drop. It's pretty good evidence of a real drop-off in voting among Gays and Lesbians" (Lisa Keen, "More Gays Stay Home: Survey Finds Sharp Drop in Gays at the Polls," *Washington Blade*, November 8, 1996, Volume 27, Number 45, pp. 1, 27).

[2]The essays in DeBold (1994) address the issue of gay-baiting in elections at all levels of government.

AT&T PAC: THE PERILS
OF PRAGMATISM

Robert E. Mutch

AT&T PAC has been shaped by three important events: the court-ordered breakup of the old Bell system in 1982, which greatly reduced AT&T's size and imposed new rules on the telecommunications industry; the 1995 revision of telecommunications law, which effects as great a change in the company's market position as the 1982 court order; and AT&T's startling announcement in the same year that it would split into three separate companies.

AT&T responded to the 1982 court order by reorganizing its PAC to increase receipts and fully integrate it with the company's lobbying arm, the Government Relations Division. The reorganized AT&T PAC soon was raising and contributing more money than any other corporate PAC.[1] As with most corporate PACs that are closely linked to lobbying operations, AT&T PAC adopted a pragmatic strategy of supporting incumbents and was orthodox in the kinds of support offered. That is, it made no in-kind contributions or independent expenditures and gave most of its contributions to Democrats.

The unexpected reversal of Democratic fortunes in 1994 brought to power a Republican majority that quickly passed a telecommunications bill quite unlike those considered by previous Congresses. The 1995 debate over telecommunications law was very important to the entire industry, especially AT&T. The PAC began the year with a double handicap: It had to make up lost ground with Republicans, most of whose freshman members it had opposed; and the new congressional leadership was intent on pursuing a deregulatory agenda that was distinctly unsympathetic to the long-distance companies.[2]

Partly in response to this agenda, AT&T stunned Wall Street with the announcement of one of the largest voluntary divestitures in the history of U.S. business (Kirkpatrick 1995, 85, 86).[3] Under this decision, which until the last moment was kept secret even from most of the company's own top executives, AT&T would split into three parts: a communications services company retaining the AT&T name; Lucent, which would continue the communications equipment manufacturing business long carried out under the name of Western Electric; and NCR, the computer company AT&T had bought just four years before. This drastic restructuring led inevitably to the reorganization of AT&T's Government Relations Division. These changes, combined with dissatisfaction with the PAC's performance on the telecommunications bill, produced a wrenching reexamination and restructuring of committee decision making in 1996.

The PAC's Origins and Growth

AT&T contributed to the business PAC explosion of the 1970s by forming political funds for its corporate headquarters and for its Western Electric division in 1977.[4] By 1979, AT&T's Long Lines division and all of the regional operating companies had created their own PACs. Had all these PACs been treated as a single unit, their receipts and expenditures would have made them the largest corporate PAC in 1980.[5] AT&T's collective top-ranked position among corporate PACs ended in 1982, when a federal court ordered the company to divest itself of its twenty-two operating companies.[6] Under the circumstances, it is not surprising that total receipts of the company's three remaining constituent PACs (Western Electric, Long Lines, and corporate headquarters) dropped in 1982.

Faced with a much smaller parent company and declining receipts, the PAC's executive committee responded by merging the three PACs into the current AT&T PAC and by expanding solicitation. The committee decided to reach deeper into management ranks, seeking contributions from all administrative personnel except those with direct responsibility for nonmanagement employees. This move accounts for most of the PAC's nearly five-fold increase in receipts from 1984 to 1986. It was in the 1986 elections that AT&T PAC first became the largest corporate PAC, raising, spending, and contributing more than the political funds of any other business corporation.

In 1976, AT&T apparently had no political contribution program at all. Ten years later it had the largest PAC in corporate America. The court-ordered divestiture was probably the most important factor in this transition. Monopolies have far less incentive to form PACs than do firms in industries with a higher-than-average concentration (Masters and Keim 1985; *Southern Economic Journal* 1991). AT&T may have seen no need to be politically active when it was still a de facto monopoly, apart from the need to protect that very monopoly status against the Department of Justice, consumer groups, potential rivals, such as MCI, and some members of Congress. By dramatically altering the telecommunications industry and AT&T's place in it, the 1982 divestiture and ensuing competition with the Bell companies and new long-distance firms may well have heightened the company's interest in political activity.

Under the old Bell system, AT&T's state and regional government affairs directors lobbied state legislatures and Congress. The postdivestiture AT&T continued this practice. Washington staff of the Government Relations Division were responsible for lobbying congressional committee staff on behalf of the company's positions, whereas state and regional directors lobbied for those same positions with members of Congress and their personal staff (Goff 1991). "We had always felt that there was considerable political benefit to having a local person, recognized as someone who was connected back to their community and their constituents, come to lobby here in Washington," said Steve Billet, AT&T PAC director (Billet 1996a). State directors, who worked for the state and regional, not the federal, government affairs organizations, spent a great deal of time in Washington, often thirty to forty weeks a year. These frequent trips to the capital allowed state directors to stay in touch with each other and with Washington office staff, while their state legislative activities kept them informed about Congress members' electoral situations back home.

State directors also made the PAC's contribution decisions. There were national executive and disbursement committees, but they distributed money not to candidates but to the PAC's own state and regional organizations. It was the state and regional disbursement committees and government affairs directors who decided how to apportion that money among their favored candidates.[7]

It was unusual for a large corporation to have a PAC with such decentralized decision making, but this too followed naturally from the old Bell system's lobbying structure. PAC officers also saw political benefit here, as the state directors not only knew members of Congress both at home and in Washington, but they also were likely to have personal knowledge of challengers and open-seat candidates in their states. Indeed, those directors were likely to have known U.S. senators and representatives when they were in state and local office.

AT&T PAC was unusual not only in its organization, but in the pragmatic cast of its contribution strategy. The PAC has always given more money to Democrats than other corporate PACs (see Table 12.1). As one AT&T PAC officer put it, the selection of candidates to support is "driven by the best assessment of what will minimize risk to the corporation and what will maximize our opportunities.... There is a disinclination to fall on our swords ideologically" (Goff 1991; 1992). This pattern is expected in light of fifteen years of PAC research showing that firms in heavily regulated industries tend to support incumbents (Burris 1987, 738–739; Eismeir and Pollack 1988, 43–47; Handler and Mulkern 1982, 29).

Table 12.1   Percentage of AT&T and Other Corporate PAC
Contributions to Democrats, 1978–1996

	1978	1980	1982	1984	1986	1988	1990	1992	1994	1996
All Corp. PACs	37.7	35.9	34.2	38.6	38.3	46.1	46.4	50.2	48.9	26.9
AT&T PAC	47.3	43.7	42.8	41.6	48.1	55.0	57.3	62.3	59.0	36.6

Source: Federal Election Commission. Figures are for all federal candidates. From 1978 through 1984, AT&T PAC means the three PACs that were later merged into the current AT&T PAC.

AT&T sought support in Congress for the entire life of the PAC to pre-serve its monopoly status and protect its interests in Congress's ten-year effort to rewrite telecommunications law. Because telecommunications bills affected an entire industry, they became the focus of nationwide lobbying campaigns that greatly influenced the PAC's contribution strategy. As one PAC officer explained it:

> One of the lobbying techniques we use to affect [these bills] before they get to the floor is cosponsorship drives. We want to get the whole House on a bill, or keep them off a bill. So having a relationship with the entire Congress is more important to us than it might be to another company whose issues are decided in a specific committee (Millert 1992).

Thus, lobbying the entire House meant not concentrating on particular committees, even on such crucial ones as Commerce and Judiciary. Those two committees were the only ones that would directly consider telecommu-nications law revision, and their members received the highest mean contri-butions from the PAC. But the economic impact of such legislation would be so broad that the PAC gave to nearly every member, including those who did not count AT&T facilities or employees among their constituents. "Contri-butions become a substitute for votes in a member's district—a surrogate" (Goff 1992).

Nevertheless, the PAC favored some members over others. In 1992, the House considered two bills the parent company opposed. Of the 405 House incumbents who won reelection in 1990, 256 decided not to cosponsor either bill. The mean AT&T PAC contribution in the 1990 elections to the major-ity who stayed off the bills was $2,862, well above the $1,967 mean contribu-tion to cosponsors (*CQ Almanac* 1995, 203–214; Mutch 1994).[8] AT&T PAC had been giving to more candidates than other PACs even before it grew large enough to give more money than other PACs (Mutch 1994, 85–86). Giving to nearly every House incumbent in a period of Democratic domi-nance meant giving mostly to Democrats.

Campaign Contributions through 1994

During the 1994 elections, AT&T PAC continued the same proincumbent, Democratic-leaning strategy it had followed previously. During the 1990s, the PAC was giving most of its open-seat contributions to Democrats (see Table 12.2). Although the PAC, like other business committees, gave noticeably less money to Democratic open-seat candidates in 1994, that drop-off is deceptive. Nearly one-third of AT&T's contributions to Republican open-seat candidates were given after the election. Counting only money given before the election, Democrats actually received 61.4 percent of the PAC's open-seat contributions.

The PAC guessed right more often than not in the fifty-two open-seat races of 1994 (see Table 12.3). Nearly all of the wrong guesses, though, were in backing Democrats. Only one of the eighteen Republican candidates it backed lost, while thirteen of the twenty-two Democrats it supported failed to gain an open seat. The PAC backed nonincumbent Democrats for much the same reason it gave to incumbents of that party: AT&T, like other corporations, uses its PAC to help the people who have helped them. In many corporations besides AT&T, most of the people are Democrats. Serious nonincumbent candidates in congressional races usually are state or city legislators, and most of the ones AT&T PAC supported probably had received backing from the company's state-level committees in state elections.

Challengers are another matter, and here the PAC guessed wrong most of the time. The drastically smaller percentage of money given to Democrats (see Table 12.4) is slightly misleading because it is calculated on all contributions in the 1994 election cycle, including those made after the election. Counting only money given before the 1994 election, AT&T PAC actually gave 48.3 percent of its challenger contributions to Democrats. In two of the four races in which it backed Democratic challengers and two of the three

Table 12.2 Percentage of Contributions to House Open-Seat Candidates, 1984–1996

	1984	1986	1988	1990	1992	1994	1996
All Corporate PACs	5.6	11.1	5.9	9.2	11.7	9.9	10.0
Percent to Democrats	23.5	28.2	31.2	33.9	38.3	31.3	26.7
AT&T PAC	9.4	10.2	5.9	5.5	8.3	6.8	5.2
Percent to Democrats	31.4	39.4	43.2	58.0	57.0	49.3	27.3

Source: See Table 12.1.

Table 12.3   Preelection Contributions to Open-Seat Candidates by Party of Winners in 1994

Open-Seat Winners	Preelection Contributions to			
	Winners Only	Losers Only	Both Sides	Neither Side
Republicans	$15,550	$14,850	$3,500	$0
(N)	(17)	(13)	(2)	(7)
Democrats	10,750	1,000	0	0
(N)	(9)	(1)	(0)	(3)
Totals	26,300	15,850	3,500	0
(N)	(26)	(14)	(2)	(10)

Source: Calculated from FEC data.

races in which it backed Republican challengers, it gave as much or more money to the incumbents.

The wrong guesses totaled $109,600 that the PAC spent on thirty-two Democratic incumbents who were toppled by Republican challengers (who received a total of $1,850). AT&T PAC was not alone in misreading the 1994 election. Asked when it had become clear that the GOP would take control of Congress, Goff replied, only half facetiously: "About 6:00 P.M. on election day." By the time PAC officers realized what was happening, it was too late.

It is difficult to see how a pragmatic PAC could have behaved differently. In the absence of clear evidence that the incumbents it had supported for years were destined for defeat, the PAC would continue to support them. This is what happens in most elections. In 1992, for example, the PAC made preelection contributions to only two of the nineteen challengers who

Table 12.4   Percentage of House Contributions to Challengers, 1984–1996

	1984	1986	1988	1990	1992	1994	1996
All Corporate PACs	11.2	3.7	3.5	3.9	6.4	6.7	3.7
Percent to Democrats	6.0	25.8	21.5	17.7	30.6	13.3	26.9
AT&T PAC	3.4	1.6	2.0	1.6	3.4	1.7	1.4
Percent to Democrats	6.1	67.9	67.1	60.9	60.3	4.2	69.0

Source: See Table 12.1.

unseated incumbents. In that election, however, debt retirement contributions made up only 46.5 percent of all money given to challengers; in the 1994 elections, it made up 79.6 percent. The difference was that every winning challenger in 1994 was a Republican and the Republicans took control of Congress.

Immediately following the election, there was a great deal of interest in providing "kiss-and-make-up" money to the Republican candidates who had won (Goff 1992). That was followed by a very systematic fund-raising effort on the part of the Republicans to consolidate their victory. Billet added that this was "a position that people at AT&T weren't used to being in, having guessed wrong on as many races as we had. We were very vulnerable, and everyone knew it. I think there was some panic."

AT&T was far from alone in having guessed wrong, but Republicans were not inclined to forgive. According to a report in the *New York Times*, Representative Newt Gingrich (R–GA), who had warned PAC directors before the election that they had better start giving more to his party, spread the word after the election that PACs had better change both their contribution patterns and their loyalties. The Republicans sought "to make up for lost time by applying what many lobbyists and business executives describe as strong-arm tactics that are blunt even by Washington standards" (Berke 1995, A1). This set the tone for the debate over what became the Telecommunications Act of 1996.

The Impact of the Telecommunications Act

The 1996 act "was one of the most significant events in the company's history, at least in the last ten to twelve years," said PAC director Billet (Billet 1997). Although Congress eventually passed a bill AT&T could support, the PAC's role in bringing about this result became a controversial topic within the company's lobbying organization. The reason for the controversy was that the PAC's 1995 contributions to House candidates were negatively correlated with floor votes in favor of AT&T's position. Doubts about the PAC's role in the telecommunications debate strengthened moves to reorganize the PAC in 1996.

The shift of party control in the 104th Congress further complicated the partisan and interest group lineup on the huge issue of telecommunications reform. The long-distance companies and the regional Bell companies disagreed on most issues, and over the years both sides entered into shifting alliances with labor, consumer, publishing, and other industry groups. The new Republican leaders in the House altered the political context of this debate in two ways: by centralizing power in their own hands to a degree unknown in recent years and by aggressively pursuing a deregulatory agenda generally seen as favorable to the Bells.

By the 1990s, the regional Bell operating companies were lobbying hard to overturn the 1982 court order, which restricted them to local phone service and AT&T to long-distance service and equipment manufacturing. Although almost no one seriously argued that the Bells should not be allowed into the lucrative long-distance market, consumers' groups joined the long-distance companies in arguing that this should not be done without first breaking the Bells' regional monopolies over local telephone service. MCI and Sprint had long since ended AT&T's de facto monopoly over long-distance service, and those three companies argued that local service should be made equally competitive before permitting the Bells to enter new markets.

Neither Republicans nor Democrats were unanimous on these issues, and both the Bells and the long-distance companies had long had powerful allies in both parties. These differences continued through the early summer of 1995, when a great deal of intraindustry horse trading resulted in a compromise bill, HR 1555. AT&T and the other long-distance companies supported the compromise bill, but the Bells were not satisfied. As public attention moved to the Senate, which was debating its own bill, House action moved into Speaker Gingrich's office.

When HR 1555 emerged again, it was a very different bill, one that reflected the Republican leaders' deregulatory agenda. It now had sixty-six pages of new amendments, not least of which was one that greatly eased the Bells' entry into the long-distance market by permitting that move even before they faced local competitors that were "comparable in price, features, and scope" (Healey 1995, 2348). The long-distance companies complained loudly, while their allies in the House denounced the backroom deal that gutted the public work of the Commerce Committee (Healey 1995, 2349). Republican leaders also imposed strict rules for debating the changes. Although the sixty-six-page "Manager's Amendment" had not been seen in final form until the day before it was debated, the rule allowed only eight new amendments, with only ten to thirty minutes of debate on each. Debate, moreover, was scheduled for an unusual late-night session and did not begin until after 10:30 P.M. on August 2. Democrats opposed the restrictive rule two to one, but near-unanimous Republican support ensured adoption. GOP support for the Manager's Amendment itself was less overwhelming, but enough to pass it over Democratic opposition. Another near-unanimous Republican vote defeated John Conyers's (D–MI) amendment to give the Justice Department the authority to link the Bells' entry into the long-distance or manufacturing markets with competition in local service.

What impact did AT&T PAC's contributions have on congressional support for the legislation? Each House member's support was measured using three roll call votes: the rule for debating the Manager's Amendment (four points), passage of that amendment (three points), and Representative Conyers's amendment to ensure competition in local markets (three points).

Scores ranged from zero (no support for AT&T's position) to ten (complete support for AT&T's position).

The substantial difference between the mean scores for Republicans and Democrats immediately suggests a more partisan contribution strategy, for Democrats were far more likely to support AT&T's position than were Republicans (see Table 12.5). Yet the GOP leadership helped produce such sharp partisan differences that, according to an AT&T PAC officer who did not want to be identified, many Republicans, including key committee chairmen, did not really support the rule or the changes but voted for them under pressure. The officer stated, "The GOP leadership really brought the hammer down. They were riding high at the time" (Dunham 1995).[9]

GOP leadership's pressure to keep the rank and file in line on a crucial vote cannot explain the PAC's poor record with Democratic members, however. Fifty-five percent of Democratic members had scores of seven and ten, while 60 percent of Republicans had scores of zero. The relationship between support for AT&T's position and contributions is even lower for Democrats than for Republicans (see Table 12.6). This pattern held true even for votes on the Conyers amendment, the only one of the three votes that affected only the long-distance and communications manufacturing business. Democrats voted 117–78 in favor of AT&T's position on this amendment, Republicans 193–33 against it. The PAC identified and supported its few Republican backers but evidently was unable to do the same for the larger number of Democrats who voted with it.

Although the relationship between Democrats' contributions and votes strongly suggests shortcomings in the PAC's own decision-making process, the PAC's overall failure to significantly affect House roll call votes on the telecommunications bill can be readily explained by external factors. Research on PAC behavior has found that contributions are likely to influence roll call votes only on issues that are neither visible nor contested and on which the long-term factors of constituency, ideology, and party are weak. None of these conditions were present in the telecommunications debate.

Table 12.5　Relationships between House Roll Call Votes and PAC Contributions to House Members

Members	Mean Scores	Correlations		
		Prevote Gifts	Aug. 95–Mar. 96	Apr. 95–Nov. 96
Republicans	1.9	.04	.03	.11
Democrats	5.8	−.06	.17	−.03
All	3.7	−.06	−.01	.01

Table 12.6 Average Contributions by Party and Vote on Conyers's Amendment

	Prevote Gifts		All 1995 Gifts	
	Yes	No	Yes	No
Republicans	$914	$715	$2,320	$1,623
Democrats	506	653	841	970

Several studies have concluded that PAC contributions can influence legislative outcomes on bills that attract little public attention and to which there is little organized opposition (Davis 1993). Both sides in the telecommunications bill debate were well financed and well organized, and the issue was followed closely outside the trade press. As noted above, research also indicates that PAC money can affect roll call votes only where the long-term factors of constituency, ideology, and party are weak (Wright 1985; Fleisher 1993; Regens, Gaddie, and Elliot 1994). Although constituency and ideology were not significant in the outcome, party was of overriding importance.

How stable was member support for AT&T's legislative agenda? Table 12.7 compares the 1992 decisions to cosponsor telecommunications bills AT&T opposed to the 1995 vote on the Conyers amendment, which the company supported. This is a particularly apt comparison, as both the 1992 and 1995 measures applied directly to the Bell companies' entry into markets reserved for AT&T under the 1982 court order. Only 36.8 percent of Democrats changed their position, and switchers were almost as likely to go in one direction as another. However, 60.8 percent of Republicans changed position, and all but a handful of them changed from support to opposition.

In the months following the House vote, the long-distance companies regained much of what they had lost when their lobbyists went to work in the Senate and in closed sessions of the Conference Committee (Hall and Wayman 1990). Assisted by friendlier GOP leaders in the Senate, Vice President

Table 12.7 Percentage of Stability and Change in House Support for AT&T's Position from 1992 to 1995

Party	Support/ Support	Support to Oppose	Oppose/ Oppose	Oppose to Support
Democrats	45.1	21.0	18.0	15.8
Republicans	11.2	56.1	28.0	4.7

Al Gore, White House threats to veto the bill, and filibuster threats from some Senate Democrats, they inserted in the conference report language that holds the Bells to a stricter definition of competition in local service. The reluctance of Senate Republicans to give their House counterparts everything they wanted also caused House GOP leaders to lift pressure on their rank-and-file members. On February 1, 1996, the final compromise passed both houses by almost unanimous votes. By that time, there was already considerable doubt within the PAC about the efficacy of its strategy in effecting this outcome.

Restructuring the PAC

AT&T PAC had given money to almost every House incumbent in the last twenty years, yet it lost the most important congressional vote in its history. Following this fiasco, it drastically changed its operations. PAC director Billet explained the thinking behind the PAC's reorganization:

> We wanted the PAC to be fully aligned with corporate strategy. But PAC strategy wasn't something that had been consciously decided upon. It just happened. One of the basic elements of the old strategy was the ubiquity of our PAC. We gave to just about any incumbent who stuck their hand out. It was a strategy by default. We're a smaller organization now and have tried to become more focused. We have to make decisions about who is and who isn't important to us (Billet 1996a).

Billet's observation captures the key elements in the decision to reassess PAC organization and strategy. Internal research that reported a negative correlation between contributions and votes on one of the most important pieces of legislation in the company's history gave powerful ammunition to those who had always opposed decentralization. Moreover, those opponents were gaining strength just when the structural feature promoting decentralization—the ubiquity of the parent company—was coming to an end. Having decided to shed its equipment manufacturing and computer businesses, AT&T would be smaller and more focused on communications. AT&T lobbyists would thus have fewer bills to track in Congress at the same time that the company needs full-time lobbyists in the states, where most regulatory decisions will be made under the new telecommunications law. With fewer resources, the PAC will have to make harder decisions about how to distribute them. Those decisions have now been centralized in a federal steering committee in Washington.

Opponents of centralization had several criticisms. One was that the structure of the Government Affairs Division under the old system actually undermined the companywide cooperation supposedly fostered by bringing state lobbyists to Washington. That division was divided into state and federal organizations, so the state lobbyists who came to work in Congress actually worked for people back home, not the federal organization in Washington. State lobbyists caught between conflicting recommendations from the federal staff and their own state organizations would choose the latter. It was their superiors back home, after all, who wrote their performance appraisals. "What we ended up with was great variation from one state and region to another in terms of what mattered and what didn't" (Billet 1997).

This situation, in the minds of many PAC officers, was responsible for their poor showing on the telecommunications bill. "We wanted to be able to say here's what matters to the corporation, and stand behind that" (Billet 1997). The smaller the number of decision makers, the easier it is to devise and consistently use a common basis for making contribution decisions. The shifting of regulatory action to the states and AT&T's own "trivestiture" strengthened the arguments for centralizing decision making in fewer hands.

Under the reorganized Government Affairs Division, state lobbyists will remain in the states. "Bringing local people to Washington is a much easier thing to do if you're a monopoly," Billet said. He added:

> When you're in a competitive situation, when you've got to be lean and keep your overhead down, you look for more cost-efficient alternatives. In the meantime, we have shifted responsibility for making basic decisions on PAC contributions to a new federal steering committee. Most members at this point are lobbyists, who are *very* political and understand exactly how this town works (Billet 1996a).

Although the steering committee still seeks advice from state directors, it has devised its own criteria for ranking members of Congress. It also seeks its own information on candidates from such Washington sources as Charles Cook and the Business–Industry PAC (BIPAC) that specialize in campaign research. In fact, BIPAC played a role in AT&T PAC's reorganization. Billet invited Bernadette A. Budde, BIPAC senior vice president, to do a study of the PAC and present it at a government affairs conference in March 1996. "She was brutally honest," said Billet. "She said there was no rhyme or reason to our giving. It was a way to wake people up" (Billet 1997).

Although waking up meant paying closer attention to BIPAC's research, it did not mean adopting BIPAC's own criteria for selecting candidates to support. BIPAC's heavy pro-Republican, antilabor tilt does not fit with AT&T's interests. "If you're a beer wholesaler or a small retail NFIB [National Federation of Independent Business] member, it's real clear," Billet explained. He further stated:

> But we're a lot different than many of the other businesses. Neither party has a monopoly on our interests. We go head-to-head with other businesses as opposed to defining unions or labor as our principal enemy. They're not our big enemy. We certainly have our differences. But our political enemies are the guys who are trying to keep us out of markets (Billet 1996b).

Beginning in April 1996, AT&T PAC began using a hastily devised tiered system in which all members of Congress were ranked by their importance to the parent company. Members in the top tier are those who sit on important committees (chiefly the Commerce Committee in the House), party leaders, and those who have helped the company in the past. The PAC's steering committee members spent much time analyzing elections, poling data, even interviewing candidates, which the federal staff had never done before. The committee will revise its rankings in 1997 for the next election cycle, breaking Congress down more finely by subcommittee.

Even with its interim ranking system, however, the PAC has made an important break with the past: telling candidates they will not get money. "We've told people that we're a much smaller PAC now," Billet said, "and we've explained to them too that if you're a freshman member on the Agriculture Committee and have no AT&T employees in your district, you're not going to get any money, and if you've never voted with us, we might help your opponent" (Billet 1996b). With fewer resources, the PAC will no longer use contributions to create surrogate constituencies.

Contributions in the 1996 Elections

AT&T PAC's reorganization had a significant impact on how it distributed contributions in 1996. The change was greatest in open-seat races, in which the PAC gave money to half as many candidates as it had given to in 1994 (see Tables 12.3 and 12.8). Moreover, over three-fourths of these contributions went to Republicans. The PAC also contributed more money to winners.

The PAC's contributions to challengers also changed substantially, but not in quite the same way. Here, too, the PAC did a much better job of pick-

Table 12.8 Preelection Contributions to Open-Seat Candidates by Party of Winners

	1995–1996 Preelection Contributions to			
Open-Seat Winners	Winners Only	Losers Only	Both Sides	Neither Side
Republicans	$25,075	$2,000	$0	$0
(N)	(10)	(2)	(0)	(15)
Democrats	7,000	4,500	0	0
(N)	(7)	(3)	(0)	(13)
Totals	32,075	6,500	0	28
(N)	(17)	(5)	(0)	(0)

Source: Calculated from FEC data.

ing winners—six of the seven challengers it backed won—but only one of them was a Republican. Six Democrats, five of whom won, received exactly two-thirds of the PAC's challenger contributions. The remaining third went to Anne Northrup of Kentucky, the only Republican challenger the PAC supported. The lone Republican not only got a larger contribution than any of the Democrats but was also the only challenger whose incumbent opponent received no money from the PAC.

The steering committee of the restructured PAC devised a tiered system for judging the importance of candidates to the company. If the 1996 contributions represent the PAC's new direction, it is concentrating more on members who sit on important committees (see Table 12.9). The importance of those committees did not change; committee rankings were the same in 1996 as in 1992. But it is clear that members of less important committees are getting less money. A rough measure of this change is the change in the difference between mean contributions to the top group, Commerce Committee members and House leaders, and the bottom group, members of other committees. In the 1992 elections, the mean contribution to the lowest group was

Table 12.9 Average Contributions by House Committee, 1992–1996

House Committee	Election Cycle		
	1991–1992	1993–1994	Apr.–Nov. 1996
Commerce/Leaders	$3,084	$3,165	$1,814
(N)	(48)	(51)	(47)
Judiciary	2,884	3,059	931
(N)	(31)	(33)	(31)
Appropriations	2,136	2,561	873
(N)	(59)	(59)	(46)
Ways and Means	1,900	2,745	667
(N)	(36)	(38)	(29)
Other Committees	1,859	1,860	475
(N)	(262)	(241)	(225)
All House Members	2,107	2,121	747
(N)	(436)	(450)	(375)
Democrats	2,151	2,256	709
(N)	(269)	(268)	(166)
Republicans	2,037	1,922	777
(N)	(167)	(182)	(209)

more than half that given to the top group; in 1996, it was only one-fourth. The PAC has also responded to the new GOP majority by giving more money to a larger number of Republicans.

The new contribution strategy is more a refinement of the old one than a radical departure from it. Perhaps, though, only a dramatic change in the PAC's decision-making process could have produced even this subtle shift in contribution patterns. Something that did not change is the relationship between contributions and the previous year's votes on the telecommunications bill. Correlations between those votes and 1996 gifts for Republicans and for Democrats are poor, as are those with prevote gifts. The reason is that the new strategy was designed to support members who sit on important committees, not punish those who voted against the company in the summer of 1995.

A policy of punishment would have been self-defeating under the circumstances. PAC officers believed that many House Republicans had voted against AT&T only because they were pressured to do so by their party leaders. Once House GOP leaders had been forced to retreat, there was no reason not to contribute to rank-and-file members who were now free to vote as they pleased. Nor was there any reason to give to Democrats, who were not expected to regain majority status in the upcoming election. So in 1996 the PAC gave even less to Democrats, who mostly supported AT&T's position, and more to Republicans, who did not.

Whether internal restructuring will succeed in making the PAC a more effective instrument of AT&T's corporate strategy is another matter, though. Changes in the lobbying laws will also affect the PAC's role in furthering corporate goals.

Effects of the New Lobbying Laws

Late in 1995, an unusual alliance of House Democrats and GOP freshmen forced a floor vote on a gift ban opposed by Republican leaders. With only six dissenting votes, the House passed H.R. 250, which prohibits House members and their staff from accepting any gifts, such as meals, trips, greens fees, or tickets to sporting events, from lobbyists. That the gift ban changed lobbying practices dramatically is clear on its face, but former AT&T PAC director and lobbyist Don Goff added some detail:

> The AT&T format was geared entirely to building personal relationships with members. Lobbyists had a credit card and a license to take members to dinner and discuss things. It was a routine thing to play golf with a member or invite them to events. Perhaps even more important than the members was the ability to augment relatively meager staff incomes with free lunches. That was the opportunity to get these harried people away and educate them for a while. Talk

through the issues, break bread, then send them back with a document that was a little thicker than the sort of thing you can get through in 10 minutes in a cramped office with phones to answer and bells ringing for votes and the member hollering for a memo. It's always been critical to get members and staff away from the Capitol to get their attention because of the sheer chaos that goes on there. The gift ban makes that much harder (Goff 1996).

What makes it harder still is AT&T's own reorganization. Under the old system, the company's state directors not only lobbied both state legislatures and Congress, they were also responsible for the state AT&T PACs. They are still responsible for state PACs and, under looser state laws, can combine PAC money with meals, trips, and other creature comforts to build close relationships with state politicians. What they can no longer do is continue those relationships with a state politician who wins election to Congress. Under the old system, first-term members of Congress might find that among the few familiar faces in Washington were those of the AT&T lobbyists they had known back home. Were that system still in place, AT&T's lobbyists could begin building personal relationships outside the new congressional restrictions. As it is, the small corps of federal lobbyists are strangers to all first-termers and can no longer get to know them by mixing business with pleasure. "The gift ban certainly diminishes the opportunity to see people in other than straight-on advocacy situations," Billet said. "Long, easy lunches at the Capitol Grille are gone" (Billet 1996a).

Goff suggested that the new law, by breaking the link between lobbyists and legislators, might also weaken the PAC. "A member who has a personal relationship with a lobbyist uses it to raise campaign money: 'We're having a little fund-raiser, old buddy, old lunch partner. Will you come to it?'" (Goff 1996).[10] Lobbyists used corporate money to buy time with a member away from the office; time spent with lobbyists being a commodity probably worth more than lunches or greens fees, the members in turn used their investment of time to raise PAC money from lobbyists. By prohibiting the use of corporate money to start such relationships, members may find that PACs, too, are strangers.

Conclusion

"Could we have turned the ocean liner around in time?" Billet asked, thinking back to the days before the 1994 election. "Maybe, but at that point we had gone through two years of contributions. We'd pretty much cast our lot" (Billet 1996a). Goff used a different simile, recalling that people in the old Bell System compared the company to an elephant lumbering down a street: "Once you get used to moving in one direction, it's very difficult to turn this big thing."

Large organizations, like elephants and ocean liners, are not noted for their ability to make sharp turns. AT&T PAC's sheer size was part of the reason it was not adept at responding to sudden change in the political status quo. Its decentralized decision-making structure, well suited in many respects to furthering the company's interests under the old status quo, may also have hindered its response to change. The new centralized PAC structure should make it easier to change direction when necessary, but it has yet to find its footing in the new status quo. As a smaller AT&T enters an uncertain economic environment, its PAC, also smaller, is deciding what it means to be pragmatic in an uncertain political environment.

Notes

[1]For a fuller discussion of AT&T PAC's origins and development, see Mutch 1994.

[2]AT&T opposed thirty-two of the thirty-four GOP House challengers who won election in 1994 and fifteen of the thirty-nine GOP House open-seat winners (data from the FEC).

[3]*Business Week* and *Fortune* both listed impending deregulation as one of the most important reasons for AT&T's voluntary breakup.

[4]Few AT&T executives are on record as having contributed to federal candidates before 1977, suggesting that the company had no organized political contribution program until it created its first PACs.

[5]AT&T PAC raised a total of $996,000 in the 1980 elections, well above the $668,000 raised by the largest single corporate PAC, that of the Chicago and Northwestern Transportation Co.

[6]The twenty-two local service companies reorganized into what are popularly known today as the Baby Bells and within the industry as regional Bell operating companies, or RBOCs.

[7]In 1991, Gregory Millert, then AT&T's vice president for governmental affairs, said that the national committee's function was "to make sure there's some constituency across the regions. But it's really up to [the state and regional directors] once they get the money" (Millert 1991).

[8]In the next Congress, the 103rd, the House passed two telecommunications bills. The votes on these were unsuited to a comparison with PAC contributions because both passed by near-unanimous votes. The two bills passed; the companies and their allies decided to make their stand in the Senate, which never brought a bill to the floor.

[9]The choice of words here may be important. House Majority Whip Tom DeLay (R–TX) is known as "The Hammer" and *Business Week* reported that DeLay "forced changes in a GOP telecom reform bill to make it more free-market" (Dunham 1995, 73).

[10]Goff further speculated on the changing relationship between PACs and parties: "One of the effects of the House GOP's consolidation of power in Speaker Gingrich's office and the growth of soft money contributions is to increase the importance of the party. And the multiplier for that is the change in the gift laws. If a member has a harder time using personal relationships to raise money, where does he go? The leadership. Because leadership is sitting on all the soft money they leveraged out of all those corporations who have been trying to kiss and make up since November 6, 1994."

THE REALTORS POLITICAL
ACTION COMMITTEE: COVERING
ALL CONTINGENCIES

Anne H. Bedlington

The National Association of Realtors (NAR) and the Realtors PAC (RPAC) represent realtors in elections and in policy making. Realtors frequently must come up with creative solutions to complex obstacles to sales and are acutely aware of the impact of local, state, and federal policies on the real estate industry. The activity of NAR and RPAC in lobbying and in elections reflects the creativity of real estate agents, as well as the firm belief that government policy affects the livelihood of realtors. RPAC is a very large committee that is active in most House races. In the 1996 elections, for example, the committee contributed money in 432 of 435 House races. Realtors have one of the most innovative of all trade association PACs. RPAC experimented for several years with a centralized system for independent expenditures before abandoning that effort after the 1992 elections. For the past two elections, it has tried a more decentralized approach that emphasizes contact between realtors and candidates.

The Realtors PAC has pursued the same goal since its creation in 1969: to promote federal policies that are healthy for the real estate business. RPAC has changed its strategy twice. From 1978 through 1986, RPAC's contributions to House candidates were guided by the assumption that federal policies affecting the real estate industry were stable, and the RPAC gave substantial support to candidates who were in favor of general probusiness policies such as lower taxes, less government spending, and deficit reduction. Many real estate analysts thought that such steps would reduce interest rates, making interest on residential mortgages low enough so that more people could purchase homes. During this period, the PAC gave significant sums to Republicans, who were more likely to support such policies. However, a Republican Senate and a Republican president helped pass the Tax Reform

Act of 1986, which repealed many real estate tax benefits. Infuriated, RPAC changed its criteria for evaluating candidates in 1987. Candidates who consistently supported NAR's position on very specific real estate issues, such as continuation of the deductibility of mortgage interest payments, could be considered for an RPAC contribution, regardless of their overall stand on business issues. This rule led RPAC to support more Democratic incumbents than before (Bedlington 1994).

In 1993 RPAC changed its methods for supporting candidates, partly in response to the possibility that campaign finance reform would eliminate or severely restrict PACs. RPAC eliminated its independent expenditures program, which had been controlled by the national PAC, and replaced it with programs that allowed local realtors greater flexibility in influencing contributions. Programs were created in 1993 and tried in 1994 so that any adjustments could be made in time for the 1996 election.

The programs were designed to cover all contingencies. If no changes are made in the current Federal Election Campaign Act, no changes need be made in RPAC's current methods. If a new law restricts PAC contributions to two thousand dollars per election cycle, then attendance at receptions held in candidates' states and in Washington, DC, would become the preferred vehicle for presenting contributions in person. If new legislation limits a PAC's donation to one thousand dollars per cycle, then RPAC would help candidates raise money by hosting fund-raising receptions, as in-kind contributions, in the states and in Washington, DC. A Special Recognition Fund Program would also be used to distribute in-kind donations of poll results and focus groups to friendly candidates involved in close races. RPAC purchases large numbers of polls at discount rates. If PACs are outlawed, the NAR would use its opportunity races and the Congressional Legislative Advocacy Program to mobilize individual realtors at the grassroots.

RPAC and NAR experimented with these programs in 1994, and they will be discussed later in the context of the 1994 and 1996 elections for the House of Representatives. It is worth noting that RPAC was one of the few PACs that created and field-tested about half a dozen contingency programs for an actual election.[1]

Organizational Characteristics

The NAR was founded in 1908 and has become the largest trade association in the country. Its purpose is to promote federal, state, and local policies beneficial to the real estate business. It has a federated structure, with the national association, state organizations, and about eighteen hundred local boards of realtors. There are approximately 730,000 real estate professionals who are members of a local board, a state association, and the national association.

The NAR has eleven political employees based in Washington: seven lobbyists and four political representatives. The latter do political analysis while in
Washington, and fieldwork when training state and local NAR and RPAC
workers. In addition, two political representatives work solely outside of the
nation's capital. The NAR periodically surveys its members to learn their
positions on public policies. It also communicates with members regularly via
a monthly trade magazine and various other reports.

RPAC was created in 1969. It also has a federated structure; there are
local board PACs and fifty state association PACs. These PACs try to influence which candidates are elected to state and local office. In states where it
is allowed, the local board or state association requests that realtors contribute to RPAC when they pay their annual dues. In other states, contributions
are solicited using a variety of methods, such as personal conversations, special events, or direct-mail requests. In 1996, 118,000 members gave money to
the PAC, a participation rate of 16 percent. RPAC received 30 percent of the
money collected at the local and state levels. This amounted to an average
annual contribution from a realtor to RPAC of slightly over ten dollars in
1995 and 1996.

Three NAR employees run RPAC: a director, a coordinator who oversees
the PAC's receipts, and another who is responsible for expenditures. They
work in Washington and constantly communicate with NAR lobbyists and
political representatives, and with the association's state and local employees.[2]
Many of the national NAR lobbyists, political representatives, and RPAC
workers are longtime employees.[3] RPAC sends monthly reports to its constituent state and local associations as well as to national, state, and local RPAC
trustees. It contributes news of its activities to the monthly NAR magazine.

PAC Activity Prior to the Republican
Takeover of Congress

During the 1992 election, RPAC and the NAR supported House candidates
by contributing money, making independent expenditures directly to advocate the election of individual candidates, and carrying out grassroots efforts
in opportunity races, in which the real estate industry had a clear stake in one
candidate's success. The first two activities were carried out by RPAC using
federally regulated hard money. The latter activity was carried out by the
NAR using unregulated soft money from its treasury.

RPAC collected its funds from state- and local-affiliated Realtors PACs,
which raise money directly from realtors. In return for their contributions to
RPAC, the state and local PACs received the opportunity to request that the
national RPAC Board of Trustees contribute money to specific candidates.
RPAC and NAR lobbyists and political representatives evaluated state

requests. They considered several factors in evaluating incumbents: voting record, committee assignments, and whether he or she was a party leader. They also assessed the competitiveness of the race and issued a recommendation. The state's request, together with the recommendations from RPAC and the NAR's lobbyists and political representatives, was presented to the RPAC Board of Trustees, a twenty-five-member committee appointed by the NAR's president. The committee met several times a year to approve or deny a request. If the trustees approved a request, then the PAC contributed amounts that typically ranged from $3,000 to $5,000 per election. Candidates in tight races, or those who served on important congressional committees or were part of the Democratic Party leadership, were likely to be given the full $10,000 amount. Contributions of $1,000 or less were routinely given and considered little more than the price of admission to a fund–raising event.

In 1992, RPAC gave more than $2.6 million to House candidates and distributed roughly 80 percent of it to incumbents. Democratic incumbents received 46 percent of contributions, whereas Republican incumbents received 33 percent. In the 1994 election, total RPAC direct contributions to the House dropped to slightly over $1.5 million. Again, contributions favored incumbents, with Democrats receiving substantially more than GOP incumbents.

RPAC made independent expenditures on behalf of seven House incumbents in 1992, who were selected by a national independent expenditure committee. Because the independent expenditures were made without any coordination with the candidates' campaigns, the expenditures were handled in secrecy. The committee commissioned polls in fifteen to twenty races to investigate citizens' opinions on important domestic issues; laws and regulations affecting real estate; and the personality, experience, policy inclinations, and competitiveness of the candidate whom RPAC was considering supporting. Once the committee selected a final list for independent expenditures, it obtained its money from the RPAC Board of Trustees.

RPAC made no independent expenditures in the 1994 elections. This was a considerable contrast to the three preceding elections, when it spent $755,885, $503,048, and $400,824. The PAC ceased making independent expenditures and disbanded its independent expenditure committee for two reasons. First, realtors objected to the secrecy of the process and their lack of input into it. Second, the diversity of realtors' political opinions and candidate preferences meant that some of them were angered by RPAC television commercials singing the praises of "Candidate Adams" because they supported his or her opponent.

RPAC gave only $1.5 million to House candidates in 1994, and the NAR spent only $183,637 to support thirteen Democratic candidates and $133,846 on eleven Republicans in opportunity races. RPAC's cash on hand at the end of 1994 was $1,100,275, a sharp contrast to the less than $200,000 it had on hand at the end of the 1992 and 1996 elections.

NAR grassroots efforts took place in election and nonelection years. In nonelection years, NAR political representatives were sent to congressional districts to instruct interested realtors in campaign techniques and how to volunteer for campaign positions that match their skills and available time. In election years, NAR, in conjunction with RPAC's director, sent political representatives to congressional districts to mobilize support for the favored candidate. They worked with politically active realtors to register real estate agents who were not registered to vote; they recruited campaign volunteers; and they worked to mobilize realtors on election day using direct mail and telephone banks.[4] Neither RPAC or the NAR anticipated the Republicans' winning control of the House in 1994, and when a Republican surge seemed possible, RPAC did not change its contribution decisions.

The 1996 Election for the House of Representatives

A month before the elections, RPAC expected that the Republicans would retain control of the House but with a reduced majority. A number of GOP freshmen were vulnerable. Additionally, the 1996 elections had several competitive open-seat races that should have been safe. The GOP candidate should have waltzed to victory in nineteen open-seat contests, but in sixteen of these, the two contenders were within one or two percentage points of each other. Similarly, there were twenty-eight races for a vacant seat usually held by a Democrat, but Republicans were competitive in eighteen of them.

RPAC budgeted 35 percent of its money for direct contributions to candidates and 65 percent to be put into a fund named the Political Advocacy Fund. This fund contained a mix of hard money and soft money consisting of corporate contributions from real estate companies. The Political Advocacy Fund paid for opportunity races, the Congressional Legislative Advocacy Program, and advocacy campaigns concerning real estate issues. For example, during the last two years NAR spent over $1,500,000 criticizing a flat tax, explaining to consumers, homeowners, and its own members why NAR thinks it would damage the real estate sector of the economy. RPAC gave 65 percent of its hard money to the Political Advocacy Fund to demonstrate the effectiveness of these new approaches. During the 1998 elections, RPAC plans to keep 90 percent of its income for hard money contributions and give the remaining 10 percent to the Political Advocacy Fund. If this fund has the same or a larger amount of money to spend, it will have a much smaller percentage of hard money in its mix.

In 1996, RPAC gave nearly $1.8 million to House candidates (see Table 13.1). It contributed significantly less than it had in the early part of the decade. RPAC gave little to nonincumbents, but the PAC made a major change in its allocation of money to incumbents. The PAC increased the

Table 13.1   RPAC Contributions to House Candidates

	1988	1990	1992	1994	1996
Incumbents					
Democrats	48%	53%	46%	49%	28%
Republicans	39	37	33	32	54
Challengers					
Democrats	1	0	1	0	0
Republicans	2	1	1	3	2
Open Seats					
Democrats	5	4	8	6	5
Republicans	5	6	10	10	10
Total Contributions	$2,732,586	$2,846,678	$2,689,830	$1,543,692	$1,797,288

Source: Federal Election Commission.

share of its House contributions to GOP incumbents from 32 percent to 54 percent and cut its share of gifts to Democratic incumbents from 49 percent to 28 percent. Two factors explain some, but not all, of the differences in the two elections. First, in 1994, 59 percent of the incumbents running for reelection were Democrats and only 41 percent were Republicans, whereas in 1996 45 percent of the incumbents running for reelection were Democrats and 55 percent were members of the GOP. Second, RPAC gives the maximum contribution of ten thousand dollars to the members of Congress who are part of the majority party's leadership. RPAC gave the maximum legal contributions to Democrats in 1994 and to Republicans in 1996.

Candidates were evaluated at the local, state, and federal levels. House incumbents were assessed using RPAC's contribution guidelines. The criteria are based on whether candidates cosponsored any key NAR federal legislation, gave a one-minute floor speech on behalf of a key issue, signed a letter of support for a key issue, and initiated additional letters of support among their House colleagues. Additional considerations include whether the candidate used congressional authority to make the White House and independent regulatory agencies respond to real estate issues, voted for a key issue on the floor or in a House committee, and provided constituent services on a real estate–related matter. Qualifications also include whether the candidate is a majority or minority party leader or a member of a committee that deals with the legislative agenda of realtors. RPAC further considers candidates' NAR voting record, the competitiveness of their primary or general election, their campaign committee's cash on hand, and the composition of their congressional district, including the number of realtors, the number of local real estate boards, and the party affiliation of registered voters.

While the national association assesses candidates on these criteria, state PAC officials also play a major role in evaluating nonincumbents because they tend to have better contacts in the district than do Washington officials. Nonincumbents who are considered for support have a personal interview with local or state PAC officers, who use RPAC's standard questionnaire to examine the candidates' political philosophy, background, financial resources, and political assets. Nonincumbents who have had local or state political experience are also rated on RPAC's fourteen contribution guidelines. NAR lobbyists also take part in making contribution decisions. One PAC official told us:

> The political representatives and all of the lobbyists will meet in this room. I'll begin with a list of thirty requests. I'll go through every one of them, and we'll argue and debate and cuss at each other. Finally, we'll come to some resolution, as to who we should give money to and how much. And the lobbyists will be open and frank about where they are. The political representatives will do the same. And we'll say okay, here is what the state wants (a state PAC requested a specific amount of money). Are we willing to take the heat if we recommend not giving this person any money? Do you feel so strongly one way or the other? The fourteen point "guidelines" are involved in our decision-making. About ten of the fourteen points are related to legislative acts—what they've done for us or against us (Richardson 1996).

RPAC groups candidates according to three factors when making contribution decisions: competitiveness, party, and incumbency. Each has an impact on the average size of gift.[5] The 91 candidates in competitive elections received an average contribution of $5,111 (including contributions given in primary and general elections); the 303 candidates who were noncompetitive were given $3,841 on the average. Republicans also received larger gifts than Democrats. For example, competitive Democratic incumbents received $3,469, while those on the opposite side of the aisle were given $5,742 (see Table 13.2). Finally, open-seat candidates in competitive races received more money than did incumbents.

RPAC made no contributions to leadership PACs and PACs formed by coalitions of PACs with similar interests in 1996. However, the PAC gave soft money at large-dollar fund-raising events and made contributions to both parties' congressional and senatorial campaign committees. The PAC contributed to forty Senate candidates running in 1996, including twenty incumbents, and to thirty other incumbents who were not seeking election in the 1996 election cycle. Republicans benefited most from RPAC contributions: Fifteen Senate Republicans received nearly 80 percent of all Senate contributions the committee made to 1996 election candidates. RPAC used similar criteria for assessing Senate candidates, although the decision-making pro-

Table 13.2   RPAC Contributions to House Candidates in the 1996
Elections[a]

	Competitive[b]		Noncompetitive[c]	
	Democrats	Republicans	Democrats	Republicans
Incumbents				
Average	$3,469	$5,742	$3,063	$4,204
Total	83,250	269,875	395,085	613,775
(N)	(24)	(47)	(129)	(146)
Open Seats				
Average	5,214	5,808	4,727	6,059
Total	36,500	75,500	52,000	103,000
(N)	(7)	(13)	(11)	(17)

Source: Federal Election Commission.
[a]Special elections are included in the analysis.
[b]Candidates in competitive races earned between 45 and 55 percent of the vote.
[c]Candidates in noncompetitive races earned less than 44 percent of the vote or more than 55 percent of the vote.

cess was more relaxed because there are fewer Senate races. RPAC gave to almost all incumbents seeking reelection in the 1996 election cycle.

New Contribution Programs

During 1993 and 1994, RPAC trustees and staff and NAR lobbyists and political representatives worked to produce a comprehensive set of interrelated programs, some using hard money to make contributions and some using soft money to make expenditures. Some were programs used in the past that were formalized and given a detailed set of rules. Others were tried for the first time in 1994, and then fully implemented in 1996. In general, the PAC replaced its centralized independent expenditure program with a variety of programs that allow local realtors to play a larger role in contribution decisions.

To facilitate communication between local realtors and House incumbents, realtors established the In-State Reception Program, which allowed key realtors in each district to attend incumbents' fund-raisers, make contributions, and convey endorsements. An incumbent may be given a contribution of up to one thousand dollars through this program.[6] No formal approval by the national RPAC trustees is needed for local realtors to attend. A completed "candidate contribution request" form, signed by the state

RPAC chair, must be given to the national RPAC's director at least two weeks prior to the scheduled date of the incumbent's fund-raising reception. These "key realtors" may also want to attend fund-raisers held by an open-seat candidate or a challenger. An open-seat candidate is governed by the same rules as an incumbent, except that the candidate may be given up to two thousand dollars during an election cycle and must be interviewed by state PAC officials. A summary of the interview with the candidate plus the request form must reach the national RPAC's director at least two weeks before the open-seat candidate's fund-raising reception. The process for handling requests for House challengers is more stringent because of the low odds of challenger success and concerns about angering powerful incumbents. The maximum amount is one thousand dollars per election. A summary of the interview with the candidate and the completed request form must be given to national RPAC's staff at least two weeks before the reception. The national RPAC trustees must formally approve or reject the request; they use conference calls and voting by fax to make their decision.

Table 13.3 shows the different types of fund-raising assistance that RPAC gave to House candidates. It demonstrates that competitiveness and party were not major factors in determining whether candidates benefited from in-state fund-raising receptions, Washington receptions, or RPAC's special recognition fund. Because of the higher contribution limit for open-seat candidates, however, candidate status is an important factor. In the 1998 campaign, the realtors plan to initiate a program of in-district, in-kind fund-raisers, in which realtors volunteer to work for the campaign of the candidate.

RPAC also has a program to allow NAR lobbyists to attend Washington, DC, fund-raisers for incumbents. They may also request approval to attend receptions for challengers and open-seat contenders. The presence of an NAR representative at a Washington fund-raising event is helpful for a candidate because it shows realtor support. House incumbents, challengers, and open-seat candidates are all eligible for a contribution of one thousand dollars or less at a Washington reception during the two-year election cycle. No requests require formal approval by the national RPAC trustees. NAR staff notify officials at the state and local level when they attend a reception or spend Washington, DC, reception money. Challengers and open-seat candidates must have held a fund-raising reception in the congressional district that attracted local and state realtors bearing contribution checks. This requirement emphasizes the importance of the local/state basis of contributions. The amounts of donations to competitive and noncompetitive incumbents were similar, and Republicans received slightly more money than Democrats on average.

Realtors may want to do more than attend a fund-raiser. Some want to host them. NAR staff who request that a Washington fund-raiser be thrown for a House candidate must submit to the national RPAC trustees a request

Table 13.3   RPAC Contributions to House Incumbents and Open-Seat Candidates Who Benefited from One of RPAC's Fund-Raising Programs

	In-State Receptions			
	Competitive		Noncompetitive	
	Democrats	Republicans	Democrats	Republicans
Incumbents				
Average	$1,141	$1,159	$931	$1,115
Total	18,250	48,675	101,425	143,775
(N)	(16)	(42)	(109)	(129)
Open Seats				
Average	1,500	2,000	1,750	2,000
Total	3,000	8,000	7,000	14,000
(N)	(2)	(4)	(4)	(7)

	Washington Receptions			
	Competitive		Noncompetitive	
	Democrats	Republicans	Democrats	Republicans
Incumbents				
Average	$1,025	$1,141	$955	$1,107
Total	20,500	52,500	107,000	155,000
(N)	(20)	(46)	(112)	(140)
Open Seats				
Average	0	0	0	0
Total	0	0	0	0
(N)	(0)	(0)	(0)	(0)

	Special Recognition Fund			
	Competitive		Noncompetitive	
	Democrats	Republicans	Democrats	Republicans
Incumbents				
Average	$3,423	$4,139	$2,592	$2,890
Total	44,500	169,700	181,410	315,500
(N)	(13)	(41)	(70)	(109)
Open Seats				
Average	4,786	5,192	5,000	5,235
Total	33,500	67,500	45,000	89,000
(N)	(7)	(13)	(9)	(17)

Source: The Realtors PAC.

form, an assessment of the candidate based on the contribution guidelines, a summary of the interview with a nonincumbent, and a proposed fund-raising goal. The event should produce at least twice the in-kind contribution costs of staging it. A simple majority vote of the national RPAC trustees is necessary to approve the request. During 1996 elections, RPAC sponsored a fund-raising reception for one Republican contender, which cost $385.

The RPAC Special Recognition Fund Program allows the PAC to give a higher level of assistance to candidates who are staunch supporters of the NAR's legislative agenda and who are running in close election contests. Assistance may be direct contributions of money, polls, and focus groups and/or independent expenditures. State or national RPAC trustees may request money for a candidate from the Special Recognition Fund. They must submit, to the national RPAC director at least two weeks before the next scheduled meeting of the national RPAC trustees, a signed request form, an examination of the candidate's rating on the contribution guidelines, and a summary of the interview if a nonincumbent. Two-thirds of the trustees must approve all requests.

Larger gifts went to incumbents in competitive races in 1996, although this was not true for open-seat candidates. Republican incumbents in close races received more money than did Democrats in similar situations, reflecting the GOP's control of Congress. Open-seat candidates consistently received more money than incumbents.

Some candidates are supported through several programs, others through only the Special Recognition Fund (see Table 13.4). A common pattern was one thousand dollars from the In-state Reception Program, one

Table 13.4 RPAC Mean Contributions to House Incumbents and Open-Seat Candidates According to the Number of RPAC Programs Involved

	Competitive		Noncompetitive	
	Democrats	Republicans	Democrats	Republicans
Incumbents				
One Program	$806	$800	$844	$929
Two Programs	2,700	3,125	2,014	2,598
Three Programs	6,250	6,543	4,830	5,245
Open Seats				
One Program	3,600	4,500	3,556	4,600
Two Programs	9,250	8,750	10,000	8,143
Three Programs	0	0	0	0

Source: The Realtors PAC.

thousand dollars from the Washington Reception Program, and one thousand dollars from the Special Recognition Fund. There were other instances of a candidate's receiving five thousand dollars from the Special Recognition Fund. While the number of programs assisting a candidate is not related to the total amount of RPAC's contribution, it is an indicator of the amount of contact between a candidate and RPAC, especially because two of the three programs involve personal contact.

RPAC's special programs have two main goals: to foster greater contact between realtors and candidates and to provide realtors with the opportunity to concentrate resources in key races. Although RPAC has not made independent expenditures since 1992, it has advanced its second goal by making issue advocacy expenditures. Campaign and lobbying activities go hand in hand as RPAC seeks to maximize its influence in Congress.

When RPAC designates an election as an opportunity race, it uses soft money to mobilize realtors at the grassroots to support its preferred candidate. RPAC carries out educational and advocacy mailings in bottom-tier opportunity races. It also carries out voter identification and get-out-the-vote telephone banks in moderate-priority races. Finally, RPAC carries out all of the preceding activities in high-priority opportunity races, and it assigns an NAR political representative to provide on-site organizational assistance.[7]

State RPAC trustees may request that a contest be designated an opportunity race by following the same procedures that are used to request an RPAC contribution, including the completion of a candidate contribution request form. The amount of money spent in opportunity races remained about the same between 1992 and 1996, but the partisan division changed (see Table 13.5). In 1992 and 1994 the Democrats had about a 10 percent edge over GOP candidates. In 1996, the Democrats' share plummeted to 27 percent, 46 percent less than the percent given to the Republicans.

Table 13.5 Distribution of NAR Communication Expenditures in Opportunity Races

	1992	1994	1996
Percent Democrats	55%	58%	27%
(N)	(16)	(13)	(7)
Percent Republicans	45	42	73
(N)	(17)	(11)	(22)
Total Spent	$386,405	$317,483	$319,465

Source: Federal Election Commission.

NAR Lobbying

In addition to their electoral activities, the realtors also lobby. The Congressional Legislative Advocacy Program is designed to mobilize realtors and, in some cases, selected members of the general public. The goal is to gain the support of senators and House members for the realtors' position on a specific piece of legislation. The importance of the issues determines the number of congressional districts targeted and whether electronic advertising, persuasion mail, ads in periodicals, telephone banks, public opinion surveys, focus group research, legislative issue educational materials, and press kits are used to communicate with realtors or the general public. All issue advocacy ads are financed with soft money.

The Congressional Legislative Advocacy Program working group, the chair and vice-chair of the national RPAC trustees, and the chair of the NAR's Public Policy Coordinating Committee oversee all issue advocacy, including communications carried out in connection with state and local elections. The national RPAC trustees notify states and local associations before a campaign is begun. The PAC spent $1,450,000 on these programs in 1996, including $650,000 from RPAC's Political Advocacy Fund and $800,000 from the NAR's discretionary fund.

When party control of the House changed in 1994 and control of the Senate changed in 1996, NAR lobbyists did not have to scramble to forge new relationships with Republican members of Congress. According to Jerry Giovaniello:

> We had the luxury of having been around these congresspeople when they were minority members. The fact that they became the majority, [that] we already knew them, [and] we already had participated in legislative strategy [and] fundraisers [meant] RPAC activities [were] planned, and [didn't] change that much. Whereas other groups suddenly ha[d] to make a lot of new friends or hire a Republican lobbyist. We ha[d] been there all along, and I think that they recognize that (Giovaniello 1997).

The NAR's and RPAC's traditional bipartisan posture served realtors well once the elections were over and the Republicans had taken control of Congress.

Conclusion

The NAR and RPAC are highly adaptive, savvy, federated interest group organizations that work together to carry out national campaign strategies. However, unlike most national interest groups, these organizations are responsive to the preferences of local realtors. Much of the groups' strength comes from their involving local realtors and real estate boards in their fund-raising, contribution, and lobbying activities. Other sources of strength are the groups' bipartisan posture and their integrated electioneering and lobbying practices. Innovation and advanced planning also strengthen the realtors' influence in Washington politics. By planning for all contingencies, the NAR and RPAC have been able to keep one step ahead of changes in federal campaign finance law, respond to changes in the balance of power in Congress, and maintain a strong influence in Washington politics.

Notes

[1] The information in this chapter was gathered during three meetings with RPAC Director Trey Richardson on the following days: August 22, 1996, October 10, 1996, March 28, 1997. Jerry Giovaniello, vice president for governmental affairs, was interviewed about lobbying on March 28, 1997.

[2] Rather than a hierarchy of more or less influential parts of this communication network, each part's impact depends on what it knows and how valuable that information is at that moment.

[3] Desiree Anderson was RPAC director from 1986 until February 1996. Trey Richardson, NAR's political director for the South, came to Washington to work for RPAC in June 1994 and became director of RPAC in February 1996. Jerry Giovaniello has been an NAR lobbyist for more than a decade.

[4] The training in the off-year was paid for by the NAR and, because the lessons did not favor any particular candidate, did not need to be disclosed. In the election year NAR's spending was a "partisan communication," money spent by the trade association urging its members to support a specific contestant. The NAR reported the costs of these "express advocacy" activities to the Federal Election Commission.

[5] RPAC organized its information for 1995 and 1996 to include: (1) all candidates on a November 1996 election ballot, (2) all candidates on a ballot for a special election to fill a vacant House seat in 1995 or 1996, and (3) all contestants who were candidates at some stage in the 1996 election process but who were defeated in a primary, eventually decided to retire, and so on. This last group is not included in this analysis because their races did not have the urgency of those that were held on November election day. There are thirty such candidates (thirteen Democratic incumbents, thirteen Republican incumbents, two Democratic open-seat candidates, one Republican open-seat candidate, and one Democratic challenger). RPAC gave contributions to eight Republican challengers, but none to Democratic challengers. These eight have been excluded from this analysis because they cannot be compared with Democratic challengers.

[6] These donation amounts are subtracted from the ten thousand dollars allowed for a primary and a general election. These projects involve a different venue or method of giving a contribution to a candidate (e.g., in-kind fund-raisers).

[7] The salary and travel costs of the NAR staff are paid by the NAR with dues money.

WISH LIST: PRO-CHOICE WOMEN
IN THE REPUBLICAN CONGRESS

Mark J. Rozell

After the election of a Republican majority to Congress in 1994, the Christian Coalition held a Capitol Hill press conference to unveil its Contract with the American Family. Numerous leading congressional Republicans and presidential aspirants attended the event to show their support. The executive director of the Christian Coalition, Ralph Reed, boldly proclaimed that by electing a Republican majority the public had sent a strong socially conservative message. The press conference, with its show of GOP support, had sent a strong message to the public: Social conservatives had become a major element in the mainstream of the new majority party.

Although the public clearly associates the GOP today with support for a socially conservative agenda, the alliance between the Christian Right and the party remains controversial. Exit polls in elections show a growing gender gap among voters, in part due to Republican women defecting from their party largely because of its antiabortion rights stand.

Prominent GOP women have started two groups with the purpose of changing the party's current abortion position. The better known is Republicans for Choice, founded in 1989 and directed by consultant Ann Stone. Less well known, but clearly gaining in stature, is Women in the House and Senate, or WISH List.

Origins and Purpose

Founded in 1992, WISH List's primary purpose is to fund pro-choice Republican women candidates for the House and the Senate, although it also provides aid to gubernatorial and state legislative candidates. WISH List does not lobby and does not involve itself in presidential election politics.

The PAC contributes only to individual candidates, not to parties or other organizations. It does not make independent expenditures or engage in issue advocacy or voter contact. Modeling itself on the success of EMILY's List, WISH List primarily engages in bundling contributions from its members to pro-choice GOP women candidates.

The organization has grown considerably during its brief history. The organization initially was located in the office of a political consultant in New Jersey, and it lacked a full-time staff or separate headquarters. It was then strictly a "volunteer-driven" effort (Goldman 1996a). In 1995, WISH List opened a headquarters in Washington, DC, and the organization now boasts a full-time staff, a president, an executive director, and a board of directors.

The organization's current president, Patricia Goldman, is both a long-time Republican leader and a feminist. She has previously served as executive director of the House Wednesday Group, an organization of moderate Republican members of the House of Representatives, and was married to the former Senator Charles Goodell (R–NY) until his death in 1987. She previously was active in the campaign to enact the Equal Rights Amendment. Like many moderates, she remains a Republican because of her views on economic issues, yet she is very uncomfortable with the GOP's move to the right on social issues (Goldman 1996b, 1996c; Mills 1996). Goldman maintains that the group's founding in 1992, "the year of the woman," was a fortuitous circumstance that enabled WISH List to attract a good deal of early attention. More importantly, she said, until WISH List entered the political scene, "there was nothing on the Republican side to raise money specifically for women candidates." WISH List founders actually contacted leaders of EMILY's List for help in setting up the GOP pro-choice group. EMILY's List founder and president, Ellen Malcolm, was instrumental in advising WISH List founders on how to set up and maintain such an organization (Rimmerman 1994, 215).

Members of WISH List make a $100 annual contribution to the PAC and then commit an additional $100 per election cycle to each of two candidates. Members are entitled to the quarterly newsletters and mailings that identify the candidates who have been endorsed by the organization. Although the majority of members contribute at least two $100 checks to candidates per election, some donors give $1,000 or more to support candidate recruitment and training.

The organization gives money through its own PAC, usually early in the election season to help candidates launch their campaigns. The PAC then lists endorsed candidates in their mailings, and members write checks directly to the candidate's campaign but mail them to WISH List, which in turn collects them into a bundle and sends them to the candidate. Executive Director Karen Raye explains that the organization does four or five candidate profile mailings per election cycle. Each mailing usually features four candidates. In an exceptional case, for a candidate the organization strongly wants to help, they will do two mailings for that candidate in one election year. WISH List accepts corporate money to help its endorsed candidates for state offices (Raye 1997a), where campaign finance laws allow for direct corporate contributions.

In its first year, WISH List supported the successful 1992 GOP House campaigns of Tillie Fowler, Jennifer Dunn, and Deborah Price. In 1993 the organization contributed over $40,000 to the successful New Jersey gubernatorial campaign of Christine Todd Whitman and $55,000 to Kay Bailey Hutchison's special election campaign in Texas for the U.S. Senate. In 1994, WISH List raised $370,000 for forty candidates. All of its incumbent candidates that year won and one additional endorsed candidate, Sue Kelly, was elected to the House; another, Olympia Snowe (R–Maine), was elected to the Senate (Raye 1997b; Goldman 1996b, 1996c; Mills 1996). In 1996 the organization contributed over $1 million to its candidates and helped Kelly win reelection in a tight race, and it also assisted former Fort Worth mayor Kay Granger in winning a House seat.

Because of its political successes and expanded fund-raising, the organization's name has become something of a misnomer. Although the organization still identifies its central purpose as helping Republican women to win election to the Congress, WISH List increasingly is putting resources into statehouse and state legislative races. In addition to assisting Whitman in 1993, for example, WISH List did a mass mailing on behalf of legislative candidates in California in 1996. The PAC also backed the four incumbent state legislators in Illinois who were challenged within the party by pro-life conservatives. All four incumbents won their races. Goldman explained that, by supporting state legislative candidates, WISH List is assisting with the recruitment of future candidates for the Congress (Goldman 1996c).

According to Goldman, "our most important role now is to give a home to those moderates in the GOP who are disaffected by the conservative direction of the party." Rather than leave the party over platform positions that "are an invasion of people's privacy," through WISH List the moderates can find others in the GOP such as themselves who continue to play a role in the party and want to change the GOP's future direction (Goldman 1996b).

The organization does not automatically support every GOP pro-choice woman candidate for Congress in her nomination quest or even general election campaign. WISH List screens its candidates and makes strategic determinations on how best to spend its resources. The board of directors has a candidate review committee that sends questionnaires to candidates who have asked WISH List for help. The committee also conducts personal interviews with the candidates and bases its decision on the results of these interviews and the questionnaires. If the committee is split in its decision, the determination goes to the full board.

Candidates must personally ask WISH List for help. Requests for WISH List support do not come from party organizations. In almost all cases, the review committee has met personally with the candidates they pledge to support. An exception may be a state legislative candidate who might meet only with a board member or members from that candidate's home state.

WISH List's primary criteria for candidate support are twofold: First, the candidate must be pro-choice. That term, of course, has a variety of meanings. James Waggoner, the executive vice president of the National Abortion and Reproductive Rights Action League, has said that he does not consider WISH List a true pro-choice organization because of its support for GOP candidates who have backed secondary restrictions on abortion rights such as parental notification requirements (Waggoner 1996).

For WISH List, the baseline is that the candidate must support the *Roe v. Wade* (1973) Supreme Court decision. The organization does insist that its endorsed candidates make very clear where they stand on the secondary restrictions, but it will not refuse to support, for example, a pro-choice Republican, such as Senator Kay Bailey Hutchison, merely because she opposes federally funded abortions.

WISH List literature details for its members the candidates' positions on family-planning funding overseas, federal funding for abortions, parental notification, and other issues. According to Goldman:

> Part of the problem is that the anti-choice forces have put on so many votes in Congress [in 1996] so that you will see some of the feminist press referring to one of our candidates as "in the mushy middle," meaning that they support choice, but not all the way.... We're probably more lenient on where the candidates stand [on the secondary issues] than some of the Democratic pro-choice groups (Goldman 1996b).

The second criterion for support is that the candidate appears likely to run a viable campaign. Goldman points out that the review committee has interviewed candidates who adopted "wonderful positions on the issues, but they don't have a campaign plan, they come here and say they don't have a treasurer but plan to get one, and so forth." In these cases, the organization has chosen not even to endorse the candidate. As Goldman put it, "We consider ourselves political venture capitalists." That is, WISH List, like a good investment adviser, recommends good choices to its clientele without, of course, any guarantee of success. But the political venture capitalist does not want to destroy credibility with investors by asking for money to support a bad selection (Goldman 1996b).

Nonetheless, WISH List will support a quality candidate in some campaigns in which it appears that the chance of victory is remote. In this case, the organization is making the long-term investment in trying to help a candidate who may have a chance of winning a future race should circumstances change.

The organization might decide, for example, to make a contribution or to mention the candidate in a newsletter, but not to do a fund-raising letter. The token mention of a candidate in a newsletter in itself will send a strong signal to the membership about the potential for victory and the contributor response will "amplify the signals that we send about which candidates to support, where to strategically place their resources" (Goldman 1996b).

Strategic use of resources also means not spending on some good candidates who are certain to win. For example, WISH List does not contribute to the campaigns of pro-choice U.S. Congresswoman Connie Morella (R–MD) because she does not need the group's help. The group and its members contributed fifteen thousand dollars in 1996 to Congresswoman Sue Kelly's (R–NY) primary campaign against a conservative challenger but did not feel it was necessary to contribute to her general election campaign.

According to the organization's vice president, Candy Straight, WISH List does not have a formal policy on campaign debt retirement. Like campaign contributions, decisions on debt retirement generally are made on a case-by-case basis. Nonetheless, in general WISH List does not devote much of its resources to debt retirement. The exception is the case of the candidate who ran a strong campaign, lost, and has a good chance at winning a future election (Straight 1996). Goldman added that on occasion the organization has paid for postelection polls for candidates who ran good campaigns and look viable for the future. Again, on those occasions, the purpose is to assist the future prospects of a good candidate by evaluating what happened in the campaign, to identify weaknesses, and to assist with issue development (Goldman 1996c).

Impact of the GOP Revolution

The 1994 Republican takeover of Congress has provided both new opportunities and challenges for WISH List. On the one hand, WISH List is a Republican organization and its members can certainly benefit by being a part of the majority party in the Congress. On the other hand, the organization is a moderate group in a more conservative Republican Party. Some of the representatives originally supported for office by WISH List now hold committee chair positions and have enough stature to promote the goals of the organization. Yet the more conservative nature of the GOP House under the leadership of Speaker Newt Gingrich has generally minimized the media coverage given to Republican centrist organizations.

For his part, Gingrich has reached out to the organization and its members in such ways as appointing a GOP women's leadership panel in the House, including WISH List–supported members Jennifer Dunn, Deborah Price, and former congresswoman Susan Molinari. Political Director Raye said that, although the result has not been dramatic, the election of the GOP Congress has helped WISH List with its fund-raising efforts.

Raye explained that having a GOP majority has not changed the candidate contribution strategy of WISH List. Regardless of the party in power, WISH remains a single-issue organization with a clear mission (Raye 1997b). The organization's media profile has benefited somewhat from the tendency of some journalists to identify WISH List as a contrast to the conservative flavor of the current GOP leadership, but the media are much more interested in focusing on partisan ideologues who generally make more interesting and colorful stories than moderates (Goldman 1996b).

The GOP takeover of Congress has provided a significant boost to the fund-raising of Democratic pro-choice groups that can attack the Republican majority, but it has only slightly helped WISH List fund-raising. EMILY's List can personalize the threat to women's rights in the name of Newt Gingrich, whose favorability ratings among women in some national polls have been in the single digits. EMILY's List can also invoke the threat of the conservative GOP majorities in Congress as a fund-raising tactic. But WISH List has to work within the GOP, which is controlled largely by the more conservative wing of the party. As Goldman put it, "we are a Republican group so we are not going to go out and attack the party" (Goldman 1996b).

According to Raye, as election day in 1994 approached, many partisan groups strategically targeted their resources to try to enhance the prospects of party control. WISH List has never used partisan control as a factor in its funding decisions. It did not, and will not, change its strategies to try to influence whether one party or another controls Congress. Naturally, as a GOP group, its efforts were and always will be allied with the electoral interests of the party. Nonetheless, before every election, regardless of broader party fortunes, "our criteria are basic.... We consider whether a candidate has a good chance and fits our issue" (Raye 1997a). Goldman added that, given that the principal way in which the organization raises its funds is mass mailings, WISH List does not have the ability to change its strategy or target its resources differently at the end of a campaign (Goldman 1996a).

WISH List in the 1996 Campaign and Beyond

WISH List identified the GOP nomination campaign of Senator Sheila Framm (R–KS) as a top priority for 1996. The former lieutenant governor had been appointed to fill the Senate post vacated by Bob Dole in June 1996. Less than two months after being sworn in as the interim Senator, Framm faced a primary challenge from the conservative pro-life Representative Sam Brownback. Despite a large lead in preference polls, Framm ultimately lost the GOP nomination, a huge setback for WISH List. Another setback was

Dolly Madison McKenna's loss in the December 10, 1996, special runoff election for the 25th House district in Texas. A prominent Republican activist, McKenna had been targeted by pro-life groups and became a symbol of the struggle by pro-choice moderates to win back "control" of the party.

WISH List placed the bulk of its efforts behind challengers and candidates for open seats, and this was true both for direct contributions and for earmarked contributions of two hundred dollars and more (see Table 14.1). That strategy suits well the group's philosophy to make a difference in the membership of the House and Senate rather than merely to inflate the victory margins of safe incumbents. In 1996 more than half of the candidates supported by

Table 14.1   Contributions by WISH List and Earmarked Contributions by Members

WISH List Contributions	1994	1996
Democrats	$0	$0
Republicans		
House		
Incumbents	12,000	7,779
Challengers	29,007	18,701
Open Seats	60,352	22,263
Senate		
Incumbents	1,798	4,907
Challengers	12,000	1,500
Open Seats	17,259	19,990

Earmarked Contributions by Members ($200 or more)		
Contributions	1994	1996
Democrats	$0	$0
Republicans		
House		
Incumbents	5,150	5,700
Challengers	5,100	31,000
Open Seats	28,250	30,350
Senate		
Incumbents	13,450	30,700
Challengers	1,500	500
Open Seats	28,250	48,900

Source: Federal Election Commission.

WISH List were in competitive general election races, and some others lost in close primary contests. Consequently, the group's record of success in 1996 was at best mixed. Although all of WISH List's endorsed candidates ran ahead of the national GOP ticket, of their forty-two endorsed candidates overall, only twelve were victorious (Raye 1997b). WISH List attributed its overall losing record to President Clinton's landslide reelection that "was more like a tidal wave in the Northeast, Midwest, and West Coast, resulting in the defeat of many superb WISH-endorsed candidates" ("Welcome to WISH List"). Goldman wrote to supporters after the campaign that "the language of some of the most vocal members of the 104th Congress and the extremism of the radical right" turned many women voters away from the GOP altogether (*The Wish List News* "From the Fourth Quarter 1996 Newsletter").

WISH List nonetheless celebrated the reelections of all its incumbent members and the U.S. Senate campaign victory of Susan Collins. With her victory, Maine became the first state in the nation to have two GOP women senators serving concurrently. For the first time, the group had contributed over $1 million in an election cycle. In the 105th Congress, of sixteen GOP women House members, nine are WISH List–endorsed. All three GOP women senators are endorsed by the group.

Even with a mixed record in 1996, WISH List has achieved considerable success in a relatively brief period and appears poised to continue to play an expanded role in elections. Rimmerman's observation of four years ago, that WISH List may become a model for other groups aspiring to electoral impact, seems even more accurate today (Rimmerman 1994, 223).

Although contributions from individual members of WISH List increased between 1994 and 1996, the group's PAC donations declined significantly in that period. According to Karen Raye, that decline in large part is attributable to the fact that a good many of WISH List's endorsed candidates did not prevail in their primary nomination contests, leaving fewer general election races in which to become involved (Raye 1997b). This suggests that WISH List must win in more intraparty nomination battles, many of which center on the abortion issue, if it is to elect more pro-choice GOP women to Congress.

In keeping with WISH List's goal of increased involvement in nonfederal elections, the organization and its members contributed over fifty thousand dollars to the reelection campaign of New Jersey Governor Christine Todd Whitman. WISH List also made small contributions to several state and local candidates in other races in New Jersey and in Virginia (Raye 1997b). The organization anticipates an expanded role as well in the midterm elections of 1998 and aspires to become not only a leading voice of moderation in the GOP but also a legitimate rival to such better-known Democratic-leaning groups as EMILY's List and NARAL.

CHAPTER 15

REVOLUTIONARY CHANGE OR MORE OF THE SAME? PACs, LOBBIES, AND THE REPUBLICAN CONGRESS

Paul S. Herrnson and Clyde Wilcox

The Republican takeover of Congress was a revolutionary change in power on Capitol Hill, but did it lead to a revolution in the ways that PACs and lobbies operate? Did PACs that had formerly given the lion's share of their dollars to congressional Democrats suddenly switch the bulk of their contributions to the Republicans in order to gain favor with members of the new majority, or did these groups continue to support Democrats and merely shift their contributions from Democratic incumbents to Democratic challengers and open-seat candidates? How did lobbyists respond? Were groups that had enjoyed strong ties to House and Senate Democrats able to kindle new relationships with Republican legislators, or did they find themselves suddenly shut out from the legislative process? The case studies in this book have addressed these and related questions. We are now in a position to determine whether there were any systematic variations in how different kinds of PACs and lobbies reacted to the Republican Revolution.

The Ins Become the Outs and the Outs Become the Ins

The reversal of roles on Capitol Hill had a dramatic impact on the influence exercised by different interest groups. Each party has its own block of supporters in the interest group community and issue networks (Ginsberg, Mebane, and Shefter 1995). During the 1980s, groups that supported the Democrats had tremendous access in Congress, but only limited access to the higher echelons of the executive branch. Two years later, after Bill Clinton was elected president, Democratic-leaning groups enjoyed opportunities to influence both the executive and legislative branches. Republican-leaning groups, by contrast, found themselves with few footholds in the federal government. Many responded by trying to influence state and local governments (Bruce and Wilcox 1998). State and local interest groups also organized grassroots mobilization campaigns to pressure Washington politicians. Money began to pour into conservative religious groups, for example, following Clinton's highly publicized stand on gays in the military. The president's reneging on his campaign promise to pass a middle-class tax cut energized antitax groups, which made their disapproval known to the public and on Capitol Hill.

Some groups also became involved in planning the Republicans' 1994 campaign. The National Taxpayers Union, the Christian Coalition, Americans for Tax Reform, U.S. Term Limits, and a variety of other antitax, antiregulation, and so-called "family values" groups helped frame the Contract with America (Gimpel 1998). These and other Republican-leaning groups also provided substantial financial and organizational support for Republican congressional candidates. Some also carried out voter registration and get-out-the-vote drives.

The GOP's 1994 victory represented a major payoff for the conservative groups. The GOP leadership changed the rules and procedures governing the House in ways that favored the new majority and the groups that comprised its coalition. Among the most important changes in procedure was the use of task forces to write controversial legislation. Republican leaders used these to bypass the normal committee process when writing several important bills. The task forces facilitated coalition building within the majority party and enhanced the input of GOP-leaning groups. However, due to their secretive meetings and the fact that no Democrats or liberal groups were invited to attend them, the task forces greatly reduced minority party input (Campbell and Davidson 1997; Sinclair 1997, esp. chapters 1 and 6). For conservative lobbyists, the GOP takeover of Congress meant that their ship had finally come in. They went from being outsiders to insiders when the new Republican majority put an end to Democratic rule in Congress. The change in control meant that, for the first time in forty years in the House and ten years in the Senate, Republicans would set the legislative agenda, control committee proceedings, and set the rules governing congressional debate and roll call votes. Rather than reacting to Democratic majority proposals, as they had during the era of Democratic hegemony, pro-Republican groups now had a place at the table where they would help write legislation, organize hearings, formulate congressional strategy, and help lawmakers build the coalitions needed to achieve their common goals.

The representatives of liberal groups, on the other hand, saw much of their influence flow out with the change in partisan tides. Among the losers were groups representing the beneficiaries of government programs, unions, environmentalists, and abortion rights supporters. Unlike conservative groups after 1992, these groups still had a foothold in the federal government because of Democratic control of the executive branch. Nevertheless, deprived of their former insider status with members of the Appropriations, Ways and Means, and other key committees, these groups found many of their cherished projects on the chopping block and tax breaks being instituted for their opponents instead of themselves. Environmental, worker safety, and other regulations that they had helped pass years earlier were suddenly being stripped from the federal code.

Many interest groups are strongly aligned with neither party. These organizations did not find themselves completely shut out from the Republican power structure, but they had to make efforts to create new relationships with GOP members. Their lobbyists worked overtime following the election to familiarize GOP legislators and congressional aides with their groups' goals and strategies for achieving them. Organizations with PACs helped build bridges to Republican members, especially first-term members, by helping them to erase the debts they had incurred during the 1994 election.

Reversal of Fortunes, Reversal of Dollars

The Republican takeover inspired a level of interest group hyperactivity in the 1996 elections unlike any that had been witnessed in recent years. Interest groups spent record sums of money through their PACs and soft money contributions to party committees. Few groups changed their goals, but many modified their election strategies and tactics, resulting in new patterns of PAC contributions. Others, such as the Realtors PAC and AT&T PAC, revamped their decision-making processes. Some groups, including the Sierra Club, the AFL-CIO, and the NFIB, broke new ground by carrying out issue advocacy campaigns that technically exist outside the federal election arena, but that in reality are designed to have a major impact on congressional and presidential elections.

One of the most important effects of the reversal of fortunes on Capitol Hill was a significant redirection in the flow of PAC money. Before and during the 1994 elections the Democrats were the major beneficiaries of PACs' largesse. During the 1996 elections, the Republicans enjoyed that distinction. Business-related PACs, which comprise mainly corporate and trade association committees, responded most strongly to the Republicans' ascendance. Between 1994 and 1996, groups such as the Realtors PAC and Federal Express's PAC switched the majority of their contributions from Democrats to Republicans. Business groups had made roughly 60 percent of their House and 43 percent of their Senate contributions to Democrats during the 1994 elections. Two years later, they gave nearly two-thirds of their House and three-fourths of their Senate contributions to Republicans. Business PACs switched their contribution patterns in order to gain access to the leaders of the new Republican majorities in the House and Senate, to help GOP incumbents in jeopardy, particularly first-termers, defend their seats, and to show support for GOP-sponsored tax cuts, reductions in federal regulations, and pro-growth economic policies (Herrnson 1997). Some of the contributions were initiated by the PACs; others were given in response to aggressive solicitations by Republican Party leaders (Maraniss and Weisskopf 1995).

Nevertheless, business PACs did not completely abandon Democratic incumbents. They continued to give roughly the same proportion of their funds to House and Senate Democrats in uncompetitive contests, most of whom occupied congressional leadership positions (Nelson 1998). Instead, business PACs distributed fewer dollars to Democratic incumbents involved in competitive contests and more funds to Republicans in similar circumstances, especially Republican House members elected in 1994. This pattern of contributions is consistent with the PACs' goals of pursuing access to powerful incumbents and maintaining a GOP majority.

Labor PACs, such as COPE and UFCR, gave the vast majority of their 1994 and 1996 contributions to Democratic candidates for the House and Senate, reflecting that party's historic ties to the labor movement. However, the tiny cracks that have always existed in labor's solidly pro-Democratic front grew somewhat after 1994 when a small number of labor committees sought to gain access with Republican incumbents. Leading the way was the American Maritime Officer's PAC, which gave Republican candidates 35 percent of its contributions in the 1994 congressional elections and 57 percent in 1996. Yet, overall, the biggest change in labor activity is that labor PACs allocated substantially more of their contributions to nonincumbents in 1996, reflecting their goal of trying to help the Democrats retake control of Congress.

Few nonconnected PACs responded to the Republicans' ascendance in Congress by transferring their support for members of one party to members of the other. Some liberal organizations capitalized on the Republican takeover by improving their fund-raising and distributing more campaign contributions. NARAL was able to reverse the decline in fund-raising it experienced following Clinton's election to the White House. The Sierra Club and the League of Conservation Voters used Republican attempts to weaken environmental protections as successful fund-raising appeals. Nevertheless, the GOP takeover and the tenuous nature of the Republicans' House majority had a bigger impact on conservative organizations. Conservative PACs raised and contributed more money in 1996 than did liberal groups. The result was a 20 percent increase in the proportion of ideological PAC contributions to Republicans and a corresponding drop-off in contributions to Democrats.

Interest group activity extended well beyond PAC contributions in the 1996 elections. Numerous PACs carried out training sessions, distributed polls, sponsored fund-raising events, and made independent expenditures on behalf of or against candidates (Herrnson 1998, 119–122). AMPAC was among those that contributed polls to incumbents. Other groups carried out numerous "independent" political activities using soft money. Several labor unions headed by the AFL-CIO carried out an unprecedented independent campaign that included voter education, registration, get-out-the-vote efforts, and issue advocacy advertisements. As is usual in U.S. politics, organization begot counterorganization. Several business groups headed by the NFIB formed "The Coalition" to carry out similar activities. Numerous environmental organizations and groups on both sides of the abortion rights debate also carried out issue advocacy and voter mobilization activities for the purpose of helping candidates who shared their views. Moreover, the Christian Coalition, which has emerged as a major force in Republican politics, distributed 54 million voter guides using church-based networks throughout the nation (Marcus 1996).

Some of the election activities carried out by interest groups in 1996 stretched the definition of what is considered legal under federal campaign finance law. Included among these are the soft money activities mentioned above and the efforts of numerous tax-exempt organizations. Tax-exempt organizations are nonprofit groups with narrowly defined missions, usually involving charitable, religious, or educational causes. Their tax-exempt status enables the groups' benefactors to deduct their donations from their federal taxes and enables the groups to avoid disclosing the sources of their funds to the FEC. In return for this special status, tax-exempt groups are not supposed to engage in partisan political activity (Corrado 1992, 80–84). However, several groups clearly did undertake efforts to influence elections in 1996. Included among these are groups with strong links to the major parties, such as Americans for Tax Reform, an antitax group with ties to Republican National Convention Chairman Haley Barbour that mobilized pro-Republican voters, and Vote Now '96, which registered individuals who belong to traditionally loyal Democratic groups (Herrnson, 1998, 94–95).

The Republican takeover of Congress also had a major impact on lobbying in the nation's capital. Labor unions, pro-choice groups, environmental organizations, and other interests with strong Democratic ties found themselves largely shut out from the legislative process. Republican Party and committee leaders, who had previously been all but ignored by liberal groups with strong ties to congressional Democrats, found themselves in the position to turn a deaf ear to these groups. Advocates for conservative interests, such as BIPAC, the NFIB, the NRA, and numerous pro-life groups, by contrast, enjoyed more access to congressional leaders than they had had since 1952, when the Republicans last controlled Congress. Groups that had practiced bipartisan politics, such as the AMA, AT&T, and the Realtors Association, were neither shut out nor greatly advantaged by the change in congressional majorities. Their strategy of cultivating relationships with Democratic and Republican legislators put them in position to work with members of Congress on both sides of the aisle.

Of course, not every conservative group enjoyed a windfall and not every liberal group was decimated by the GOP's ascendance on Capitol Hill. WISH List had some success in fulfilling its goal of electing pro-choice Republican women but then faced a Congress that was decidedly more hostile to its position on abortion rights than before the Republican takeover. NARAL, the Sierra Club, the Gay and Lesbian Victory Fund, and numerous unions found a new bogeyman in Republican House Speaker Newt Gingrich. These groups painted Gingrich and his congressional colleagues as partisan extremists and used the GOP's agenda to mobilize their members at the grassroots level and boost their fund-raising.

Meet the New Boss, Same as the Old Boss

The Republican takeover had a major impact on the distribution of power on Capitol Hill, the flow of PAC money, and the election-related activities of numerous other groups. It also influenced the level of access enjoyed by different lobbying organizations. But, the Republicans' ascendance did not essentially change how PACs and lobbies do business in Congress. The findings reported in the case studies and the aggregate patterns described previously show that Washington fat cats grew neither gills nor fins after the Republicans took the center stage of the Washington big top. Rather, the change was subtle, like a zebra turning its black stripes to white and its white stripes to black. The takeover reshuffled the billing of the top to players in Congress, but it did not result in much turnover among those lobbyists and PAC managers who play important supporting roles in Washington politics.

Despite their reformist rhetoric, Republicans did not "clean up" Washington following their historic victory in the 1994 elections. Instead, groups paid sums to the party in exchange for the right to help draft the implementing legislation for the Contract with America (Judis 1995). Lobbyists stepped up their efforts to influence the new congressional leaders and committee and subcommittee chairs that the Republicans had installed. In 1996 the sums that PACs spent directly in federal elections and that corporations, trade associations, and unions withdrew from their treasuries in order to influence those contests reached record proportions. The fierceness of the battle for control over Congress and influence on Capitol Hill intensified rather than abated the election and lobbying efforts of interest groups following the GOP takeover.

The Republican takeover was not really a revolution because it did not change how either the federal government or the groups that lobby it conduct their business. However, it did constitute a major shake-up in the Washington establishment. Moreover, as is the case with actual revolutions, the takeover produced immediate winners and losers in the struggle for influence and left the future of other groups to be determined.

REFERENCES

Active Ballot Club Handbook. UFCW. Washington, DC. n.d.

AFL-CIO. 1996a. "The Real Money Story: Business Outspends Labor 7 to 1." *AFL-CIO Political Department Document.* November 12.

———. 1996b. "1996 Election Results: Labor '96." *AFL-CIO Political Department document.* November 12.

———. 1996c. "Labor '96 Report." *AFL-CIO Political Department Document.* November 15.

Aldrich, Howard E. 1979. *Organizations and Environments.* Englewood Cliffs, NJ: Prentice-Hall.

Alexander, Herbert E. 1992. *Financing Politics: Money, Elections, and Political Reform.* Washington, DC: CQ Press.

American Medical Association. 1995. "A Matter of Trust." *American Medical News.* October 16.

———. 1996. "Making Sure Your Voice Is Heard." *American Medical News.* November 4.

———. 1997. "About Grassroots Political Action." www.AMA-ASSN.com.

American Society of Association Executives (ASAE). 1996. *Associations in a Nutshell.* Washington, DC: American Society of Association Executives.

Andelman, David A. 1997. "Prescription for a Powerful Lobby." *American Management Association Review.* 86: 28–35.

Babson, Jennifer and Kelly St. John. 1994. "Momentum Helps GOP Collect Record Amounts from PACs." *Congressional Quarterly Weekly Report.* December 3.

Barbour, Haley. 1996. "Excerpts of Remarks by RNC Chairman Haley Barbour on November 11." *U.S. News Wire.* November 12: 1–2.

Baumgartner, Frank R. and Jeffery C. Talbert. 1995. "From Setting a National Agenda on Health Care to Making Decisions in Congress." *Journal of Health Politics, Policy, and Law.* 20: 437–443.

Bedlington, Anne H. 1994. "The National Association of Realtors PAC: Rules or Rationality?" In *Risky Business? PAC Decisionmaking in Congressional Elections,* ed. Robert Biersack, Paul S. Herrnson, and Clyde Wilcox. New York: M. E. Sharpe.

Berke, Richard L. 1995. "Congress's New GOP Majority Makes Lobbyists' Life Difficult." *New York Times.* March 20: A1.

———. 1996. "Lawsuit Says Christian Coalition Gave Illegal Help to Candidate." *New York Times.* July 31: A1.

Biersack, Robert, Paul Herrnson, and Clyde Wilcox. 1993. "Seeds for Success: Early Money in Congressional Elections." *Legislative Studies Quarterly.* 18: 535–552.

———. 1994. *Risky Business? PAC Decisionmaking in Congressional Elections.* Armonk, NY: M. E. Sharpe.

Billet, Steve. 1996a. PAC Director, AT&T. Personal Interview. April 17.

———. 1996b. PAC Director, AT&T. Personal Interview. October 15.

———. 1997. PAC Director, AT&T. Personal Interview. January 2.

Birch, David L. 1987. *Job Creation in America: How Our Smallest Companies Put the Most People to Work*. New York: Free Press.

Birnbaum, Jeffrey H. 1996. "Beating the System: This Year More Than Ever, Candidates Get Help from Special Interest Groups That S-T-R-E-T-C-H the Rules." *Time*. February 1.

Bosso, Christopher J. 1995. "The Color of Money: Environmental Groups and the Pathologies of Fundraising." In *Interest Group Politics*, 4th ed., ed. Allan J. Cigler and Burdett A. Loomis. Washington, DC: CQ Press.

Braun, Gerry. 1996. "Bilbray in the NRA's Doghouse; Nine Other Incumbents Rated 'A'." *San Diego Union-Tribune*. November 1.

Bruce, John and Clyde Wilcox. 1998. *The Changing Politics of Gun Control*. Lanham, MD: Rowman and Littlefield.

Budde, Bernadette. 1996a. Senior Vice President, BIPAC. Personal Interview. May 31.

———. 1996b. Senior Vice President, BIPAC. Personal Interview. October 17.

———. 1997. Senior Vice President, BIPAC. Personal Interview. January 21.

Bukro, Casey. 1996. "Donors Wield Big Vote Punch; Small Business, Unions, Others Back Candidates in Record Amounts." *Chicago Tribune*. October 14: 1.

Bull, Christopher and John Gallagher. 1996. *Perfect Enemies: The Religious Right, the Gay Movement, and the Politics of the 1990's*. New York: Crown.

Burris, Val. 1987. "The Political Partisanship of American Business: A Study of Corporate Political Action Committees." *American Sociological Review*. 52: 738–739.

Business and Health. 1991. "Fax Poll Results: Readers Say Its Time for Health Care Reform Involving the Government, a Canadian-Style System, and More Utilization." December 12.

Campbell, Colton C. and Roger H. Davidson. 1998. "Coalition Building in Congress: The Consequences of Partisan Change." In *The Interest Group Connection: Electioneering, Lobbying, and Policymaking in Washington*, ed. Paul S. Herrnson, Ronald G. Shaiko, and Clyde Wilcox. Chatham, NJ: Chatham House.

Campion, Frank D. 1984. *The AMA and U.S. Health Policy Since 1940*. Chicago: Chicago Review Press.

Center for Responsive Politics. 1996. "Political PAC-analia." *Center for Responsive Politics Report*. October 17.

Chibbaro, Lou, Jr. 1997. "Gay PACs Gave Over $1 Million to Campaigns." *Washington Blade*. February 7: 28: 16.

Citizen Action. 1996. "It's the Money: House of Representatives Fundraising, January 1995–June 1996." *Citizen Action Report*. June.

Clines, Francis X. 1996. "Abortion Rights League Plans to Challenge 15 Freshmen." *New York Times*. July 14: 18.

Clymer, Adam. 1995. "Health Lobby Starts Taking Aim at G.O.P. Plan." *New York Times*. October 10: A1.

Connelly, William F., Jr. and John J. Pitney, Jr. 1994. *Congress' Permanent Minority? Republicans in the U.S. House*. Landover, MD: Rowman and Littlefield.

Connolly, Ceci. 1993. "Mrs. Clinton Strikes Back." *Congressional Quarterly Weekly Report*. November 6.

Cook, Elizabeth Adell, Sue Thomas, and Clyde Wilcox. 1994. *The Year of the Woman: Myths and Realities.* Boulder, CO: Westview Press.

Cooper, Helene. 1997. "GOP to Rebuke Companies for Bipartisan Donations." *Wall Street Journal.* January 9: A14.

Corrado, Anthony. 1992. *Creative Campaigning: PACs and the Presidential Selection Process.* Boulder, CO: Westview Press.

CQ Almanac. 1995. Washington, DC: Congressional Quarterly.

Crabtree, Susan. 1996. "Big Labor Is Spending Big Bucks on Elections." *Washington Times.* November 4: A14.

Danner, Donald. 1996. Vice President of Federal Government Relations, NFIB. Personal Interview. January 14.

———. 1997a. Vice President of Federal Government Relations, NFIB. Personal Interview. February 17.

———. 1997b. Vice President of Federal Government Relations, NFIB. Personal Interview. March 1.

Davis, Frank L. 1993. "Balancing the Perspective on PAC Contributors: In Search of the Impact on Roll Calls." *American Politics Quarterly.* 21.

DeBold, Kathleen, ed. 1994. *Out for Office.* Washington, DC: The Gay and Lesbian Victory Fund.

Dine, Philip. 1996a. "Labor, Business Groups Battle, Try to Advance Their Agenda." *St. Louis Post-Dispatch.* November 6: A20.

———. 1996b. "Nudged by Labor's Effort, Business Group Decides to Get Political." *St. Louis Post-Dispatch.* November 15: 1C.

Drew, Elizabeth. 1997. *Whatever It Takes.* New York: Viking.

Dugan, I. Jeanne. 1996. "Washington Ain't Seen Nothin' Yet." *Business Week Report.* May 13: 3.

Dunham, Richard S. 1995. "The Enforcer Isn't Blinking." *Business Week.* October 2: 73.

Edsall, Thomas B. 1996. "Issues Coalitions Take on Political Party Functions: Alliances on Left, Right Gain Power." *Washington Post.* August 8: A1.

Eismeir, Theodore J. and Philip H. Pollack. 1988. *Business, Money, and the Rise of Corporate PACs.* New York: Quorum Books.

Epstein, Edwin M. 1969. *The Corporation in American Politics.* Englewood Cliffs, NJ: Prentice-Hall.

Fasig, Lisa Biank. 1996. "Small Business' Big Clout." *Cincinnati Enquirer.* September 15: I 01.

Feder, Barnaby J. 1993. "Medical Group Battles to Be Heard Over Others on Health Care Changes." *New York Times.* June 10: A22.

Fein, Rashi. 1986. *Medical Care, Medical Costs: The Search for a Health Insurance Policy.* Cambridge, MA: Harvard University Press.

Fleisher, Richard. 1993. "PAC Contributions and Congressional Voting on National Defense." *Legislative Studies Quarterly.* 18: 391–409.

Garceau, Oliver. 1941. *The Political Life of the American Medical Association.* Cambridge, MA: Harvard University Press.

Gardner, Jonathan. 1997. "Solo Practitioner: The American Medical Association Often Goes It Alone in Washington, Which Leaves Other Lobbyists Unhappy." *Modern Healthcare.* February 17.

Gilbert, Patrice. 1996. "Pressuring for Dollars." *Legal Times.* September 16: 4.

Gimpel, James G. 1996. *Fulfilling the Contract: The First 100 Days.* Boston: Allyn & Bacon.

———. 1998. "Grassroots Organizations and Equilibrium Cycles in Group Mobilization and Access." In *The Interest Group Connection: Electioneering, Lobbying, and Policymaking in Washington,* ed. Paul S. Herrnson, Ronald G. Shaiko, and Clyde Wilcox. Chatham, NJ: Chatham House: 100–115.

Ginsberg, Benjamin, Walter R. Mebane, and Martin Shefter. 1995. "The Presidency and Interest Groups: Why Presidents Cannot Govern." In *The Presidency and the Political System,* 3rd. ed., ed. Michael Nelson. Washington, DC: CQ Press.

Giovaniello, Jerry. 1997. Vice President of Governmental Affairs, RPAC. Personal Interview. March 28.

Goff, Donald L. 1991. PAC Director, AT&T. Personal Interview. October 11.

———. 1992. PAC Director, AT&T. Personal Interview. June 23.

———. 1996. PAC Director, AT&T. Personal Interview. May 2.

Goldman, Patricia. 1996a. President, WISH List. Personal Interview. June 27.

———. 1996b. President, WISH List. Personal Interview. September 12.

———. 1996c. President, WISH List. Personal Interview. November 26.

Greenhouse, Stephen. 1996. "Some Republicans Condemn House Leadership's Attacks on Labor as Divisive." *New York Times.* May 11: A9.

Gruenwald, Juliana and Robert Marshall Wells. 1996. "The Odds with Some Workers, AFL-CIO Takes Aim at GOP." *Congressional Quarterly.* April 13: 993–998.

Gusmano, Michael K. and Robert M. Tennant. 1993. "Health Care Reform and Campaign Financing in 1992: Proactive Politics and Policy Shaping." Paper presented at the annual meeting of the Northeast Political Science Association, Newark, NJ, November 11–13.

Hall, Richard L. and Frank W. Wayman. 1990. "Buying Time: Moneyed Interests and the Mobilization of Bias in Congressional Committees." *American Political Science Review.* 84: 797–820.

Handler, Edward and John R. Mulkern. 1982. *Business in Politics.* Lexington, MA: Lexington Books.

Healey, Jon. 1995. "Leaders' Last-Minute Additions Offers Morsels for Everyone." *Congressional Quarterly.* August 5: 2348–2349.

Henry, Ed. 1996. "Everyone Needs Friends—Especially These Friends. Roll Call Looks at Ten of Washington's Top Interest Groups, No Matter Who's in Power." *Roll Call.* September 23.

Herrnson, Paul S. 1995. *Congressional Elections: Campaigning at Home and in Washington,* 1st ed. Washington, DC: CQ Press.

———. 1997. "Money and Motives: Spending in House Elections." In *Congress Reconsidered,* ed. Larry C. Dodd and Bruce I. Oppenheimer. Washington, DC: CQ Press.

———. 1998. *Congressional Elections: Campaigning at Home and in Washington,* 2nd ed. Washington, DC: CQ Press.

Herrnson, Paul S. and Clyde Wilcox. 1994. "Not So Risky Business." In *Risky Business? PAC Decisionmaking in Congressional Elections.* ed. Robert Biersack, Paul S. Herrnson, and Clyde Wilcox. Armonk, NY: M. E. Sharpe.

Hirschman, Albert O. 1970. *Exit, Voice, and Loyalty.* Cambridge: Harvard University Press.

Hutter, Jean. 1997. Chief Lobbyist, United Food and Commercial Workers Union. Personal Interview. January 17.

Jacobson, Gary C. and Samuel Kernell. 1983. *Strategy and Choice in Congressional Elections*, 2nd ed. New Haven: Yale University Press.

Jacoby, Mary. 1996. "ANRA Rethinks Support for Salvi Ad Campaign." *Chicago Tribune*. October 4.

Johnson, Paul. 1991. "Organized Labor in an Era of Blue-Collar Decline." In *Interest Group Politics*, ed. Allan J. Cigler and Burdett A. Loomis. Washington, DC: CQ Press.

Judge, Don. 1996. Personal Interview. November.

Judis, John B. 1995. "The Contract with K Street." *New Republic*. 4: 18–25.

———. 1996. "K Sera." *The New Republic*. November 18: 6.

Keen, Lisa. 1996. "More Gays Stay Home." *Washington Blade*. November 8: 27: 1, 27, 29.

Kirkpatrick, David. 1995. "AT&T Has the Plan." *Fortune*. October 16.

Kriz, Margaret. 1996. "In Oregon, They've All Turned Green." *National Journal*. January 13: 74.

Landers, George. 1996a. Assistant Director of Legislative and Political Affairs, United Food and Commercial Workers Union. Personal Interview. June 19.

———. 1996b. Assistant Director of Legislative and Political Affairs, United Food and Commercial Workers Union. Personal Interview. September 5.

League of Conservation Voters. 1996a. "Dirty Dozen Television Ads."

———. 1996b. "Dirty Dozen's Campaigns at a Glance."

Light, Donald W. 1991. "The Restructuring of the American Health Care System." In *Health Politics and Policy*, 2nd ed., ed. Theodore J. Litman and Leonard S. Robins. Albany, NY: Demar Publishers.

Loyless, Betsy. 1996a. Political Director, League of Conservation Voters. Personal Interview. July 2.

———. 1996b. Political Director, League of Conservation Voters. Personal Interview. October 11.

———. 1997a. Political Director, League of Conservation Voters. Personal Interview. January 27.

———. 1997b. Political Director, League of Conservation Voters. Personal Interview. January 28.

Luft, H. S. 1981. *Health Maintenance Organizations: Dimensions of Performance*. New York: John Wiley.

Lundegaard, Karen. 1996. "Small Biz Group to Give $1 Million-Plus to Candidates." *Austin Business Journal*. October 11: 4.

Mack, Charles. 1996. President, BIPAC. Personal Interview. May 31.

Malbin, Michael J. 1984. *Money and Politics in the United States: Financing Elections in the 1980's*. Washington, DC: American Enterprise Institute.

Maraniss, David and Michael Weisskopf. 1995. "Speaker and His Directors Make the Cash Flow Right." *Washington Post*. November 27.

Marcus, Ruth. 1996a. "FEC Files Suit Over Christian Coalition Role; Work With Republicans in Campaigns Alleged." *Washington Post*. July 31.

———. 1996b. "Outside Groups Pushing Election Laws into Irrelevance." *Washington Post*. August 8: A9.

Masters, Marick F. and Gerald D. Keim. 1985. "Determinants of PAC Participation among Large Corporations." *Journal of Politics.* 47: 1158–1174.

McBurnett, Michael, Christopher Kenny, and David J. Bordua. 1996. "The Impact of Political Interests in the 1994 Elections: The Role of the National Rifle Association." Paper presented at the 1996 annual meeting of the Midwest Political Science Association, Chicago, IL.

McDaniel, Diane. 1996. Personal Interview. November 9.

Metaksa, Tanya. 1996a. Executive Director of the Institute for Legislative Action, NRA. Personal Interview. July 18.

———. 1996b. Executive Director of the Institute for Legislative Action, NRA. Personal Interview. November 12.

Millert, Gregory. 1992. PAC Officer, AT&T. Personal Interview. June 23.

Mills, Kay. 1996. "Patricia Goldman: Still Trying to Link 'Pro-Choice' and Republican." *Los Angeles Times.* January 7.

Montgomery, Lori. 1996. "Disarming Gunfighters: Researchers Blame Political Pressure from the National Rifle Association for Shooting Down Studies of Fun-Related Injuries at the Centers for Disease Control." *Tampa Tribune.* May 6: 6.

Moore, J. Duncan, Jr. 1996. "AMA in Drive to Keep Industry Role." *Modern Healthcare.* October 7: 52–55.

Mother Jones. 1996. July/August.

Murphy, Kim. 1996. "Oregon's New Senator Credits Environmental Vote for Victory." *Los Angeles Times.* February 1: A12.

Mutch, Robert E. 1994. "AT&T PAC: A Pragmatic Giant." In *Risky Business? PAC Decisionmaking in Congressional Elections,* ed. Robert Biersack, Paul S. Herrnson, and Clyde Wilcox. Armonk, NY: M. E. Sharpe.

NARAL. 1996. *NARAL News.* Spring.

National Federation of Independent Business. 1985. "NFIB: A History, 1943–1985." Washington, DC: National Federation of Independent Business.

———. 1994. "Who Will Pay the Bill for Charges Made on This Card?" Washington, DC: National Federation of Independent Business.

———. 1995a. "America's Small Business Report Card for the 103rd Congress." Washington, DC: National Federation of Independent Business.

———. 1995b. "Campaign '96: How Small Business Can Impact the 1996 Elections." Conference Registration Form. Washington, DC: National Federation of Independent Business.

———. 1996. "Small Business Voice Heard in Mandate Ballot: Important in NFIB Lobbying Efforts." *Capitol Coverage: Report from the Front Lines.* Washington, DC: National Federation of Independent Business: 4.

Nelson, Candice J. 1997. "Money in the 1996 Elections." In *America's Choice,* ed. William Crotty. Guilford, CT: Brown and Benchmark: 113–120.

———. 1998. "The Money Chase: Partisanship, Committee Leadership Change, and PAC Contributions in the House of Representatives." In *The Interest Group Connection: Electioneering, Lobbying, and Policymaking in Washington,* ed. Paul S. Herrnson, Ronald G. Shaiko, and Clyde Wilcox. Chatham, NJ: Chatham House: 52–64.

Nichols, Frederic. 1997. National Association of Manufacturers. Personal Interview. January 6.

Olson, Mancur. 1965. *The Logic of Collective Action*. Cambridge, MA: Harvard University Press.

Pear, Robert. 1993a. "White House Shuns Bigger A.M.A. Voice in Health Changes." *New York Times*. March 5: A1.

———. 1993b. "Doctors at A.M.A. Meeting Are Divided Over Strategy on Health Proposals." *New York Times*. December 6: A7.

———. 1994. "A.M.A. and Insurers Clash over Restrictions on Doctors." *New York Times*. May 24: A12.

———. 1995a. "Doctors' Group Backs Plan of Republicans on Medicare." *New York Times*. October 11: A1.

———. 1995b. "Doctors' Group Says G.O.P. Agreed to Deal on Medicare." *New York Times*. October 12: A1.

Peterson, Mark A. 1993. "Political Influence in the 1990s: From Iron Triangles to Policy Networks." *Journal of Politics, Policy and Law*. 18: 395–438.

Pianin, Eric. 1997. "How Business Found Benefits in Wage Bill." *Washington Post*. February 11: A1, A8.

Pressman, Steven. 1984. "Physician's Lobbying Machine Showing Some Signs of Wear." *Congressional Quarterly*. January 17: 15–19.

Rayack, Elton. 1967. *Professional Power and American Medicine: The Economics of the American Medical Association*. Cleveland, OH: World Publishing.

Raye, Karen. 1997a. Executive Director, WISH List. Personal Interview. February 28.

———. 1997b. Executive Director, WISH List. Personal Interview. October 25.

Regens, James L., Ronald Keith Gaddie, and Euel Elliot. 1994. "Corporate PAC Contributions and Rent Provision in Separate Elections." *Social Science Quarterly*. 75: 152–165.

Richardson, Trey. 1996. RPAC Director, RPAC. Personal Interview. October 10.

Rimmerman, Craig. 1994. "New Kids on the Block: The WISH List and the Gay and Lesbian Victory Fund in the 1992 Elections." In *Risky Business? PAC Decisionmaking in Congressional Elections*, ed. Robert Biersack, Paul S. Herrnson, and Clyde Wilcox. Armonk, NY: M. E. Sharpe.

———. 1996. *Gay Rights, Military Wrongs: Political Perspectives on Lesbians and Gays in the Military*. New York: Garland.

Rozell, Mark J. and Clyde Wilcox. 1998. *Interest Groups in American National Elections*. Washington, DC: CQ Press.

Sabato, Larry J. 1984. *PAC Power: Inside the World of Political Action Committees*. New York: W. W. Norton.

Salant, Jonathan D. and David S. Cloud. 1995. "To the '94 Election Victors Go the Fundraising Spoils." *Congressional Quarterly Weekly Report*. April 15.

Sammons, James H. 1991. *Inside Medical Washington*. Knoxville, TN: Whittle Books.

Sapolsky, Harvey, Drew Altman, Richard Greene, and Judith Moore. 1981. "Corporate Attitudes Toward Health Care Costs." *Milbank Memorial Quarterly*. 59(4): 561–585.

Schear, Stuart. 1996. "The Ultimate Self-Referral: Medicare Reform, AMA-Style." *American Prospect*. March–April: 71.

Schlozman, Kay Lehman and John T. Tierney. 1986. *Organized Interests and American Democracy*. New York: Harper & Row.

Seelye, Katharine. 1997. "An Ailing Gun Lobby Faces a Bitter Struggle for Power." *New York Times*. January 30: A1.

Shaiko, Ronald G. 1991. "More Bang for the Buck: The New Era of Full-Service Public Interest Organizations." In *Interest Group Politics*, 3rd ed., ed. Allan J. Cigler and Burdett A. Loomis. Washington, DC: CQ Press.

———. 1998. "Interest Groups and Lobbying in Washington: A Contemporary Perspective." In *The Interest Group Connection: Electioneering, Lobbying, and Policy making in Washington*, ed. Paul S. Herrnson, Ronald G. Shaiko, and Clyde Wilcox. Chatham, NJ: Chatham House.

Shribman, David M. 1995. "By Principle, Black Republican." *Boston Globe*. February 3: 3.

Sierra Club. 1995. Sierra Club Political Committee Compliance Guidelines. 1995. Autumn.

Sinclair, Barbara. 1997. *Unorthodox Lawmaking*. Washington, DC: CQ Press.

Skrzycki, Cindy. 1995. "How Small Business Won Congress's Heart." *Washington Post*. June 6: B1.

Smucker, Bob. 1991. *The Nonprofit Lobbying Guide*. San Francisco: Jossey-Bass.

Southern Economic Journal. 1991. "The Industrial Organization of Corporate Political Participation." *Southern Economic Journal*. 57: 727–739.

Spitzer, Robert J. 1995. *The Politics of Gun Control*. Chatham, NJ: Chatham House.

Starr, Paul. 1982. *The Social Transformation of American Medicine*. New York: Basic Books.

Stevens, Jane Ellen. 1994. "Treating Violence as an Epidemic." *Massachusetts Institute of Technology Alumni Association Technology Review*. 97: 22.

Stone, Peter H. 1996a. "Answering the GOP SOS." *National Journal*. May 25: 1155.

———. 1996b. "From K Street Corridor." *National Journal*. 28: 1910.

Straight, Candy. 1996. Vice President, WISH List. Personal Interview. November 26.

Sverdlik, Alan. 1997. "Blasts Rock Atlanta Abortion Clinic; At Least 7 People Slightly Injured in Explosions 45 Minutes Apart." *Washington Post*. January 17: A3.

Taft, Philip. 1964. *Organized Labor in American History*. New York: Harper & Row.

Thomas, Steve. 1994. "The National Abortion Rights Action League PAC: Reproductive Choice in the Spotlight." In *Risky Business? PAC Decisionmaking in Congressional Elections*, ed. Robert Biersack, Paul S. Herrnson, and Clyde Wilcox. Armonk, NY: M. E. Sharpe.

Thorpe, Kenneth. 1996. "The Health Care System in Transition: Implications for Health Care, Cost and Coverage." Paper prepared for Health Care into the Next Century: Markets, States, and Communities. *Journal of Health Politics, Policy, and Law*. Spring 1996 Conference. May 3–4, Durham, NC.

Truman, David B. 1951. *The Governmental Process: Political Interests and Public Opinion*. New York: Alfred A. Knopf.

Turner, Tom. 1991. *Sierra Club: 100 Years of Protecting Nature*. New York: Henry N. Abrams.

UFCW Action. 1996. May/June: 18: 2.

Waggoner, James. 1996. Executive Vice President, NARAL. Personal Interview. October 29.

Waybourn, William. 1993. Director, Gay and Lesbian Victory Fund. Personal Interview.

Weisbrod, Burton A. 1988. *The Nonprofit Economy*. Cambridge, MA: Harvard University Press.

Weisman, Jonathan. 1996. "Union Leaders Predict Victory Even Before Votes Tallied." *Congressional Quarterly*. November 2: 3163–3165.

Weiss, Dan. 1996. Political Director, Sierra Club. Personal Interview. October 26.
———. 1997. Political Director, Sierra Club. Personal Interview. February 5.
Weissenstein, Eric. 1996. "Washington Report: Hefty Health Lobbying Expenditures Reported." *Modern Healthcare*. October 7: 60–62.
Weissert, Carol S. and William G. Weissert. 1996. *Governing Health: The Politics of Health Policy*. Baltimore: Johns Hopkins University Press.
Weisskopf, Michael. 1995. "To the Victors Belong the PAC Checks." *Washington Post National Weekly Edition*. January 2–8: 13.
———. 1996. "Campaign '96—Small Business Lobby Becomes a Big Player in Campaigns." *Washington Post*. August 9: A1.
Wilcox, Clyde. 1989. "Organizational Variables and the Contribution Behavior of Large PACs: A Longitudinal Analysis." *Political Behavior*. 11: 157–173.
———. 1994. "Coping with Increasing Business Influence: The AFL-CIO's Committee on Political Education." In *Risky Business*, ed. Robert Biersack, Paul S. Herrnson, and Clyde Wilcox. Armonk, NY: M. E. Sharpe.
Wilson, James Q. 1995 (1973). *Political Organizations*. Princeton, NJ: Princeton University Press.
WISH List. "Welcome to the WISH List." *WISH List web site* (www.thewishlist.org).
———. "From the Fourth Quarter 1996 Newsletter." *WISH List web site* (www.thewishlist.org).
The Wish List News. Selected quarterly newsletters.
Wolf, Linda F. and John K. Gorman. 1996. "New Directions and Developments in Managed Care Financing." *Health Care Financing Review*. 71(3): 243–267.
Wolinsky, Howard and Tom Brune. 1994. *The Serpent on the Staff: The Unhealthy Politics of the American Medical Association*. New York: G. P. Putnam.
Wright, John R. 1983. "PACs, Contributions, and Roll Calls: Evidence from Five National Associations." (Doctoral Dissertation, University of Rochester).
———. 1985. "PACs, Contributions, and Roll Calls: An Organizational Perspective." *American Political Science Review*. 75: 400–414.

Court Cases Cited in Text

Federal Election Commission v. Christian Action Network, 92 F. 2nd 1178 (4th Circ. 1996).
Planned Parenthood of Southeastern Pennsylvania v. Casey, 505 U.S. 833 (1992).
Roe v. Wade, 410 U.S. 113 (1973).
Webster v. Reproductive Health Services, 492 U.S. 490 (1989).

INDEX